The Best
AMERICAN
SPORTS
WRITING
1994

The Best AMERICAN SPORTS WRITING 1994

EDITED AND WITH
AN INTRODUCTION BY

Tom Boswell

Glenn Stout, SERIES EDITOR

HOUGHTON MIFFLIN COMPANY
BOSTON • NEW YORK   1994

ISSN: 1056-8034
ISBN: 0-395-63326-5
ISBN: 0-395-63325-7 (pbk.)

Printed in the United States of America

AGM 10 9 8 7 6 5 4 3 2 1

Contents

Foreword

SPORTS IS IN trouble.

At least it sure seems that way. Any quick scan of the headlines this past year seems to confirm that feeling. In a year when the United States' women's national figure skating champion can make the entire sport appear as the poor stepchild of roller derby, and where the victim can discover that her misfortune is absolutely, positively the best thing that ever could have happened to her because the bottom line is money, sports certainly seems to be in trouble. All too often, the "big stories" seem to have little to do with what happens on any field, or what any particular athlete actually accomplishes. It's easy to get the idea that sports is simply the subplot to an ongoing orgy of celebrity and greed. From this perspective, sports is merely the hook that draws us into something more sensational, the way a lurid headline in a national tabloid at the newsstand on the grocery line leads us to read the spurious account of the two-headed bat-faced boy. It's about the ratings, baby!

As our native media culture seems ever more enamored of such sound-bite reportage, I like to think that *The Best American Sports Writing* provides a healthy antidote to this approach. The stories that appear in *The Best American Sports Writing*, without shying away from the sometimes more troubling aspects of sports, never settle for a facile treatment. In my annual survey of the sports writing that appears each year, I find plenty of writing that does settle for less. These stories are promptly bagged and put into my closet for later donation to a charitable organization. But several hundred other stories remain in which the writer has resisted the cheap and easy for something more substantial, and sometimes even profound. These writers seem to recognize something I've recently come to realize. "Sports" is not in trouble at all. Rather, those who are involved in sports are sometimes in trouble, just as any of us sometimes are. "Sports" is neutral on the subject. To any given individual, it can help bring out both the best and the worst. The writer's job is to tell us which, and to what degree.

I think this book helps temper the cacophony and allows readers to view sports as it is, as this "neutral" agent within which each man or woman learns something about themselves and reveals that to others. I know this is the function that working on this series provides for me.

In some sense, I feel that my experience reading thousands of stories each year makes me sort of an "everyman" for the readers of this book. Like me, the reader has read thousands and thousands of words about sports. Just as I must find in the stories themselves a reason to select some for inclusion in this book, each reader must find his or her own reason, after already having read thousands of words about sports each year, to want to read still more in this book.

The only answer is to learn and enjoy. Early last spring, as I was making my selections for *The Best American Sports Writing 1994*, I began to see sports as something joyless and remote. I have always been particularly attached to baseball, and now in spring, of all seasons, I found myself singularly uninterested in the chatter of spring training and speculation about the upcoming season. For baseball, which had always been a central part of my character, to become suddenly boring was something I found frightening.

I wondered what to do, for to abandon baseball was to abandon part of myself. I examined my feelings, and over the course of several weeks came to a startling conclusion. I needed to play.

I realized that ever so slowly, I had been drifting along a path from participant to spectator, then from spectator to something else, something that had damned little to do with the game as it is played and a lot more to do with the game as simply some product. The trouble wasn't with baseball. The trouble was with me.

So I started playing again. I joined a team of similar over-thirties and *played*, actually pitched baseballs again. That was what had been missing; the remembrance that all sports begins with play. Between sore arms and stiffness, I discovered something essential.

Now, I don't expect the reader of this book to drop everything and run out into the backyard and start playing again. But as you read *The Best American Sports Writing 1994,* I do ask that you remember that at its very essence, sports is play. The stories that make up this book, in one way or another, seem to me to be explorations within this gulf, along the path between sports as pure play and sports as something else. They are stories about where people are along this journey. The writers whose stories are reprinted herein, have all, I think, marked eloquently and precisely where their subjects currently reside.

And now a few words about the process that leads to the selection of a story to appear in *The Best American Sports Writing.*

Each year, I personally survey every issue of about three hundred sports and general interest magazines in my search for stories that I feel might merit inclusion in this series. I also read every issue of nearly fifty Sunday supplement magazines from daily newspapers around the country, and the Sunday sports sections of a like number of newspapers. While I feel this gives me a good jump on the best writing to appear each year, I am equally dependent upon the submissions of authors, editors, and readers to make up for any possible gaps in my search. To insure that all interested parties are aware of my interest in reading as much as is humanly possible, I also send letters to more than three hundred magazine editors and more than three hundred sports editors of daily and weekly newspapers and encourage them to submit any stories of merit for consideration. My eye — and level of attention — are far from perfect, and I depend on the input of others. As much as anyone can, I try to keep an open mind and read the work of the unknown writer for the unread small magazine with the same sense of suspended judgment as I do the Very Important Writer for the Very Big Publication. In other words, no free lunches. I try to be fair, and the best seventy-five or so stories are forwarded to the guest editor, who then selects the twenty-five that are included in the book.

I think this is the best possible way to approach a project like *The Best American Sports Writing,* and I believe the success of this series provides some proof of the wisdom of this technique. But this past year, for the first time, I received a letter from the Very Important Sports Editor of a Very Big Newspaper berating me for not selecting a story by his Very Important Writer. I then called this particular editor and explained to him that while his Very Important Writer may well have done some Very Wonderful Writing last year, *I didn't see it.* I explained to him that I try to read as much as possible and reminded him that I solicited a submission from him some weeks before. He grumbled that he does not have time to respond to such requests, if one even was received, and that his Very Important Sports Section deserves to be read by me every day.

This is, of course, impossible. There are too many papers to read each of them every day, and it would be patently unfair for me to preselect those publications that I feel are worth reading. I read what I can find — what I receive in subscription form, what I can get at the newsstand, what I find at the Big Public Library, and what I am sent. I explained this, and after a moment or two of continued grumbling on the part of the Very Important Sports Editor, our conversation ended, but only after I encouraged him to please send me submissions for this year's volume. In November, he even received his annual entreaty from me asking for such.

I suspect that this same editor will soon pick up this copy of *Best American Sports Writing,* glance at the contents, resume grumbling, and maybe write me another letter. But I hope the editor has taken the time to read my little parable, and that this year, instead of taking up his valuable time by writing to me and asking where the story by Very Important Writer is, that he please simply send me a copy of the Memorable Work Itself. In other words, the lesson is that I cannot choose what I do not read, and I cannot read what I do not see. And it should be obvious by now that I try to see as much as possible.

Fortunately, many hundreds of writers, editors, and interested readers did choose to submit stories for consideration for this edition of *The Best American Sports Writing,* and I welcome their contributions to *The Best American Sports Writing 1995.* As before, to be considered for inclusion in *The Best American Sports Writing 1995,* each nonfiction story must have been published in 1994 in the United States or Canada and must be column length or longer. Reprints or excerpts from published books are not eligible. All stories must be received by me by February 1, 1995. This is a real deadline.

All submissions must include the author's name, date of publication, and publication name. Either clear photocopies, tearsheets, or the complete publication is fine. Submissions cannot be returned, and I do not feel that it is appropriate for me to comment on or critique individual submissions. Publications that want to make certain their contributions will be considered for the next edition should make sure to include this anthology on their subscription list. Submissions or subscriptions should be sent to Glenn Stout, The Best American Sports Writing, P.O. Box 40, Back Bay Annex, Boston, Massachusetts 02117. Please note that this is a change from previous years. Copies of previous editions of *The Best American Sports Writing* can be ordered through most book stores. The staff and collections of the Boston Public Library again provided immense help with this project, and I also thank Doe Coover, Steve Lewers, Marnie Patterson, and Kristin Robbins for their role in the success of this series. My teammates on the Hyde Park Athletics provided welcome relief. So did Siobhan. Guest editor Thomas Boswell fulfilled all expectations and did an admirable job in his role. But the writers, as usual, deserve the greatest credit for this series. It is their book, and no one else's.

GLENN STOUT

Introduction

THESE DAYS, if you say you're a sports writer, nobody looks away with embarrassment. You're so legit it hurts.

Perhaps your best work will end up between dignified hard covers in *The Best American Sports Writing 1995*. Maybe you'll appear on TV in a suit worthy of a banker or hold court on a radio show. You're one writer who probably doesn't have to starve. You're so much in the mainstream, dealing with subjects common to so many tongues, you seldom have to explain yourself.

It hasn't been this way long. To get a sense of what's in this book, and to meet some of the people who wrote it, take a trip backward with me.

Sports writing offered little status, less respectability, and ninety dollars a week when I chose it with half my heart twenty-five years ago as the job I disliked least.

Then, before Watergate, before our age of media, journalism had limited cache. Within newspapers, sports writing was a niche for some of us who, while perhaps not lost, were seldom entirely found. We had everything from alienated artists to cheerful goof-offs. Sports writing promised us a modestly paid but entertaining escape from the slavery of a career. I was home.

Back then, nobody called sports writing a profession. It was just a job. One with well-defined minimum standards. Get the facts straight. Work hard when hard work is needed. Don't blow deadlines. Beyond this it was pretty loose, even at a paper like the *Washington Post*, which had a high opinion of itself.

If a desk man came to work with a hangover, nobody bothered to notice. Playing golf was sufficient excuse for tardiness. Girlfriends or wives, calling to seek information about the inmates, were stonewalled. Only one reporter claimed to take hallucinogens. However, one news aide did remain stoned for years. Screaming arguments were commonplace — led with gusto by the sawed-off sports editor — and were quickly forgotten. Supposedly, an obnoxious reporter was once bound, gagged, and stuffed in a locker. Possible. As long as the section came out and nobody sued us, we could remain at large for another day.

One day the Senators reliever Darold Knowles called the sports department from the bullpen at RFK Stadium to get the latest Aqueduct race results. Naturally, I read him the wires. How many bookies dialed that bullpen direct?

Today, Knowles would have a $5-million contract. He wouldn't bet the nags; he'd own several. For results, he'd buzz his agent by cellular phone. Tell a sports department he was a gambler? Dream on. If a newspaper got such a call today, we'd be too pious to give a result over the phone (it's illegal) and the sports staff's investigative reporter might ring up a source at the FBI.

Only yesterday we were content to be dubious characters involved in a spurious pursuit. Nobody wore a tie unless an assignment required it. Nobody thought sports writing was a stepping-stone toward a TV career, a six-figure talk radio gig or a big book contract. Nobody was going anywhere too special, and few worried about it. Shirley Povich, our silk-suit paragon, and Bob Addie, our egg-on-his-shirt reprobate, had been the columnists for decades. If you were in a rush, you were in the wrong racket.

Once, I covered the same high school football game six seasons in a row. Nobody thought my "career" was off track. Besides, even I knew I needed several years to peel away my education to get my own voice. In the seventies, a sports department was a superior place to peel. To molt. Years on the "lobster shift," 5 P.M. to 2 A.M., let me consume more books than I'd probably have touched in graduate school.

The department's crabby, volatile atmosphere produced strong friendships and feds. We formed our own grudge-match golf league. We infiltrated a printers-only bowling league on Monday mornings — who says you can't start drinking beer at 10 A.M.? Nobody had a separate "office." Everybody under forty answered the phones. Everybody under thirty fetched coffee. Desks touched.

You were elbow-to-elbow. One year, you could have covered Shelby
Coffee, now the editor of the *Los Angeles Times,* Kenneth Turan,
now an all-purpose scriptwriting film critic Hollywood guy, and me
with a blanket.

Turan once found two 400-pound Mongolian immigrant brothers who were being exploited as professional wrestlers. The
Monguls were living in borderline squalor in a flat hardly big
enough for them to turn around in. Kenny's piece was hysterical,
sad, authentic and had boffo art, too. That was our kind of story.
When I found a college basketball team that held practice in the
storage room of a shoe store, I almost had him topped. When I un-
earthed a high school football coach who spied on the practices of
rival teams from the back of a bread truck, even Kenny thought his
title was in danger. Not quite. Not the Monguls.

If somebody tried to throw a boomerang around the Washington Monument, or hold a golf tournament in the dark at midnight
with phosphorescent balls, we were there. Certainly none of us
had an agent. None of us could *name* an agent.

Joe the Slot Man was vicious, hard-drinking, and passionately re-
actionary — exactly the old-boy qualities needed to get the union-
ized composing-room workers to shape up on deadline. Greg the
Aging News Aide was a hippie, talking about drugs, peace in Vietnam, and all his women. Joe and Greg, separated by thirty years,
abused each other relentlessly yet worked better together closing a
page on deadline than any pair. Both were demons for work.

Bill arrived on his motorcycle with his pool cue laced through
his belt so he could go hustle on his dinner hours. Our Navy-beat
man had a Swarthmore education, hair over his shoulders, a beard
over his chest, and wore a butterfly necklace around his neck. He
and the Naval Academy adored each other. "Nice people," he'd
say. "Out of their minds. Probably blow up the world. But nice."

Then, it all changed. Sometime between the late sixties and the
mid-seventies, sports departments became a kind of cultural guerrilla battleground all across the country. Of course, many American institutions could be described the same way in those days.
The eclectic, eccentric, live-and-let-live atmosphere in our department was leaving. The Joes and the Gregs couldn't really stay
friends as the Joes got too old and the Gregs came of age.

The old guard cared about who the new backfield coach might

be at State U. The insurrectionists wanted to "blow out the page" with a brainy feature on Barishnikov as Athlete, plus a mammoth photo of the ballet dancer — even if it ate seventy inches out of the day's pinched news hole.

Few papers suffered more sports department identity angst than the *Post*. We changed editors — and basic approaches to everything from layout to What Is News — about once a year. At one point, we had *seven* people with the title Sports Editor. And they all took it personally. Every day was a Balkan war of backstabbing intrigue. One editor was simply nicknamed Captain Fuck Up.

Reports of similar upheavals in other departments were the norm. Sports department turf that had hardly seemed worth fighting over a few years before was now seen as valuable. The reason, of course, was the astronomical growth of sports on TV. The whole country watched the same games and then wanted to read and talk about them the next day.

Gradually, sports writing became both more and less important. Or self-important, depending on your view. The entire process probably took a decade.

In their relationships with people inside the games, sports writers became somewhat less influential. Television celebrities like Howard Cosell, with their big audiences and salaries, made their print counterparts look smaller. The vain Cosell loved it. The slighted writers, like Dick Young, who once bossed the beats, hated it.

However, because of America's TV-induced addiction, sports writers discovered that while they were getting a somewhat smaller piece of the pie, it was now a hell of a big pie. During the eighties, newspapers had bidding wars for sports writers. Sports books began appearing on the bestseller lists. Soon, sports writers could dream of being as prosperous as small-town lawyers.

So, we became respectable. These days, the *Post* sports department is bigger than an airport. Some offices are glass enclosed on all four sides, like gigantic specimen cages. Nobody thinks — as Thomas Jefferson did — that newspapers owe it to the public to take such strong positions upon occasion that they run the risk of being irresponsible. The ultimate standard, perhaps the only standard, is Be Fair. Nobody has screamed in anger in many years.

Scruffiness hasn't left the business entirely, of course. No generalization could cover so many people. However, more and more sports writers resemble dentists or stockbrokers. They tend to have brains, ambition, organization, dedication, degrees from good colleges, straightforward writing styles, and upright private lives. Some of us, who never aspired to such traits, have acquired them out of self-defense so as not to be trampled.

There's peer pressure to be nice. And productive. And responsible. And politically correct. Some of my colleagues write three hundred or even four hundred stories in a year. I thought I was killing myself at two hundred. As a group, they're easy to like. They can even spell. But, sometimes, I don't feel so at home any more.

In moments when I long for the old days, I ask myself, "When did excellent writers, as a group, tend to be such efficient, fairminded paragons?"

Passion, eccentricity, and even arrogance are often a writer's friends. In private life, you may prefer to keep these unsociable traits handcuffed. But when you sit down to write, you handicap yourself severely if you do not invite them to join you at the table.

Is there one sports writer left in America who, before signing a contract as the lead columnist in a major market, would insist that a clause be put in his deal that *not one word* of his copy could be changed by anybody for any reason unless he was consulted? John Schulian did, at the *Chicago Sun-Times*.

"If they could write, they wouldn't be editors," John often raged, believing that editors, on the pretext of clipping a hangnail, would usually manage to sever an artery. I wish there were more Schulians who'd run the risk of taking their work too seriously.

Eventually John went to Hollywood, writing scripts to TV shows, including the *Slap Maxwell* series. Yes, the Old Slapper, the jerk sports columnist from the unregenerate school.

Whenever Charles P. Pierce, whose work also appears in this collection, crosses my path, we always address each other with Slap's favorite salutation to a fellow sports writer, "Hello, my semi-literate kimosabi."

It's tempting to say that something brilliant, irreverent, and unpredictable has been lost in sports writing. But I can't honestly say I believe it. To me, sports writing's gift to the public is a steady stream of good writing, occasionally interspersed with very good writing. In the nineties, there's been vastly more of the good stuff than twenty-five years ago; respectability attracts solid talent.

Emerson said that talent writes with coffee, genius writes with wine. When sports writers aren't satisfied with coffee, common sense, legwork, detail and the poetry of everyday speech, they often go astray. For better and for worse, almost nobody goes astray these days.

Without question, rotten sports writing has improved enormously. There's so little of it left that it's hard to find anybody to laugh at anymore. For years, the *Augusta Chronicle* sports page during Masters Week was The Worst. We visiting sophisticates would howl each morning at the obsequious, clinched, grammar-mangling rustics. Now, we read the tiny industrious *Chronicle* to make sure we haven't missed a good angle.

Luckily, there's still one big-city columnist who offers the rest of us the reassurance of knowing that we can never be dead last. Once he wrote a piece that seemed stilted and bizarre even by his standards. It turned out he was cheating on his wife with a new girlfriend and, as a kind of ode to her, the first letter of each paragraph spelled out her name. Worst, he told the story proudly on himself.

In another twenty-five crotchety years, I'll probably have convinced myself that there will never be another ballplayer as great as Ken Griffey, Jr., or a sports writer to put alongside Gary Smith, Frank Deford, or Roger Angell. But I'm not there yet. I still believe that the best sports writing has little to do with generations or social trends or journalistic/literary fashion.

Just as individual writers seldom know when their best work will appear, or what sparked it, so a field like sports writing doesn't deliberately set out to manufacture its best practitioners. It just enjoys them when they appear. Red Smith is sui generis. We'll never run out. Just when you think Jim Murray can't be replaced as a humorist, you look twenty feet away and your old buddy Tony Kornheiser looks like he's steadily grown into the job.

Tagging and docketing writers by generations or decades works very poorly in sports. We enjoy falling out of our pigeonholes.

For example, George Plimpton came along well before me but his work, like "Fishing On the FDR," is so fresh and full of sharp appetite that you might say it contains both a mature man's and a young man's point of view. Usually, it's the cub reporter who chooses a subject as humble as interviewing the folk who fish the

East River, hoping not to hook a floating corpse. However, that's typical of Plimpton. His ability to remain bemused and indifferent toward his own celebrity has been an object lesson for some time.

John Ed Bradley ("Get A Load of Me!") came along so far behind me that, the first day he ever held a newspaper job, the large former LSU football co-captain shyly introduced himself to "Mr. Boswell." Now, as both novelist and journalist, he's a writer with the nerve to put himself at risk for the sake of insight.

Before carrying myself completely over the edge in my enthusiasm for my craft and my colleagues, I'd like to admit, just once, that it's easy to overestimate the quality of the best sports writing because, of all our American genres, it may be the most seductively engaging. For example, I promise that you will enjoy this book even if you *dislike* sports.

Why? Because sports writers tend to be wonderfully energetic, playful, argumentative companions who walk beside the reader, quipping and philosophizing, as they consider a subject together. Sports writers are unashamed lapel-grabbers who are proud to claim that they can hook any reader, regardless of the subject matter. Raymond Chandler was once asked his theory for plotting his mystery novels. "When in doubt," said Chandler, "have a man come through a door with a gun." A sports writing anthology may hold the record for men-with-guns-per-page.

Leigh Montville ("Triumph on Sacred Ground") and Bud Collins ("Boxing Grieves Loss of 5th Street Gym") exemplify that anything-to-hook-'em style. In this collection, Montville has a wonderfully reported and gentle story about what happens to a small country after its entire national soccer team dies in a plane crash. Leigh, however, is also the guy who once interviewed the left field wall in Fenway Park.

Reading Bud is like talking to him over dinner after Wimbledon. He's got a pink sweater thrown around his neck. He can't wait to discuss politics or food. And he's mad to rise at dawn the next morning to see some Hungarian player, number 178 in the world, whom nobody at the table has ever heard of. He's "been there, done that," but still loves it all as much as ever.

Almost all of us possess, or cannot be cured of, that desire to talk to Green Monsters or gather exotic delicious irrelevant expertise about games. Sometimes, I think that sports writers love experience, and have the knack of enjoying it, too much to judge the world as deeply, and perhaps as harshly, as more lasting writers. If you have seen Bill Nack ("The Rock") dance to rock 'n roll, you know the syndrome. Basically, he looks like a seal being electrocuted. He's having too much fun to worry about potential injury to himself or others. My wife, herself a clear-the-decks hoofer, kissed Nack, declared him the world champion and made him swear never to ask her to dance again.

Sports writers, as this collection certainly shows, have an acute sense of pathos. Yet, even when dealing with the saddest or most painful topics, it's a rare sports writer who does not have some hidden therapeutic agenda. Read Ira Berkow on Ferguson Jenkins or Davis Miller on Muhammad Ali. The torments of the protagonists may make you cry. But, if you think of Jenkins or Ali reading those stories, it's easy to imagine that both would find their burdens slightly lighter as a result. Something in the way the stories are framed makes them cathartic. Jenkins and Ali gain, rather than lose, dignity from the telling.

Almost the first lesson a sports writer learns is that what he writes is read, and felt, deeply by those about whom he writes. Sometimes — and I've heard other sports writers say this with a shudder — people actually begin to see themselves in the way that we write about them.

So, within a few years, you become very careful. You sense that you have more power than you deserve or want. Because we write about real people, not fictional characters, sports writers almost always develop an instinctive generosity toward their subjects when the issue is serious. On botched plays or contract haggles, we chew 'em up or mock 'em. But on the kinds of stories that occupy much of this book, we know how much damage we can do. So, we leave behind much of the ruthlessness that characterizes the artist.

It's rare to find a complete, and effective, public evisceration of a person, such as Bruce Buschel's bleak vision of a disintegrating Lenny Dykstra in "Lips Get Smacked." What a brilliant assassination!

Buschel is not, I believe, a sports writer. Which may explain why I have no interest in meeting him, but consider his piece my favorite of the year.

The Best
AMERICAN
SPORTS
WRITING
1994

BRUCE BUSCHEL

Lips Gets Smacked

FROM PHILADELPHIA MAGAZINE

YOU DON'T often see a contortionist wearing a black leather Redskins cap in the baccarat pit playing around with $20,000 at 1 A.M. on a Tuesday morning. You stop and watch. Though seated, his body is arced like a swimmer on a starting block, his chin resting on the large oblong table, his face hidden behind two upright cards, a cigarette burning between two fingers. The guy's a southpaw. A single stack of orange chips is piled neatly before him — each one is worth $1,000 here at Resorts. Baccarat players generally shy away from orange chips, even though baccarat is the elegant game of tuxedos and turbans and high-priced cleavage, the game of James Bond and jet-setters on the French Riviera.

You'll have to pardon this guy's French: After toying with his two cards interminably, he finally looks at them, is appalled by their markings, leaps to his feet, throws the losing cards high into the air and bellows, "Fuck me! This is brutal! Fucking brutal! Fuck me!"

It's Lenny Fucking Dykstra. What a mouth on this guy — not just the utterances that pass through it, but the actual physical mouth. Never closed, even when its owner is ruminative or silent, it is the control center for heavy traffic. Things go in (filtered tips of cigarettes and clear liquids and fingers, one or two at a time) and things come out (a stream of profanity and filtered tips and gusts of smoke and fingers and a tongue). His tongue loves his lips. You can't blame it. They are fine lips, bountiful, shapely, ideal for pursing or pouting. Women receive injections to achieve such lips. On the baseball field, where Dykstra spends the other seven months of the year, they are protected by coats of lip gloss, something with a double-digit SPF rating. While his tongue may flap or jut or merely hang about, its favorite activity is to travel lambently along the upper lip, sometimes leisurely, sometimes scurrying from corner to corner like a dazed lizard.

The croupier collects Dykstra's three orange chips and passes the shoe — the card dispenser — to the far end of the table to the only other gambler, a bald, mild-mannered fellow.

Lenny the Lips locates his rolling chair, extinguishes his cigarette, watches a brunette exchange his soiled ashtray for a fresh one, lights another Salem with a thin gold lighter and counts his orange wafers: twenty-one. He decides to slide three more onto the space marked BANKER and offers encouragement to his hairless compadre. "Let's go, dude. You're the fucking man. Show me something." His voice carries like a high fly caught in a swift wind. As the cards skim along the baize, Dykstra releases his face to a series of ticks and twitches, freezing his gaping yap as if to address an endodontist. It remains stretched wide until he sees his cards. He likes what he sees. He takes a deep drag. He expels abruptly.

"I love you, dude," he says to the bald gambler, who nods meekly in acknowledgment. Dykstra compulsively smoothes out his slender spire of chips; he keeps adding to the stack like a child testing how high his building blocks will climb before gravity intrudes.

"We're on a fucking roll, dude."

And so are we. Watching Lenny Dykstra gamble is like having an orchestra seat at a one-character David Mamet tragicomic-psychodrama. You are appalled and delighted by the language and the largesse, the exposed and tortured soul. You enjoy the ride. You know it will end badly.

A dozen strangers are loitering at the entrance to the pit, watching the littlest Phillie go through his off-season regimen: tossing cards to keep his arm in shape, honing hand-eye coordination by betting, smoking, stacking and drinking simultaneously. He never does nothing. After performing before tens of thousands of screaming meemies, a handful of hushed spectators won't inhibit his hyper reverie; degenerate gamblers are in heaven when in action, and Dykstra has been known to wager on tennis and golf and dice and football and poker and the accuracy of his own expectorated tobacco juice.

The Banker is hot. The center fielder settles into a giddy super-
stitious spree, talking to himself, taking short circular walks, con-
tinually licking those luxurious lips like a nervous ingenue
confronting a camera. Everyone knows the outcome of each hand
the instant he does. No poker face, he is easier to read than a roadside billboard. In baccarat, it doesn't matter.

The rules of the game are simple. The gambler with the shoe
deals two cards each to another participant (Player) and to himself
(Banker). The closest to nine points wins. Tens and face cards
count as zero, aces as one. A third card may be drawn, if needed.
The gambler makes one decision: bet on Banker or Player. You
win whatever you bet, dollar for dollar; the casino takes a five percent fee — vigorish — on Banker wins. In France, the game is
called *chemin de fer* (railroad) because it moves at great speeds,
money changing hands every minute, 60 or 70 times an hour. The
game requires no talent at all. If you bat .400, you're a stone loser.

Losing does not concern Lenny the Lips. Having won a dozen
hands in a row, the streak hitter keeps ponying up the orange on
Banker and the Banker keeps paying. Every so often, Dykstra removes his cap, mops his brow, strokes his thick brown hair, shoos
invisible insects from his cheeks, fiddles with the sleeves of his
black sweatshirt. The routine is familiar to baseball fans. Each
hand is approached with the same intensity as a bases-loaded at-
bat. You'd have no trouble spotting him at a masquerade ball. It's
impossible, in fact, to imagine him behaving any differently in any
setting at any time.

*Santa Ana, California, 1968. Kindergarten. After milk and cookies,
Miss Crabapple announces naptime. Little Lenny flits about, nervous as a
mayfly. "Lenny Dykstra — it is naptime," insists Miss Crabapple. "Go
tuck yourself," says little Lenny, who crashes into the blackboard, knocks
over the Lego castle, races through the halls spitting milk. Miss Crabapple
can only step back and say, "He's impossible, but he's so adorable."*

"You're the best, dude!" yells Lenny across the long table, wag-
ging his index finger and winking. Exhilarated by his success —
his tower of orange power has reached $40,000 — one forgets
about the Mercedes he wrapped around a Main Line tree, forgets
about the year probation meted out by the baseball commissioner's office after Dykstra lost $78,000 to shady crackers in a
shady Mississippi poker game, forgets about the busted collarbone

and broken wrist and large chunks of the past two seasons lost to self-destruction. But forgetting is the point.

"He puts on a great show," says a voice in the crowd.

"Better than Cher. I saw her last week."

"He's the Wayne Newton of baccarat — the hardest-working gambler I ever saw." They all laugh.

Laughter comes easily as long as Lenny F. Dykstra is winning. He's breaking no laws, not imbibing like the Babe or scuffling like the Georgia Peach or abusing women, children or imported vehicles. Just a fun-loving jock doing what jocks have always done to fill the long months between games. A competitor needs competition. Perhaps his good fortune foreshadows that of the Phils. You root for him, the cute bugger, somehow finding your own joy in his.

A casino rep in a sharp suit and expensive haircut descends into the baccarat pit. He whispers to Lenny and lays a room key next to his orange stack. Word has reached important ears, and the casino has reacted swiftly, predictably. Merv Griffin's Resorts doesn't want Lenny Dykstra leaving any time soon, not with their lucre. They encourage him to stick around. He is a soft player: With patience, and a little flattery, he'll return his winnings. And more. Last week, he lost a bundle at Caesars. He did not go gently into that good night. But casinos are as tolerant as saints when you're a high roller at low ebb. They will overlook boorish behavior, the legality of your habits, the source of your money, the date on your birth certificate. They will indulge, acquiesce, coddle. They will, in effect, treat you like a baseball team does. Such enterprises are shamelessly accommodating when you deliver the goods, be they line drives or hard cash. If you bet big enough, casinos will provide suites, Sinatra, credit, champagne, jewelry, cruises, cars, Super Bowl parties, private jets, ringside seats at prizefights. When a renowned high and holy roller had trouble getting away from his wife a few years ago, one casino flew the missus to Paris on a shopping trip; she was bought fancy dresses even as her husband was losing his shirt. If Lenny Dykstra had a sudden urge for a gigantic wad of chewing tobacco, Merv Griffin himself might whip out the Red Man and shine up the spittoon.

After treading water for a while, two losses turn into four. Dykstra keeps banging away on Banker, though the streak is over. Four losses turn into eight. He avoids Player like the plague. He is betting five thou a pop now. He is not winning. He is walking more and cursing louder and slamming the table. As if to make certain these hexed cards will not be used again, he bends them, tosses them, launches them like Frisbees. The casino is only too happy to pass him more cards for mutilation. After one close loss, he tries to throw the card shoe onto some distant table; it is attached by a chain and boomerangs back. He smacks it like a disobedient dog.

Suddenly, you know all the money will disappear. The orange tree will be chopped down. You know it and the casino knows it and the bald guy knows it and maybe Lenny knows it too. He scales down his bets to two thou. All levity is gone. "Fuck me's" shower the baccarat pit like hailstones. His facial expressions now appear as painful disfigurements. The roll has taken a new direction, a downward, unstoppable spiral.

Having lost $40,000, the orange mountain is a molehill. The Banker and the Lips have lost ten hands in a row. After ten consecutive curve balls, what kind of hitter would still be looking fastball?

Cards keep coming, coming. Wordlessly, Dykstra bolts for the men's room. The half-dozen croupiers and dealers step back, giving him a wide berth. It is his third such break in the last 30 minutes. He is not drinking enough to require such frequency. The croupiers roll their eyes, sigh with relief; they relax in his absence. "Always exciting when Mr. Dykstra is here," confides one. "We see him every other week and we never know what he'll do next. He's a real trip." Maybe Mr. Dykstra uses the lavatory as a meditation room; maybe he punches a stall and splashes his face and feels better; maybe he looks at himself in the mirror and feels worse.

The crowd outside the baccarat pit has grown in size and animation. The identity of the gambler is whispered down the lane.

"That's right, Dykstra, the guy on TV who warns kids about drinking and driving."

"Shit — he just lost more money than most people make in a year."

"Phillies better trade his ass, pronto. This guy's out of control."

Mr. Lenny F. Dykstra returns. Looks renewed. Lights a Salem.

"Let's get down to fucking business. All right, dude?"

Down is the key word: down to ten chips. Ten G's. The once unmanageable stack is very stable. Two chips are placed on Banker. Lenny the Lips deals himself two cards. He throws over a red queen. He throws over a black four. He is given a red eight. He loses. He curses. He rubs out one Salem and ignites another. He pushes another two chips onto Banker.

The bald guy at the other end of the long table, who has held his counsel throughout, now asks softly, with heartbreak in his voice, "What are you doing, Lenny?"

Lenny is taken aback. Way back. Someone has actually spoken to him, said what needed to be said, and you realize how alone Dykstra has been. No wife, no entourage, no buddies. Self-flagellation is a gambler's best friend.

"Why you want to show me, dude?" he beseeches. "Why?"

Dykstra rises now, as does his anger.

"I give a fuck about the money! I know how much fucking money I'm losing. It's my fucking money! I know how much fucking money I'm fucking losing! I give a fuck! I give a fuck! FUCK YOU!" It is the first invective aimed at someone other than himself. His rage has turned outward. His body follows. He takes off after the guy, dashing around the table, nostrils flaring, fists clenched, cap flying off like Willie Mays darting for a sinking liner.

If the bald man were lucky, really lucky, if all his planets were in alignment, Mr. Dykstra would land one good portside punch, break the guy's nose, maybe a jawbone, and the bald man would see stars and then a lawyer. Oh, what glorious litigation! Against Dykstra, against Resorts, the croupiers, the casino commission, Merv! This could have been his greatest night ever at a casino: medical bills, mental anguish, public humiliation, time lost from work, recurring baseball nightmares. Thwack! A one-punch windfall.

No such luck. Three croupiers jump between the marauding center fielder and the startled gambler, forming a human wall. Mr. Dykstra bounces off the wall. He is quickly restrained by four casino employees, like teammates halting an inchoate fracas with an umpire. It's an old-fashioned rhubarb; a lot of feckless jostling. Mr. Dykstra regains his composure. He stands there, menacingly, glowering at the top of the bald man's bare head. Unaccustomed to such physical threats, the poor fellow is scared just this side of cardiac infarction. (That would be another lollapalooza lawsuit, though far less appealing and harder to prove.) His hands and his cards shake visibly. Mr. Dykstra is escorted back to his seat, his squinty eyes fixed on the trembling object of his scorn.

If, at this point, you expect the pit boss to eject the little lout, to wave his right arm and bark a thunderous "You're outta here!," you don't know the rules of the casino league. No reprimands, no suspensions — Mr. Dykstra still has a few thousand bucks on the table, and it would be imprudent to expel him just yet.

"I give a fuck," Mr. Dykstra keeps muttering, "I give a fuck." Now thoroughly distracted, chips are wagered and lost without reaction. It's the bottom of the ninth and no one's on base and he's down 47,000 to nothing. Mr. Dykstra slides his last three orange wafers onto Banker. Strike three. Game over.

He ascends from the hellish pit. As he walks by, you want to reach out to him and say, "Hey, Lenny, hey dude — can I do something to help?"

You don't dare.

You already know the answer.

He does too. That's why Mr. Dykstra bet every last penny on the Banker and not one on the Player. Not one.

Concrete Charlie

FROM SPORTS ILLUSTRATED

HE WENT down hard, left in a heap by a crackback block as naked as it was vicious. Pro football was like that in 1960, a gang fight in shoulder pads, devoid of the high-tech veneer its violence has taken on today. The crackback was legal, and all the Philadelphia Eagles could do about it that Sunday in Cleveland was carry a linebacker named Bob Pellegrini off on his shield.

Buck Shaw, a gentleman coach in this ruffian's pastime, watched for as long as he could, then he started searching the Eagle sideline for someone to throw into the breach. His first choice was already banged up, and after that the standard 38-man NFL roster felt as tight as a hangman's noose. Looking back, you realize that Shaw had only one choice all along.

"Chuck," he said, "get in there."

And Charles Philip Bednarik, who already had a full-time job as Philadelphia's offensive center and a part-time job selling concrete after practice, headed onto the field without a word. Just the way his father had marched off to the open-hearth furnaces at Bethlehem Steel on so many heartless mornings. Just the way Bednarik himself had climbed behind the machine gun in a B-24 for thirty missions as a teenager fighting in World War II. It was a family tradition: Duty called, you answered.

Chuck Bednarik was thirty-five years old, still imposing at six foot three inches and 235 pounds, but also the father of one daughter too many to be what he really had in mind — retired. Jackie's birth the previous February gave him five children, all girls, and more bills than he thought he could handle without football. So here he was in his twelfth NFL season, telling himself he was taking it easy on his creaky legs by playing center after all those years as an All-Pro linebacker. The only time he intended to move back to defense was in practice, when he wanted to work up a little extra sweat.

And now, five games into the season, this: Jim Brown over there in the Cleveland huddle, waiting to trample some fresh meat, and Bednarik trying to decipher the defensive terminology the Eagles had installed in the two years since he was their middle linebacker. Chuck Weber had his old job now, and Bednarik found himself asking what the left outside linebacker was supposed to do on passing plays. "Take the second man out of the backfield," Weber said. That was as fancy as it would get. Everything else would be about putting the wood to Jim Brown.

Bednarik nodded and turned to face a destiny that went far beyond emergency duty at linebacker. He was taking his first step toward a place in NFL history as the kind of player they don't make anymore.

The kids start at about 7 A.M. and don't stop until fatigue slips them a Mickey after dark. For twenty months it has been this way, three grandchildren roaring around like gnats with turbochargers, and Bednarik feeling every one of his years. And hating the feeling. And letting the kids know about it.

Get to be sixty-eight and you deserve to turn the volume on your life as low as you want it. That's what Bednarik thinks, not without justification. But life has been even more unfair to the kids than it has been to him. The girl is eight, the boys are six and five, and they live with Bednarik and his wife in Coopersburg, Pennsylvania, because of a marriage gone bad. The kids' mother, Donna, is there too, trying to put her life back together, flinching every time her father's anger erupts. "I can't help it," Bednarik says plaintively. "It's the way I am."

The explanation means nothing to the kids warily eyeing this big man with the flattened nose and the gnarled fingers and the faded tattoos on his right arm. He is one more question in a world that seemingly exists to deny them answers. Only with the passage of time will they realize they were yelled at by Concrete Charlie, the toughest Philadelphia Eagle there ever was.

But for the moment football makes no more sense to the kids than does anything else about their grandfather. "I'm not *one* of the last 60-minute players," they hear him say. "I am *the* last." Then he barks at them to stop making so much noise and to clean up the mess they made in the family room, where trophies, photographs and game balls form a mosaic of the best days of his life. The kids scamper out of sight, years from comprehending the significance of what Bednarik is saying.

He really was the last of a breed. For 58¼ minutes in the NFL's 1960 championship game, he held his ground in the middle of Philly's Franklin Field, a force of nature determined to postpone the christening of the Green Bay Packers' dynasty. "I didn't run down on kickoffs, that's all," Bednarik says. The rest of that frosty December 26, on both offense and defense, he played with the passion that crested when he wrestled Packer fullback Jim Taylor to the ground one last time and held him there until the final gun punctuated the Eagles' 17–13 victory.

Philadelphia hasn't ruled pro football in the thirty-three years since then, and pro football hasn't produced a player with the combination of talent, hunger and opportunity to duplicate what Bednarik did. It is a far different game now, of course, its complexities seeming to increase exponentially every year, but the athletes playing it are so much bigger and faster than Bednarik and his contemporaries that surely someone with the ability to go both ways must dwell among them.

Two-sport athletes are something else again, physical marvels driven by boundless egos. Yet neither Bo Jackson nor Deion Sanders, for all their storied shuttling between football and baseball, ever played what Bednarik calls "the whole schmear." And don't try to make a case for Sanders by bringing up the turn he took at wide receiver last season. Bednarik has heard that kind of noise before.

"This writer in St. Louis calls me a few years back and starts talking about some guy out there, some wide receiver," he says, making no attempt to hide his disdain for both the position and the player. "Yeah, Roy Green, that was his name. This writer's talking about how the guy would catch passes and then go in on the Cardinals' umbrella defense, and I tell him, 'Don't give me that B.S. You've got to play *every* down.' "

Had Green come along thirty years earlier, he might have been turned loose to meet Bednarik's high standards. It is just as easy to imagine Walter Payton having shifted from running back to safety, or Lawrence Taylor moving from linebacker to tight end and Keith Jackson from tight end to linebacker. But that day is long past, for the NFL of the nineties is a monument to specialization.

There are running backs who block but don't run, others who run but only from inside the five-yard line and still others who exist for no other reason than to catch passes. Some linebackers can't play the run, and some can't play the pass, and there are monsters on the defensive line who dream of decapitating quarterbacks but resemble the Maiden Surprised when they come facemask to facemask with a pulling guard.

"No way in hell any of them can go both ways," Bednarik insists. "They don't want to. They're afraid they'll get hurt. And the money's too big, that's another thing. They'd just say, 'Forget it, I'm already making enough.' "

The sentiment is what you might expect from someone who signed with the Eagles for $10,000 when he left the University of Pennsylvania for the 1949 season and who was pulling down only seventeen grand when he made sure they were champions eleven years later. Seventeen grand, and Reggie White fled Philadelphia for Green Bay over the winter for what, $4 million a year? "If he gets that much," Bednarik says, "I should be in the same class." But at least White has already proved that someday he will be taking his place alongside Concrete Charlie in the Hall of Fame. At least he isn't a runny-nosed quarterback like Drew Bledsoe, signing a long-term deal for $14.5 million before he has ever taken a snap for the New England Patriots. "When I read about that," Bednarik says, "I wanted to regurgitate."

He nurtures the resentment he is sure every star of his era shares, feeding it with the dollar figures he sees in the sports pages every day, priming it with the memory that his fattest contract with the Eagles paid him $25,000, in 1962, his farewell season. "People laugh when they hear what I made," he says. "I tell them, 'Hey, don't laugh at me. I could do everything but eat a football.' " Even when he was in his fifties, brought back by then coach Dick Vermeil to show the struggling Eagles what a champion looked like, Bednarik was something to behold. He walked into training camp, bent over the first ball he saw and whistled a strike back through his legs to a punter unused to such service from the team's long snappers. "And you know the amazing thing?" Vermeil says. "Chuck didn't look."

He was born for the game, a physical giant among his generation's linebackers, and so versatile that he occasionally got the call to punt and kick off. "This guy was a football athlete," says Nick Skorich, an Eagle assistant and head coach for six years. "He was a very strong blocker at center and quick as a cat off the ball." He had to be, because week in, week out he was tangling with Sam Huff or Joe Schmidt, Bill George or Les Richter, the best middle linebackers of the day. Bednarik more than held his own against them, or so we are told, which is the problem with judging the performance of any center. Who the hell knows what's happening in that pile of humanity?

It is different with linebackers. Linebackers are out there in the open for all to see, and that was where Bednarik was always at his best. He could intercept a pass with a single meat hook and tackle with the cold-blooded efficiency of a sniper. "Dick Butkus was the one who manhandled people," says Tom Brookshier, the loquacious former Eagle cornerback. "Chuck just snapped them down like rag dolls."

It was a style that left Frank Gifford for dead, and New York seething, in 1960, and it made people everywhere forget that Concrete Charlie, for all his love of collisions, played the game in a way that went beyond the purely physical. "He was probably the most instinctive football player I've ever seen," says Maxie Baughan, a rookie linebacker with the Eagles in Bednarik's whole-schmear season. Bednarik could see a guard inching one foot backward in preparation for a sweep or a tight end setting up just a little farther from the tackle than normal for a pass play. Most important, he could think along with the best coaches in the business.

And the coaches didn't appreciate that, which may explain the rude goodbye that the Dallas Cowboys' Tom Landry tried to give Bednarik in '62. First the Cowboys ran a trap, pulling a guard and running a back through the hole. "Chuck was standing right there," Brookshier says. "Almost killed the guy." Next the Cowboys ran a sweep behind that same pulling guard, only to have Bednarik catch the ballcarrier from behind. "Almost beheaded the guy," Brookshier says. Finally the Cowboys pulled the guard, faked the sweep and threw a screen pass. Bednarik turned it into a two-yard loss. "He had such a sense for the game," Brookshier says. "You could do all that shifting and put all those men in motion, and Chuck still went right where the ball was."

Three decades later Bednarik is in his family room watching a tape from NFL Films that validates what all the fuss was about. The grandchildren have been shooed off to another part of the house, and he has found the strange peace that comes from seeing himself saying on the TV screen, "All you can think of is 'Kill, kill, kill.'" He laughs about what a ham he was back then, but the footage that follows his admission proves that it was no joke. Bednarik sinks deep in his easy chair. "This movie," he says, "turns me on even now."

Suddenly the spell is broken by a chorus of voices and a stampede through the kitchen. The grandchildren again, thundering out to the backyard.

"Hey, how many times I have to tell you?" Bednarik shouts. "Close the door!"

The pass was behind Gifford. It was a bad delivery under the best of circumstances, life-threatening where he was now, crossing over the middle. But Gifford was too much the pro not to reach back and grab the ball. He tucked it under his arm and turned back in the right direction, all in the same motion — and then Bednarik hit him like a lifetime supply of bad news.

Thirty-three years later there are still people reeling from the Tackle, none of them named Gifford or Bednarik. In New York somebody always seems to be coming up to old number 16 of the Giants and telling him they were there the day he got starched in the Polo Grounds (it was Yankee Stadium). Other times they say that everything could have been avoided if Charlie Conerly had thrown the ball where he was supposed to (George Shaw was the guilty Giant quarterback).

And then there was Howard Cosell, who sat beside Gifford on *Monday Night Football* for fourteen years and seemed to bring up Bednarik whenever he was stuck for something to say. One week

Cosell would accuse Bednarik of blindsiding Gifford, the next he would blame Bednarik for knocking Gifford out of football. Both were classic examples of telling it like it wasn't.

But it is too late to undo any of the above, for the Tackle has taken on a life of its own. So Gifford plays along by telling what sounds like an apocryphal story about one of his early dates with the woman who would become his third wife. "Kathie Lee," he told her, "one word you're going to hear a lot of around me is Bednarik." And Kathie Lee supposedly said, "What's that, a pasta?"

For all the laughing Gifford does when he spins that yarn, there was nothing funny about November 20, 1960, the day Bednarik handed him his lunch. The Eagles, who complemented Concrete Charlie and Hall of Fame quarterback Norm Van Brocklin with a roster full of tough, resourceful John Does, blew into New York intent on knocking the Giants on their media-fed reputation. Philadelphia was leading 17–10 with under two minutes to play, but the Giants kept slashing and pounding, smelling one of those comeback victories that were supposed to be the Eagles' specialty. Then Gifford caught that pass.

"I ran through him right up here," Bednarik says, slapping himself on the chest hard enough to break something. *"Right here."* And this time he pops the passenger in his van on the chest. "It was like when you hit a home run; you say, 'Jeez, I didn't even feel it hit the bat.' "

Huff would later call it "the greatest tackle I've ever seen," but at the time it happened his emotion was utter despair. Gifford fell backward, the ball flew forward. When Weber pounced on it, Bednarik started dancing as if St. Vitus had taken possession of him. And as he danced, he yelled at Gifford, "This game is over!" But Gifford couldn't hear him.

"He didn't hurt me," Gifford insists. "When he hit me, I landed on my ass and then my head snapped back. That was what put me out — the whiplash, not Bednarik."

Whatever the cause, Gifford looked like he was past tense as he lay there motionless. A funereal silence fell over the crowd, and Bednarik rejoiced no more. He has never been given to regret, but in that moment he almost changed his ways. Maybe he actually would have repented if he had been next to the first Mrs. Gifford after her husband had been carried off on a stretcher. She was standing outside the Giants' dressing room when the team physician stuck his head out the door and said, "I'm afraid he's dead." Only after she stopped wobbling did Mrs. Gifford learn that the doctor was talking about a security guard who had suffered a heart attack during the game.

Even so, Gifford didn't get off lightly. He had a concussion that kept him out for the rest of the season and all of 1961. But in '62 he returned as a flanker and played with honor for three more seasons. He would also have the good grace to invite Bednarik to play golf with him, and he would never, ever whine about the Tackle. "It was perfectly legal," Gifford says. "If I'd had the chance, I would have done the same thing to Chuck."

But all that came later. In the week after the Tackle, with a Giant–Eagle rematch looming, Gifford got back at Bednarik the only way he could, by refusing to take his calls or to acknowledge the flowers and fruit he sent to the hospital. Naturally there was talk that Gifford's teammates would try to break Concrete Charlie into little pieces, especially since Conerly kept calling him a cheap-shot artist in the papers. But talk was all it turned out to be. The Eagles, on the other hand, didn't run their mouths until after they had whipped the Giants a second time. Bednarik hasn't stopped talking since then.

"This is a true story," he says. "They're having a charity roast for Gifford in Parsippany, New Jersey, a couple of years ago, and I'm one of the roasters. I ask the manager of this place if he'll do me a favor. Then, when it's my turn to talk, the lights go down and it's dark for five or six seconds. Nobody knows what the hell's going on until I tell them, 'Now you know how Frank Gifford felt when I hit him.' "

He grew up poor, and poor boys fight the wars for this country. He never thought anything of it back then. All he knew was that every other guy from the south side of Bethlehem, Pennsylvania, was in a uniform, and he figured he should be in a uniform too. So he enlisted without finishing his senior year at Liberty High School. It was a special program they had; your mother picked up your diploma while you went off to kill or be killed.

Bednarik didn't take anything with him but the memories of the place he called *Betlam* until the speech teachers at Penn classed up his pronunciation. Betlam was where his father emigrated from Czechoslovakia and worked all those years in the steel mill without making foreman because he couldn't read or write English. It was where his mother gave birth to him and his three brothers and two sisters, then shepherded them through the Depression with potato soup and secondhand clothes. It was where he made ninety cents a round caddying at Saucon Valley Country Club and two dollars a day toiling on a farm at the foot of South Mountain, and gave every penny to his mother. It was where he fought in the streets and scaled the wall at the old Lehigh University stadium to play until the guards chased him off. "It was," he says, "the greatest place in the world to be a kid."

The worst place was in the sky over Europe, just him and a bunch of other kids in an Army Air Corps bomber with the Nazis down below trying to incinerate them. "The antiaircraft fire would be all around us," Bednarik says. "It was so thick you could walk on it. And you could hear it penetrating. *Ping! Ping! Ping!* Here you are, this wild, dumb kid, you didn't think you were afraid of anything, and now, every time you take off, you're convinced this is it, you're gonna be ashes."

Thirty times he went through that behind his .50-caliber machine gun. He still has the pieces of paper on which he neatly wrote each target, each date. It started with Berlin on August 27, 1944, and ended with Zwiesel on April 20, 1945. He looks at those names now and remembers the base in England that he flew out of, the wake-ups at four o'clock in the morning, the big breakfasts he ate in case one of them turned out to be his last meal, the rain and fog that made just getting off the ground a dance with death. "We'd have to scratch missions because our planes kept banging together," he says. "These guys were knocking each other off."

Bednarik almost bought it himself when his plane, crippled by flak, skidded off the runway on landing and crashed. To escape he kicked out a window and jumped 20 feet to the ground. Then he did what he did after every mission, good or bad. He lit a cigarette and headed for the briefing room, where there was always a bottle on the table. "I was eighteen, nineteen years old," he says, "and I was drinking that damn whiskey straight."

The passing of time does nothing to help him forget, because the war comes back to him whenever he looks at the tattoo on his right forearm. It isn't like the CPB monogram that adorns his right biceps, a souvenir from a night on some Army town. The tattoo on his forearm shows a flower blossoming to reveal the word MOTHER. He got it in case his plane was shot down and his arm was all that remained of him to identify.

There were only two things the Eagles didn't get from Bednarik in 1960: the color TV and the $1,000 that had been their gifts to him when he said he was retiring at the end of the previous season. The Eagles didn't ask for them back, and Bednarik didn't offer to return them. If he ever felt sheepish about it, that ended when he started going both ways.

For no player could do more for his team than Bednarik did as pro football began evolving into a game of specialists. He risked old bones that could just as easily have been out of harm's way, and even though he never missed a game that season — and only three in his entire career — every step hurt like the dickens.

Bednarik doesn't talk about it, which is surprising because, as Dick Vermeil says, "it usually takes about twenty seconds to find out what's on Chuck's mind." But this is different. This is about the code he lived by as a player, one that treated the mere thought of calling in sick as a betrayal of his manhood. "There's a difference between pain and injury," Maxie Baughan says, "and Chuck showed everybody on our team what it was."

His brave front collapsed in front of only one person, the former Emma Margetich, who married Bednarik in 1948 and went on to reward him with five daughters. It was Emma who pulled him out of bed when he couldn't make it on his own, who kneaded his aching muscles, who held his hand until he could settle into the hot bath she had drawn for him.

"Why are you doing this?" she kept asking. "They're not paying you for it." And every time, his voice little more than a whisper, he would reply, "Because we have to win."

Nobody in Philadelphia felt that need more than Bednarik did, maybe because in the increasingly distant past he had been the town's biggest winner. It started when he took his high school coach's advice and became the least likely Ivy Leaguer that Penn has ever seen, a hard case who had every opponent he put a dent in screaming for the Quakers to live up to their nickname and de-emphasize football.

Next came the 1949 NFL champion Eagles, with halfback Steve Van Buren and end Pete Pihos lighting the way with their Hall of Fame greatness, and the rookie Bednarik ready to go elsewhere after warming the bench for all of his first two regular-season games.

On the train home from a victory in Detroit, he took a deep breath and went to see the head coach, who refused to fly and had one of those names you don't find anymore, Earle (Greasy) Neale. "I told him, 'Coach Neale, I want to be traded, I want to go somewhere I can play,' " Bednarik says. "And after that I started every week — he had me flip-flopping between center and line-backer — and I never sat down for the next fourteen years. That's a true story."

He got a tie clasp and a $1,100 winner's share for being part of that championship season, and then it seemed that he would never be treated so royally again. Some years before their return to glory, the Eagles were plug-ugly, others they managed to maintain their dignity, but the team's best always fell short of Bednarik's. From 1950 to '56 and in '60 he was an All-Pro linebacker. In the '54 Pro Bowl he punted in place of the injured Charlie Trippi and spent the rest of the game winning the MVP award by recovering three fumbles and running an interception back for a touchdown. But Bednarik did not return to the winner's circle until Van Brock-lin hit town.

As far as everybody else in the league was concerned, when the Los Angeles Rams traded the Dutchman to Philadelphia months before the opening of the '58 season, it just meant one more Eagle with a tainted reputation. Tommy McDonald was being accused of making up his pass patterns as he went along, Brookshier was deemed too slow to play cornerback, and end Pete Retzlaff bore the taint of having been cut twice by Detroit. And now they had Van Brocklin, a long-in-the-tooth quarterback with the disposition of an unfed Doberman.

In Philly, however, he was able to do what he hadn't done in Los Angeles. He won. And winning rendered his personality deficien-cies secondary. So McDonald had to take it when Van Brocklin told him that a separated shoulder wasn't reason enough to leave a game, and Brookshier, fearing he had been paralyzed after making a tackle, had to grit his teeth when the Dutchman ordered his carcass dragged off the field. "Actually Van Brocklin was a lot like me," Bednarik says. "We both had that heavy temperament."

But once you got past Dutch's mouth, he didn't weigh much. The Eagles knew for a fact that Van Brocklin wasn't one to stand and fight, having seen him hightail it away from a postgame beef with Bob Pellegrini in Los Angeles. Concrete Charlie, on the other hand, was as two-fisted as they came. He decked a teammate who was clowning around during calisthenics just as readily as he tried to punch the face off a Pittsburgh Steeler guard named Chuck Noll.

Somehow, though, Bednarik was even tougher on himself. In '61, for example, he tore his right biceps so terribly that it wound up in a lump by his elbow. "He just pushed the muscle back where it was supposed to be and wrapped an Ace bandage around it," says Skorich, who had ascended to head coach by then. "He hardly missed a down, and I know for a fact he's never let a doctor touch his arm." That was the kind of man it took to go both ways in an era when the species was all but extinct.

The San Francisco 49ers were reluctant to ask Leo Nomellini to play offensive tackle, preferring that he pour all his energy into defense, and the Giants no longer let Gifford wear himself out at defensive back. In the early days of the American Football League the Kansas City Chiefs had linebacker E. J. Holub double-dipping at center until his ravaged knees put him on offense permanently. But none of them ever carried the load that Bednarik did. When Buck Shaw kept asking him to go both ways, there was a championship riding on it.

"Give it up, old man," Paul Brown said when Bednarik got knocked out of bounds and landed at his feet in that championship season. Bednarik responded by calling the patriarch of the Browns a ten-letter obscenity. Damned if he would give anything up.

All five times the Eagles needed him to be an iron man that season, they won. Even when they tried to take it easy on him by playing him on only one side of the ball, he still wound up doing double duty the way he did the day he nailed Gifford. A rookie took his place at center just long enough to be overmatched by the Giants' blitzes. In came Bednarik, and on the first play he knocked the reddogging Huff on his dime. "That's all for you, Sam," Bednarik said. "The big guys are in now."

And that was how the season went, right up to the day after Christmas and what Bednarik calls "the greatest game I ever played." It was the Eagles and Green Bay for the NFL championship at Franklin Field, where Bednarik had played his college ball, and there would be no coming out, save for the kickoffs. It didn't look like there would be any losing either, after Bednarik nearly yanked Packer sweep artist Paul Hornung's arm out of its socket.

But there was no quit in Vince Lombardi's Pack. By the game's final moments, they had the Eagles clinging to a 17–13 lead, and Bart Starr was throwing a screen pass to that raging bull Jim Taylor at the Philadelphia 23. Baughan had the first shot at him, but Taylor cut back and broke Baughan's tackle. Then he ran through safety Don Burroughs. And then it was just Taylor and Bednarik at the 10.

In another season, with another set of circumstances, Taylor might have been stopped by no man. But this was the coronation of Concrete Charlie. Taylor didn't have a chance as Bednarik dragged him to the ground and the other Eagles piled on. He kicked and cussed and struggled to break free, but Bednarik kept him pinned where he was while precious seconds ticked off the clock, a maneuver that NFL rulemakers would later outlaw. Only when the final gun sounded did Bednarik roll off him and say, "O.K., you can get up now."

It was a play they will always remember in Philadelphia, on a day they will always remember in Philadelphia. When Bednarik floated off the field, he hardly paid attention to the news that Van Brocklin had been named the game's most valuable player. For nine-of-20 passing that produced one touchdown — an ordinary performance, but also his last one as a player — the Dutchman drove off in the sports car that the award earned him. Sometime later Bednarik caught a ride to Atlantic City with Retzlaff and halfway there blurted out that he felt like Paul Revere's horse.

"What do you mean by that?" the startled Retzlaff asked.

"The horse did all the work," Bednarik said, "but Paul Revere got all the credit."

*

In the mornings he will pick up his accordion and play the sweet, sad "etnik" music he loves so much. As his football-warped fingers thump up and down the keyboard, he often wishes he and Emma and the girls had a family band, the kind Emma's father had that summer night he met her at the Croatian Hall in Bethlehem. Not what you might expect, but then Bednarik is a man of contradictions. Like his not moving any farther than his easy chair to watch the Eagles anymore. Like his going to 8 A.M. Mass every Sunday and saying the Rosary daily with the industrial-strength beads that Cardinal Krol of Philadelphia gave him. "I'm a very religious person, I believe in prayer," Bednarik says, "but I've got this violent temper."

Sixty-eight years old and there is still no telling when he will chase some joker who cut him off in traffic or gave him the finger for winning the race to a parking place. If anybody ever thought he would mellow, Bednarik put that idea to rest a few years back when he tangled with a bulldozer operator almost forty years his junior. As evening fell the guy was still leveling some nearby farmland for housing sites, so Bednarik broke away from his cocktail hour to put in a profane request for a little peace and quiet. One verb led to another, and the next thing Bednarik knew, he thought the guy was going to push a tree over on him. He reacted in classic Concrete Charlie fashion and got a fine that sounded like it came from the World Wrestling Federation instead of the local justice of the peace: $250 for choking.

That wouldn't change him, though. It slowed him down, made him hope that when he dies, people will find it in their hearts to say he was a good egg despite all his hard edges. But it couldn't stop him from becoming as gnarly as ever the instant a stranger asked whether he, Chuck Bednarik, the last of the 60-minute men, could have played in today's NFL. "I wasn't rude or anything," he says, "but inside I was thinking: I'd like to punch this guy in the mouth."

Of course. He is Concrete Charlie. "You know, people still call me that," he says, "and I love it." So he does everything he can to live up to the nickname, helping to oversee boxing in Pennsylvania for the state athletic commission, getting enough exercise to stay six pounds under his final playing weight of 242, golfing in every celebrity tournament that will invite Emma along with him, refusing to give ground to the artificial knee he got last December. "It's supposed to take older people a year to get through the rehab," he says. "I was done in four months." Of course. He is the toughest Philadelphia Eagle there ever was.

But every time he looks in the mirror, he wonders how much longer that will last. Not so many years ago he would flex his muscles and roar, "I'm never gonna die!" Now he studies the age in his eyes and whispers, "Whoa, go back, go back." But he can't do it. He thinks instead of the six teammates from the 1960 Eagles who have died. And when he sees a picture of himself with six other Hall of Fame inductees from 1967, he realizes he is the only one still living.

It is at such a moment that he digs out the letter he got from Greasy Neale, his first coach with the Eagles, shortly after he made it to the Hall. "Here, read this out loud," Bednarik says, thrusting the letter at a visitor. "I want to hear it."

There is no point in asking how many times he has done this before. He is already looking at the far wall in the family room, waiting to hear words so heartfelt that the unsteady hand with which they were written just makes them seem that much more sincere.

Neale thought he hadn't given Bednarik the kind of introduction he deserved at the Hall, and the letter was the old coach's apology. In it he talked about Bednarik's ability, his range, his desire — all the things Neale would have praised if his role as the day's first speaker hadn't prevented him from knowing how long everybody else was going to carry on.

"If I had it to do over again," he wrote in closing, "I would give you as great a sendoff as the others received. You deserve anything I could have said about you, Chuck. You were the greatest."

Then the room is filled with a silence that is louder than Bednarik's grandchildren have ever been. It will stay that way until Concrete Charlie can blink back the tears welling in his eyes.

LEIGH MONTVILLE

Triumph on Sacred Ground

FROM SPORTS ILLUSTRATED

YOU START with the graves. You have to start with the graves. You stand in the middle of the arid African landscape on a warm afternoon, surrounded by the thirty mounds of earth, not knowing where to look first. The dust blows into your face. The sun beats onto your head. You try to catalog all of the feelings, try to capture the sight and the emotions in words, but how can you do that? You stand and mostly you gape.

"This was the goaltender," a security guard says. "Efford Chabala. Oh, Chabala, he was very good. Very, very good."

You stare at the black-and-white picture of Chabala that is attached to a thin wooden stick behind one of the mounds. A head shot. You read the printing underneath the picture, his name and the fact that he lived from 1960 to 1993 and played for the Mufulira Wanderers and for Zambia. You squint to read the smaller writing, maybe from a half-dozen hands, messages that have been scribbled in pencil or ballpoint pen, messages of condolence, messages of farewell. "You have left us alone," one of them says. "What are we to do now?"

You look at all the pictures, one picture behind each of the thirty mounds. Many of the black faces are so young, faces that could be from a yearbook, from a college football program on a Saturday afternoon, eighteen soccer players and then the coaches and the trainer and then the officials of the Zambia national team and then the crew of the de Havilland DHC-5 Buffalo airplane that dropped into the Atlantic Ocean just before midnight on April 27 off the coast of the tiny African country of Gabon. How can this be? All these people?

The dust and sun have turned the edges of the pictures a faded brown in five months' time. Everything seems faded. The remnants of burial wreaths cover each of the graves, the colors of the satin ribbons faded, the real flowers long gone, the artificial flowers also faded. Plastic sheets have been laid over some of the graves, helping to keep the presentations intact. Cinder blocks have been set upon the sheets to keep them in place. The cinder blocks are chipped and broken, the plastic colored brown, again from the dust. Everything is brown.

"There is going to be a memorial here," the security guard says. "Something permanent. There will be grass and terraces and stone. But we have to wait until the rains come at the end of November, when the ground is soft, to begin."

There is no rain now. Nothing close. The guard says that for three months there was little security, and children would come here and play among the graves. They would take the flowers, climb on the mounds, deface the pictures. They would play soccer right here, play soccer in their bare feet, children as young as four and five years old, playing with a ball made from newspapers crammed tightly inside a paper or plastic bag, the way all children learn how to play soccer in Zambia. This could not continue. That is why there is more security now.

"This is sacred ground," the guard says. "These are our national heroes."

You stand on this desolate and memorable sacred ground, no more than a few hundred yards from Independence Stadium, the biggest stadium in the country, a ramshackle structure on the outskirts of the capital, Lusaka, that seats 30,000 spectators and resembles a tired minor league baseball park. You are quietly overwhelmed. How do you describe all that has happened, the death of this one team, followed by the rise of a new, replacement team that has done so much more than anyone expected, that has brought pride and hope to an impoverished country where hope is rationed in only the smallest doses? How do you combine the happiest happy this country has ever known with the saddest sad it has ever known, everything played out against a backdrop of the miseries of modern sub-Saharan Africa? What do you do? A Zambian television broadcaster, Dennis Liwewe, has said, "From the

ashes of disaster, our soccer program is headed for glory, glory hal-
lelujah." You start with the ashes.

"I was going out for a run," Kalusha Bwalya says. "It was around
noon. I was all dressed for running. The phone rang. Since I was
playing in Holland, the plan was for me to fly down to Senegal the
next day from Amsterdam to join the national team. The caller
was the accountant from our football association in Lusaka. This
was different, since usually the secretary from the association calls
me, but I figured the call had to do with my trip.

"The accountant sounded strange, though. He asked, 'How are
you, Kalusha?' I said I was fine. 'How are you feeling?' he asked. I
said I was fine. 'Nothing wrong?' Nothing. He kept going along
like this, and I didn't know what was happening. He couldn't tell
me the bad news. Finally, he said I would have to delay my trip.
'Why is that?' I asked. He said the boys on the team didn't arrive in
the Ivory Coast, where they were supposed to spend last night.
'Didn't arrive?' I asked. 'How is that possible?' He said there was
something with the plane. 'Something with the plane?' I asked. He
said they had confirmed reports that the plane had crashed and
everyone was dead.

"I couldn't believe it. I said this couldn't be true. But then I
turned on BBC and CNN, and there it was. The plane had
crashed. Everyone was dead."

Everyone dead. Kalusha, the team's star forward, was spared because he was in Holland, and two other players were also supposed
to fly in from Europe, but everyone else selected to play against
Senegal in Dakar in the opening game of second-round qualifying
for the World Cup perished. The depth of the tragedy was almost
unimaginable. Making an analogy to a similar accident in America
is impossible. The death of the entire U.S. Olympic hockey team?
The death of the entire basketball Dream Team? This, hard to believe, was an even deeper loss. This was the disappearance of a
country's biggest national treasure.

Soccer, football, is far and away the sport of Zambia, a land-
locked country the size of Texas, located in the south of the continent. Turn a corner in Lusaka and you see a game. The ball might
be made of paper and rope, the goals designated by sticks or rocks,

the players in bare feet, but the game is everywhere. The British brought soccer with them when the country was a colony known as Northern Rhodesia, and along with language and tradition, soccer has remained, long after the British were ousted. In a poor country it is virtually the only team game. Who has the money even for the sneakers and equipment of basketball? Soccer is the game that all boys play, a basic component of their upbringing, even more basic than baseball in the U.S., which must battle for attention against the computer games and swimming pools and round-the-clock television of an affluent society. There is no battle in Zambia.

"You play . . . everybody plays the same way as a boy," Aggrey Chiyangi, a fullback on the new Zambian team, says. "Someone makes the ball, which lasts two or three days, depending on how long you play each day. If you are good, you make a team somewhere and play with a real ball. All with bare feet. I think I was in grade seven when I received my first pair of boots. I remember the first time I ever played with them, I took them off at halftime. They seemed so heavy to me. I could not move."

This Zambian national team was the distillation, the end result, of all of that soccer. It was not some put-together outfit for a wide-eyed shot at notoriety. It was a veteran team, mostly players in their late twenties and early thirties, players who had performed together for five and six and seven years. Six of them were on the squad that shocked Italy 4–0 and finished tied for fifth in the 1988 Olympics, the brightest moment in Zambian soccer history. That was when the players were kids, unknowns. They had experience now. This team, the winner of its earlier World Cup qualifying round, was favored to reach the final Cup tournament next year, in the United States.

For a country in which malaria and cholera are everyday worries, a country where capitalism and democracy have emerged only in the past two years after the twenty-seven years of socialism under Kenneth Kaunda, which followed independence in 1964, a country with virtually no industry except a string of copper mines in the north, this team was a statement to the outside world: *See what we can do? This is our potential.* No country from this far south on the continent had ever qualified for the final Cup round. This would be the first. This was the team that would separate Zambia from Zimbabwe and Namibia and Angola and Madagascar and Uganda and all the rest of the countries that always seem to be confused in the cluttered minds of the West.

This was the team that died.

"I was supposed to go with them," Goliath Mungonge, a thirty-year-old sports writer for the *Zambia Daily Mail,* says. "I had an argument with my wife because she didn't want me to go. We have a young son, and she told me I already had been to Senegal once, so I didn't have to go. I didn't care. I still was going. I even had packed my clothes. The problem was that they were scheduled to leave at four in the morning. I had trouble getting money, no banks open at that time. As it turned out, the plane was eight hours late in leaving — it didn't go until around noon — and I would have had time to get the money. But I didn't know that."

The twenty-year-old Canadian-built plane was a Zambian military transport that had been refurbished three years before. The team often used military planes, as recently as a day earlier to return from a game on the island nation of Mauritius, 1,900 miles away. Commercial airline travel is expensive in Africa because there are few direct routes between cities. As with everything else in Zambia, a country that has no professional soccer simply because professional soccer would be too expensive, the use of that plane was an economy measure.

The route to Dakar was a series of hops determined by the need to refuel. The first hop went to Brazzaville, in Congo, the second to Libreville, on the coast of Gabon. The third hop was scheduled to go to Abidjan, in the Ivory Coast, where the team would spend the night before a final hop to Dakar the next day. After the initial eight-hour delay, the trip proceeded.

What happened next is confusing. Some radio reports said that the 44-year-old pilot, Captain Fenton Mike Mhone, wanted technicians to check a mechanical problem in Brazzaville. The BBC reported that a technician worked on the plane in Libreville. And there are other accounts that Mhone had no complaints at all. Whatever, the plane took off and reached a height of 6,000 feet; radio contact ceased a minute after departure. The takeoff path went out over the ocean and the pilot began to ease the plane into its flight pattern toward Abidjan. Witnesses said they saw an explosion. Or was it two explosions? One witness said she saw a beam of light shoot through the air, followed by two explosions. A beam of light? The plane dropped into the ocean.

"It was confusing then, and it is confusing now," says Mungonge, who went to Libreville after the crash. "The fuselage landed ten kilometers off the coast, where the mud at the bottom of the sea is very thick. The fuselage still is there. There was no black box because this was a military aircraft, and Gabon has refused to release the tapes of conversations back to the tower. It has become an incident between the governments. What happened? You think that something went wrong with the plane, but we may never know.

"Every day there seem to be new rumors," says Mungonge. "One is that the plane was shot down by a missile from a former French base by a Gabonese national guard unit in training. That would explain the beam of light. This was a military plane, remember, that had arrived late and maybe wasn't expected. Another rumor is that there was a bomb on the plane. Another, and this one is everywhere, is that the team is still alive. That they are being held captive in Gabon, that the bodies that were found really were the bodies of political prisoners in Gabon. I don't believe this at all, but that doesn't mean people don't talk about it."

News of the disaster was held off Zambian television for more than twelve hours while officials tried to make sure that a crash had really occurred. When the first reports started to surface on other networks, the government released what it knew at quarter past one in the afternoon. The entire country was dropped into grief. Liwewe, the broadcaster, cried for twenty minutes on the air, shouting the name of each player, uncontrollable in his misery. The grim news was a flashbulb that froze a moment forever.

"I was shopping, and this woman came up to me on the street," Peggy Wilma Mwape, wife of Michael Mwape, the late chairman of the Football Association of Zambia, says. "She said, 'Peggy, did your husband go with the team to Senegal?' I said that he left yesterday, 'Are you sure that he went?' she said. I said I was sure. She didn't say anything else but asked if she could give me a ride home. She never told me, just gave me a ride home — she was afraid that I would hear the news on the radio if I drove myself — and she dropped me off. It was my daughter who told me. She said when I came in, 'Daddy's gone.' "

"I was buying cement building blocks for our new house on that sad Wednesday," Doreen Mankinka, whose husband, Debby, was a starting midfielder, says. "I was tired and went into a store for a drink with my brother. The news was on the radio. We looked at each other. We thought it was some kind of lie. We went home and listened to the radio at home, and it was not a lie. From then on, I was just unconscious. I remember thinking, How will I ever wake up again in the morning?"

Her husband was twenty-six years old. She is the mother of two daughters, five and three years old. Her son, Davy John, was one month old when his father died. The 30 men on the plane were fathers to 90 children.

There was never much doubt that another team would be formed to play out the World Cup qualifying schedule. There was never really an argument against continuing. The idea that a new team should be built seemed as natural as the idea that the old team — everyone on the plane — should be buried together in the open land beside the stadium. The second round of World Cup qualifying would be a three-team round-robin, home and home against Morocco and Senegal, the winner qualifying to play in the U.S. The first Zambia–Senegal game, naturally, was rescheduled. The team was given time to rebuild.

"We have to go on," Kalusha told reporters as he arrived for the memorial service and funeral. "I don't know whether we will be able to build another team, but we must not give up."

The thirty coffins were shipped back from Libreville, and the drive from the Lusaka airport to the stadium, usually a 15-minute trip, took three hours as people gathered along the roads in tears. The coffins were stretched the length of the soccer field, and the stadium was left open all night for the public to pay its respects. On May 3, a third and final national day of mourning, the stadium was filled, and at least 100,000 people gathered outside as President Frederick Chiluba tearfully delivered his eulogy. HEROES LAID TO REST, the headline in the *Daily Mail* read. The paper reported that 130 people at the funeral fainted and two women went into labor.

"For that entire week I wasn't worth anything," Morris Gwebente, a thirty-year-old mechanic, a Zambian soccer fan, says. "I didn't want to talk with anyone. I just wanted to be alone. I sat in that stadium at the memorial and wondered if I ever could watch soccer again. I thought about all those guys. . . . I knew them all. How could it be that I would never see them again?"

The effort to build a new team evolved in the next month. Invitations were given to 30 players from the midlands, which is the area around Lusaka, and to 30 more from the cities of the Copper Belt, to the north. Tryouts were held at both locations. Kalusha and his brother, Joel, who plays in Belgium, and a couple of others from professional teams outside Zambia were automatic choices, and a handful of other players who had been dropped from the national team earlier were strong possibilities, but the rest of the talent was young and without international experience. Freddie Mwila, a Zambian native who once played for the Atlanta Chiefs in the North American Soccer League, was asked to assemble and guide the new team. He was working as the national coach in Botswana, but how could he resist this call from his country at a time like this? He was allowed by Botswana to get out of his contract.

He knew many of the players, had known some of them since they were children in various youth leagues, but he had no idea what kind of team he could build. He made cuts and then more cuts, working his roster down to thirty players. The neighboring country of Malawi offered to play a series of three benefit matches to help in the process. The benefits, played in late May in Zambia, gave Mwila the first idea that there might be some possibilities.

"We tied the first game 1–1," he says. "Then we lost the second 1–0. The final game we won easily, 4–2. What I tried to emphasize, from the beginning, was that what has happened has happened and that we had to move ahead. We could not be the *other* team. Those guys were together for five, six years. They had some brilliant individual players, a brilliant style. We had to find our own style. We had to do it without emotion. We had to just play."

Help came from various sources. Money arrived, donated not only to help the families of the departed players but also to help rebuild Zambian soccer. The world soccer community was involved. Offers of expense-paid training trips were made by various countries. The offer from Denmark was accepted. Mwila felt this was the best way to remove emotion from the equation. Go to Denmark for a month.

"There was too much going on here," Mwila says. "Getting away was just what we needed. We had kids who had never traveled. Some of them were scared of color, of playing against white people. Some were scared of environment, playing away from home. We went to Denmark, played some games against some very good club teams, and pretty soon these kids weren't scared anymore."

For the first time, through sad circumstance, this Third World team had New World, Old World advantages. For the first time there was money. No team from Zambia had ever trained like this in a foreign country. A Danish coach, Roald Poulsen, added some strategic assistance in Denmark. The British offered the services of Ian Porterfield, a Scotsman who had been fired as coach of Chelsea in the British Premier League. Porterfield would coach through the second round of World Cup qualifying, all expenses paid. The offer was accepted, Mwila becoming an assistant. The individual skills learned barefoot in the dirt would be merged with high-level professional coaching experience from Europe.

How well would all this work? The second qualifying round began at Independence Stadium against Morocco on July 4, just as Porterfield arrived. Nobody really knew what to expect.

"I hadn't played with three quarters of the team before it was put together," Kalusha says. "I'd been in Europe while these kids were growing up. I didn't even know them."

"If Zambia had an advantage," says Porterfield, "it was that Morocco didn't know what to expect because it never had seen this team."

The team's entrance onto the field was amazing. The day was amazing. The stands were filled, the people on the top rows able to look out and see a procession of police vehicles and cars and motorcycles coming down the road to the stadium. At the rear was the team bus. The procession drove around the outside of the stadium, paused briefly next to the graves, then entered the stadium and drove a long route around the running track. In one of the cars were President Chiluba and various state officials, who headed for the presidential box. The team bus stopped, and the team ran onto the field, headed by Kalusha, the star of both the old team and the new team. Did Morocco have a chance? A moment of silence was held for the departed players.

"It's a fact," Gwebente, the fan, says. "We Africans, we are Christian, most of us, but we also are believers in the spiritual. Morocco took a 1–0 lead in the first half, and you could see people standing, down at the end of the stadium that is near the graves. They were turned in the direction of the graves. They were shouting to the departed players, calling their names, asking for help. *Where are you now that we need your help? What are you going to do about this? We need your help now.* I was shouting along with everyone else. Then Kalusha scored on a direct kick and then we scored again. . . . I don't know about spirits. I just say what happened."

The word *miracle* was mentioned more than once. Zambia 2, Morocco 1. The Moroccan players openly discussed the presence of spirits in attendance, the feeling from the crowd. Had the timing of any win anywhere ever been better? One small ration of hope had suddenly been returned.

"The load has become bigger and bigger," Chiyangi, the fullback, says. "At first we were expected to do nothing, just to fill out the form. Now we are expected to win all the time."

The date is September 27, a day after the Zambians have belted Senegal 4–0 at Independence Stadium before another giddy crowd. The game was no contest, a rout. The win has given them a one-point lead in their qualifying group. They have one game left, on October 10 against Morocco in Casablanca. If they tie or win, they qualify for the Cup final-round tournament next year, in the U.S. If they lose, alas, they are done.

The new team is undefeated in official matches. That first win over Morocco in July was followed by a scoreless tie with Senegal a month later, and then another month of expenses-paid training in France and the Netherlands. In games to qualify for the African Nations Cup, also to be played next year, the team beat South Africa and tied Zimbabwe to reach the final round. Half of Zambia seemed to follow the team to the match in Harare, Zimbabwe, spilling into the streets after the 0–0 tie, chanting, *'Chipolopolo, yo! Chipolopolo, yo!'* That is the slogan for this team. It comes from the tribal dialect Nyanja and means "strong, impervious, unbeatable." *Chipolopolo, yo!*

"It has been an unbelievable experience being here for all of this," Porterfield, the coach, says. "When we've played at home, it's been as if only one team was meant to win. After the tragedy and all, this team has been sort of the focal point for the entire country. I've seen some amazing things, some very good talent, raw talent. I saw a local game the other day, just kids, no shirts, no shoes on. I saw things that made you stand up. I saw a kid dribble down the side and smash one in, 35 yards off the goal, unbelievable. If you ever could put together the financing, the proper structure, the teaching in a place like this . . . some African country is going to come very close to winning the World Cup very soon."

The new team has been far different from the old team, the system entirely different, the personalities as well. The stress has been on teamwork, unity, more than on individual brilliance. Kalusha, thirty-one, and striker Gibby Mbasela, who plays professionally in Germany, have been the offensive standouts. Goalkeeper James Phiri, previously untested internationally, has been a surprise. Another goaltender, the first choice, had been left off the old team at the last moment for that fatal trip to Senegal. He was so shaken by the tragedy that he quit, refusing to join the new team. Phiri has been the answer.

"Actually, I also had practiced with the other national team," he says. "There is a chance I would have played with them, would have been on the plane, except my mother died. Malaria. I was at her funeral when I heard the news of the team. All of that at once, my mother, the team, my friends. I was twisted inside, but I am all right now."

The other continuing stories from the disaster have not been so nice. The words between the Zambian government and the Gabonese government become more harsh with each exchange. The fuselage continues to sit at the bottom of the ocean, and there still is no explanation of what happened. A problem has also arrived for the widows and children of the victims. Many of them have been disowned by their former in-laws, wrangles erupting over property and the cash settlements that have arrived for survivors.

"It is an African concept of family," Debby Mankinka's widow, Doreen, says. "A wife is not considered part of her husband's family. Some terrible things have happened. Wives have been thrown out of their homes. In-laws have claimed that the wives never were married to their sons. My own in-laws came to my house the day of the funeral — the day of the funeral! — and took everything. The television. The stereo. They unscrewed light bulbs from the ceiling. They took the picture hooks from the walls. What could I do? The money we received was supposed to buy food and clothing for our children, but instead we have had to spend it to replace household goods that were taken. They took the beds. We have lawyers now, working on all of this."

"My husband had two sons when I married him," Peggy Mwape says. "They were three years old and one. I raised those children as my own. The oldest now is twenty-three. All those years, I raised those children. I see my in-laws now and they will not even offer me a cup of tea. It is all very sad."

There have been no psychiatrists involved, no grief counselors to help with pain. The wives have even been discouraged from visiting the graves with their children. It is not their place. Everyone must move forward. The national psychiatrist, the national grief counselor, has seemingly been this new soccer team as much as anyone or anything.

"Oh, how am I supposed to watch soccer?" Mankinka says. "I watched soccer because my husband played. I watched him. Who am I supposed to watch now? For me, soccer died on that airplane. I hope this new team does well, but for me. . . ."

The newspapers follow all of the stories, but the soccer team draws some of the biggest headlines. No Zambian team has ever come so close. One more point. Only a tie in Casablanca. The finals in America. Is that too much to ask? Every practice is ringed by spectators. Every subtlety is discussed. Kalusha is cheered if he walks down a street.

"We'll go there and do our best," he says. "Already it has been so much better than I thought it would be. We may not be so technically advanced, but we play this game from the heart."

"I have seen better teams, perhaps," Mwila says, "but never a team with this determination."

You visit the graves one more time on the day you leave Zambia. You travel to the site with Kalusha in a Third World taxi, a battered Datsun with a cracked windshield and a transmission that grinds and whines through every gear change, the sounds of metal rubbing directly upon metal. You pass the open markets of Lusaka, racks and racks of secondhand clothes. You pass the trucks filled with workers, maybe fifty men packed into the open end, everyone standing, pressed together. You pass the women sitting at the side of the road, a display of maybe six oranges or five bags of maize in front of them for sale. You pass the children, all the children, children wandering everywhere, packs of barefoot children from the imagination of Dickens, drawn here in the black ink of a different continent.

You walk with Kalusha among the thirty mounds of earth. He, too, reads the messages that have been written next to the faded pictures, the pictures of his teammates and friends. He, too, is quiet and reflective. What is he thinking? How many conflicting feelings must run through him? The problem remains. How to describe all of this? Africa. Poverty. Death. Hope. Soccer.

"I still think these guys are going to show up one of these days," Kalusha says. "These were boys with ambition. All of them. The back line had played together, intact, forever. The keeper, Chabala. My friends. I see their families suffering now, and it bothers me so much. All of them."

He sighs.

"It will be all right," Kalusha finally says. "In Africa we believe that the spirits must be satisfied. If someone dies, everything must be done properly for that person. Everything has been done properly here. These are the spirits behind us. They are not forgotten."

Less than two weeks later, far removed from all of this, you call the sports department of your local American newspaper on a Sunday afternoon. The baseball playoffs are in progress and the NFL is going strong and the number 1 and number 3 teams in college football played each other on Saturday. You ask for the score that interests you most, the one from Casablanca.

"Morocco 1, Zambia 0," an anonymous voice answers.

You take a moment to digest the news. The most dramatic story of the World Cup is finished before it reached the American stage. You share the heartbreak, long distance.

Cherry Bombs

FROM SPORTS ILLUSTRATED

HE KNOWS the end will come someday. Maybe someday soon. Maybe tonight. He is pushing, pushing, pushing the limits too far, saying too much. One final piece of outrage will bubble from Don Cherry's high-volume mouth, and that will be that. *Ka-boom!* He will self-destruct in full public view, the carnage strewn across the living rooms of an entire country, from the Maritimes to British Columbia. *Ka-boom!*

"I can't keep saying these things," he says. "How can I keep saying these things?"

Things like what?

"Like asking someone to break [Pittsburgh Penguin defenseman] Ulf Samuelsson's arm," he says. "How can I say that on television? I asked someone to break Ulf Samuelsson's arm between the wrist and the elbow."

Ka-boom!

He cannot help himself. The lights come on, four and a half minutes to fill on a Saturday night, a tidy little show called "Coach's Corner" between the first and second periods of *Hockey Night in Canada,* and he might as well be holding a lighted stick of dynamite while he gives his commentary. How can four and a half minutes, once a week, be so dangerous? He will say anything, do anything. He will tweak noses, pick fights. He will ask for the arm — if not the head — of a Penguin defenseman he doesn't like.

Four and a half minutes. One week he suddenly unfurled an eight-foot-long Canadian flag and talked about the "wimps and creeps" who opposed Canada's participation in the gulf war. Another week he was wearing sunglasses and an earring in his left earlobe and talking with an exaggerated effeminate lisp. Wasn't the subject supposed to be the opposition of Los Angeles King star Wayne Gretzky and King owner Bruce McNall to hockey violence? Wasn't the subject supposed to be hockey? Couldn't he simply say what he thought? An earring. A lisp.

Cherry still can't believe he did that. He could not help himself. "I come off after wearing the earring, and I'm just shaking, eh?" he says. "I was just so pumped up. Scared. I was just shaking."

Everything has become so much bigger than he ever expected. He says these things — says anything that comes into his head — and the entire country seems to stop and listen. He is fifty-nine years old, moving hard on sixty, and he has become Canada's Rush Limbaugh and Canada's Howard Cosell. All in one. He is George C. Scott and Willard Scott and Randolph Scott. He is John McLaughlin and Dick Vitale and Bobby (the Brain) Heenan and Roseann Roseannadanna and Cliff Clavin, mailman, and George Will and Henry David Thoreau and maybe a little bit of Mighty Mouse, here to save the day.

Polls have shown that he is the most recognizable figure in the country, more recognizable than any pop star, any politician, even any of the hockey players he discusses. He is so big that he cannot walk on any street in Canada without drawing a crowd. He is so big that he doesn't do banquets anymore, can't, because the demand is so great. He is so big that there have been petitions to put him on the ballot to replace the retiring Brian Mulroney as prime minister. Prime minister? How did this happen?

"Tomas Sandstrom," he said once on the air about the Kings' forward. "A lot of people think he is Little Lord Fauntleroy, but Tomas Sandstrom is a backstabbing, cheap-shot, mask-wearing Swede." Actually, he's a Finn, not a Swede.

Is that something a prime minister would say? The words just came out.

"I was watching from the stands in the first period," he said another week. "There was a tipped shot, and I had to get out of the way, and it went over my head and hit this poor lady in the face. I'm telling you, when you come to the game, ladies, keep your eye on the puck. I've seen some awful smacks, and it's always a woman, just talking away, not paying any attention."

Is that any way to get the women's vote?

"The NHL is expanding to Anaheim and Miami," he said on yet another week. "Disney is in Anaheim, and the video guy [Wayne Huizenga, owner of Blockbuster Video and the Miami franchise] is in Miami. O.K., two heavy hitters like that come knocking, you'd better open the door. But TELL ME THIS. WHERE ARE THEY GOING TO GET THE PLAYERS? Would you mind telling me? You already got Ottawa. OTTAWA! Tampa Bay. San Jose, sinking fast. WHERE ARE THEY GOING TO GET THE PLAYERS?"

Did he have to shout?

Educators decry his misuse of English, his fractured syntax, his mangled pronunciations, worrying that he will breed a future generation that says "everythink" and "somethink" and won't have any idea how to make verbs agree with nouns. Hockey executives often paint him as a Neanderthal, out of touch, arguing for violence and against style, trying to defend a frontier that already has been opened wide to the arrival of international talent. Interest groups pick out one outrage after another, the shelves beginning to shake as soon as he speaks, carefully constructed politically correct ideas falling to the ground one after another as if they were so many pieces of cut glass or bone china. Oops, there goes another one.

None of this matters. The Canadian public simply can't get enough of him. He points. He shouts. He sneers. He laughs. His clothes come from the wardrobe of some road company of *Guys and Dolls,* flashy suits and fat-checked sport jackets, custom-tailored, elongated shirt collars starched to the consistency of vinyl siding, riding high above his Adam's apple. His head juts out like a hood ornament in search of a collision. Put on a small screen, he is a larger-than-life terror.

"My wife, Rose, wants me to quit," he says. "She stays home and just worries. She hates the show, hates it. She knows I'm going to say something sometime that's going to send everything up in flames. Probably some of the political stuff. She hates the political stuff. You know, though, she's my best critic. If I go home and she won't talk to me, that's when I know the show has been really good. The best ones are the ones she hates most."

It is a problem. The best things he says are the worst things he says. The danger is everything. The danger is the attraction for the public. What next? What will he do? He always is one F word, one outrage away from extinction. What will he do? He holds on to the stick of dynamite and watches the wick burn shorter and shorter. This is his eleventh season. He cannot let go as the inevitable approaches. *Ka-boom!*

The first time he was paid to be on television was during the 1980 Stanley Cup playoffs. He had been fired following the regular season after a one-year run as coach of the now-defunct Colorado Rockies. His mouth had hastened his dismissal, an acrimonious ending. A year earlier he had resigned as coach of the Boston Bruins, another acrimonious ending, another problem with his mouth. He wasn't really looking for a job, but when the Canadian Broadcasting Company, the producers of *Hockey Night in Canada*, offered $1,500 a shot, plus expenses, he took a chance. Why not? He might as well make some money with his mouth instead of losing it because of his mouth.

He was on his way. His champion was Ralph Mellanby, then the executive producer of *Hockey Night*. Mellanby liked the way Cherry filled out a television screen, the way he talked in blunt terms, naming likes and dislikes, naming names. Cherry was different. He was a guy from the corner stool at the neighborhood bar, from the back room at the firehouse. His bad grammar was a plus, not a minus. His passion was a definite plus. He was people.

"I met him when he was in his last year as coach of the Bruins," Mellanby says. "That was when I first started thinking about him for TV. The Bruins were playing the Canadiens in the semifinals. He was coaching, and I was producing the games. After the second game he came up to me all mad. There had been a fight. Stan Jonathan of Boston had beaten up someone from Montreal. Cherry had seen a tape of the game and saw that we hadn't replayed the fight. He wanted to know if it was because a Bruin had won the fight. I told him it was our practice; we didn't replay fights. The Boston station did, but our policy was not to replay fights, to hold down the violence.

"During the fourth game there was another fight. This was at the Montreal Forum. Mario Tremblay won the fight. He beat up someone from the Bruins. We're doing the game from this little production room at the Forum, and suddenly we can see on one of the monitors that Cherry isn't behind the bench anymore. Where'd he go? This looks like it might be a story. Suddenly he's in the production room. In the middle of a Stanley Cup game. He's talking to me, telling me that we'd better not replay this fight either. He was worried because a Montreal guy had won. I remember thinking, The middle of a game. This guy is interesting."

The truth was that he always had been interesting, always had been flamboyant, wearing the flashy clothes and speaking his mind, but until he coached the Bruins, no one had noticed very much. He was a minor league guy, condemned to the back roads of hockey for most of his life. The logbook of former Montreal general manager Sam Pollock, filled with notations on every player ever under contract to the Canadiens, even listed him that way: "Confirmed minor leaguer."

As a slug-it-out defenseman and high school dropout from Kingston, Ontario, he played sixteen years in the minors. He played in just about all the way stations to the top. His career ran from 1954 to '72. This was the era of the old NHL: six teams, 120 players, everyone else locked into the netherworld at the bottom. The money in the minors was short, maybe $4,500 a year, the conditions awful. Cherry played in Hershey and Springfield and Sherbrooke and Spokane and Jacksonville and a long list of other places. He estimates now that he and Rose moved 53 times in the first 26 years of their marriage. For most of the time, they kept their possessions to a minimum. Unplug the stereo. Unplug the television. Put them in the back seat of the car next to Don's clothes. Gone. Don't mess up the clothes.

He played one game, total, in the NHL. It was a playoff game. He played for Boston, actually getting on the ice for a few minutes against the Canadiens in 1955. He thought then that he would be in the NHL forever. Alas, he separated a shoulder during the off-season, playing baseball, and never was in the big league again. His talent wasn't the greatest — and his mouth never helped.

"I guess I always had something to say," Cherry says. "I remember one time I was with Montreal in its camp. I was dressing with all of those great players. Jean Beliveau. Boom Boom Geoffrion. All of them. All the guys were complaining about the cab ride to the practice rink in Verdun. The club was picking up the cab fare, but the guys had to provide the tips. That was fifty cents each way, a buck round-trip. Everybody was complaining. Toe Blake, the coach, came in the locker room one day. Toe Blake won all those

Stanley Cups. He asks if everything is all right. Not a word. I get up, a nobody. 'Well, Mr. Blake, all the guys have been wondering about the cabs. . . .' I was gone the next day."

He retired after the 1968–69 season, but two years later he started working out again and tried playing for one last season with the Rochester (New York) Americans. Midway through the season an amazing thing happened. Doug Adam, the Americans' coach, resigned. Cherry was named as Adam's replacement. Three years later he was in Boston, coaching Bobby Orr.

Rose remembers thinking, How can we go to Boston? We're confirmed minor leaguers. I'm going to be sitting next to Bobby Orr's wife? I have nothing to wear. Don didn't have that problem. He always had the good wardrobe. Now he finally had a proper place to wear it.

His five years with the Bruins were some of the happiest times of his life. His strategy called for simple, workmanlike hockey: throw the puck into a corner, beat up anyone in your path, get the puck out of the corner, shoot the puck at the goalie as hard as you can. He had a team of big players who could do that. The Big Bad Bruins. He was the ringmaster at their hockey circus but also a star performer. He walked the dasher as if it were a tightrope, pumped on adrenaline, howling at all perceived injustices. He quoted Lord Nelson and Popeye to the press. He treated each game as if he were sending knights of honor off to an icy plain to defend the honor of the poor city of Boston. He had fun.

"I don't think any team had more fun than that one," he says. "I remember one night we're playing L.A., and Hilliard Graves hits Bobby Orr from behind. I went crazy. I grab a guy, Hank Nowak, send him over the boards, screaming, 'Get him, Get him, Get him.' Poor Nowak, he skates to the blue line and turns around. 'Get who?' he asks."

There was the time when Stan Mikita of the Chicago Blackhawks committed some transgression. Cherry threatened to have the Bruins "send him back to Czechoslovakia in a pine box." Reporters wrote that down. Put it in the papers.

There was the time when Bruin winger Rick Middleton arrived at training camp overweight. Cherry said that Middleton "looked like Porky Pig." Reporters wrote that down, too. There was the time . . . there were a lot of times.

By the end, when he was feuding with then general manager Harry Sinden and assistant general manager Tom Johnson, calling them Ben and Willard, after the cinematic rodents; when he was decrying management for using "cheap pucks, no logo on the top, dime-store pucks that a rookie would be ashamed to keep if he scored his first goal in Boston Garden," he had developed a full-blown notoriety. His pet English bullterrier, Blue, subject of so many of his stories, had become famous. Blue was even doing commercials. The Bruins might not have won a Stanley Cup during his time, but they always were in the hunt, finishing first in the division four times.

Then Cherry was off to Colorado to coach the expansion Rockies. He was working with a ghostwriter on his autobiography. "Three years ago I couldn't spell *author*," he said on the first page when the book was published at the end of that expansion season. "Now I are one."

He was ready for television.

"There was controversy about him from the beginning," Mellanby says. "We decided that being a color commentator wasn't the right vehicle. He had too much force. It was too much of him. We came up with *Coach's Corner*. In and out. Don't overwork it. A lot of people didn't think he was right at all, wanted to get rid of him right away. Luckily, I was in a position to have some control. He stayed."

The first shows were scripted and rocky. Cherry soon threw away the scripts and simply talked. Another broadcaster at the anchor desk fed him straight lines and subjects. Cherry talked. Talked? Cherry shouted, ranted, commanded the screen. An interesting statistic evolved: CBC executives noticed that between the first and second periods of *Hockey Night* in French-speaking Quebec, the ratings were going down for the French version of the broadcast while the ratings for the English broadcast were going up. What was happening? People were switching channels. They wanted to hear Cherry.

"I go with him to Montreal," says Ron MacLean, the broadcaster who now shares the CBC anchor desk with Cherry. "This is 1986. I had just started. This is our first trip together. We come out of the airport to catch a cab to the city. The first cab in line is this little

cab. It's one of those Russian cars. A Lada. The starter tells us to
get in. Cherry looks at the cab and goes crazy. What kind of cab is
this? He isn't going to ride in a cab like this . . . this Communist
piece of crap. He is screaming. There's a whole big scene. We get a
new cab. A bigger cab.

"Same trip," MacLean continues. "We're at the studio. Don likes
to arrive late. He likes everything to be spontaneous. I'm doing
some work, and I notice the director is speaking in French. He's
counting down, '*dix, neuf, huit, sept*. . . .' O.K., we're in a place
where the people speak French. Their language. No problem.
Don comes in. The director starts the same thing. Cherry goes
crazy. 'What is this einz-freinz crap? English! This is a program in
English.' The director begins again: 'Ten, nine, eight.' "

The original four and a half minutes have grown. They are still
the foundation — four and a half minutes every Saturday night,
plus other nights during the playoffs — but now Cherry also does
a weekly taped half-hour interview show on The Sports Network,
the Canadian equivalent of ESPN, and a daily three-and-a-half-
minute radio show that is heard on more than one hundred stations. He writes a monthly column, longhand, for twelve newspapers. He writes columns for two hockey magazines. He has done
a commercial for a government-sponsored hockey lottery in three
provinces.

The bars are another success. The set of a bar was used for the
first season of the taped show. And someone suggested that maybe
a real bar with Cherry's name on it would be a good business venture. There now are fifteen franchised Don Cherry's Grapevine
bars across Canada, three more soon to open. Then there are the
videos. For four years he has issued annual highlight videos, featuring KOs and random collisions. There have been more than
half a million copies sold. Then there is the rap video. The rap
video? Cherry did it for charity, wearing a red trench coat, black
fedora and sunglasses, saying, among other things. "Probert, Probert, what a man; we see him, it's slam-bam. Let's go." Cherry
wrote those words about Detroit Red Wing enforcer Bob Probert.
The video was shown on Much Music, the Canadian equivalent of
MTV.

"People always ask me what he's like off the air," MacLean says.
"I tell them, he's no different. What is on the screen is what he is."

His passions are as visible as his neckties. That is his attraction. He is a neon light on a bland landscape. How many men say what they think, what they really think? How many are strong enough, maybe even crazy enough, to disregard possible consequences? How many are able to do it on TV? He is real, a real face from a real world. That is what makes him unique. He says what he thinks.

"I thought I'd do this two or three years, and then I'd fade away," Cherry says. "That's what happens to guys when they leave the game. Two, three years on television, then they're gone. This . . . I don't know. For some reason, people respond to me. I had a letter from the parents of this five-year-old girl who is hearing-impaired. She never had talked, never said a word. Every week, though, she watched the games, watched the show. One week, for some reason, I wasn't on. She turned to her parents and said, 'Where's Don?' The first words out of her mouth. 'Where's Don?' "

The essence of his blustery message is his love of tradition. Why can't things be the way they always were? Where is the honor? What has happened to the virtues of hard work? His is the voice calling for the return of Latin to the Sunday Mass, for the preservation of the neighborhood variety store, for the past against the troublesome future. If hockey is his country's national religion, then he is the keeper of the faith.

His two main crusades are for Canadian kids' keeping jobs in the NHL and for fighting to remain in the game. Keep everything the same. Why change something that has worked for all these years? Every week he talks about the increasing number of foreign players on the league rosters. Who needs them? Every week he talks about the people who would change the game to a wide-open, violence-free exhibition of skating and puck-handling skills. This is supposed to be hockey?

"They talk about all the things the foreign players have brought to the game," Cherry says. "Well, let's see, what have they brought? The helmet. The visor. The dive. Lying there and letting on that you're hurt, the way soccer players always do. I guess, you look at it that way, these people are right. The foreign players have brought a lot to the game."

What is better now? New NHL commercials are being filmed, backed by classical music, to portray "the majesty of the game." Cherry scoffs. What majesty? The game is hits and grunts and hard work. Majesty? How many touchdowns does the NFL show in its commercials in relation to hits and grunts? The game of hockey is a question of valor, of not being afraid. The majesty of the skating and the puck handling is that they are executed in an atmosphere of violence. This should be a man's world, men dealing with men. The new world is a world of parking tickets and regulations and show business.

"It used to be, you'd get cut, you'd finish your shift, no matter what," Cherry says. "A guy like Tim Horton of Toronto, the blood would be coming down his face, and he'd finish his shift. You'd want to get up there to the NHL to be like Tim Horton. Now, you have a guy like Jaromir Jagr of the Penguins. Jaromir Jagr [who not coincidentally is Czech] is everything that's wrong with the NHL. He gets hit, he goes down and stays there. Get up!"

Who are these people who would change the game? Cherry has called McNall, the Kings' owner, Bruce McNutt. He points out again and again that Gil Stein, the league's interim president from June 1992 until Gary Bettman became commissioner on February 1, instituted various rules changes in the past year but "never saw a hockey game until he was thirty-nine years old." Should someone who never saw the game until he was thirty-nine be allowed to tinker with something that has been a part of people's lives from birth? Is that right? These are people "who wouldn't know a hockey player if they slept with Bobby Orr." Bettman is a basketball man, the former senior vice president and general counsel of the NBA. Cherry says he is withholding judgment on Bettman, but is there any doubt about which way he is leaning? He noticed that Bettman recently said he wants to "enhance the puck" so it can be seen better on television. What does that mean?

"They all want to change something," Cherry says. "They think if they change — if they take out the fights, do something different — hockey is going to become big in the U.S. The big TV contract. It just isn't going to happen. Face it, people in the U.S. would rather watch *The Rifleman* than a hockey game. It's almost sad the way our people try to market this game. Let it stand for itself. Let it be what it is."

The league boasts that fighting is down thirty-three percent this year and that the number of foreign players still is rising. As of last Friday a total of 767 players had appeared in at least one NHL game this season. There were 49 players from the former Soviet Union on the list, 29 from the former Czechoslovakia, 24 from Sweden, 9 from Finland and 13 from other countries outside North America. The 508 Canadians and a surging group of 135 Americans — U.S. players are all right with Cherry because they grew up under a similar hockey system — still were in the majority, but the freedom of hockey movement clearly is in full force. There will be more Europeans before there will be fewer.

"Don Cherry is like Humphrey Bogart in the wrong movie," Winnipeg Jet assistant coach Alpo Suhonen, a Finn, says. "He's real, but he doesn't fit in all the different situations he's in."

"He's a total idiot," Calgary Flame defenseman Frank Musil, a Czech, says. "He's a goof. I ignore him. He accuses all European players of not playing physically, but not all Canadian and U.S. players have the same skills as the Europeans. You can't criticize these players for not fighting, because they never did it back home. If they grew up here, maybe they would be more willing to do that. What can you say? He's a goof."

"I think Don is very predictable," says Stein, who is now the NHL's number 2 man. "I think he's fun, but he's always been who he is. I guess he likes goon hockey. Well, the public doesn't, and the league doesn't, and the people running the game don't. The league has a wonderful group of Europeans now, and an international character has already been established. That isn't going to change."

Cherry responds the way he always responds. Directly.

"That's really stupid," he says into the camera. "Isn't that stupid?

"The fans love fighting. The players don't mind. The coaches like the fights. What's the big deal? The players who don't want to fight don't have to fight. Do you ever see Wayne Gretzky in a fight? What's the big deal? I saw Winnipeg and New Jersey the other night, and they were just skating around. Skating around. It was like a tea party, like watching Sweden and Finland play."

Ka-boom! Ka-ka-ka-boom?

Cherry's friends worry about him. Mellanby, now working with the planning committee for the 1996 Olympics in Atlanta, says he is glad he no longer is in charge at *Hockey Night in Canada.* He would not want to be the one who eventually will have to deal with Cherry's future. Cherry is beating on the two themes too much, the foreigners and the fighting. He is moving into politics too often. Something will happen. Cherry has a deal with MacLean. "I don't tell him [MacLean] what I'm going to say. . . . I don't want him to go down with me when it all blows apart." This is all right with MacLean. He has his own career.

"I was thinking about Don the other night," MacLean said recently. "I went to the movies and saw *A Few Good Men*. Every time Jack Nicholson came onto the screen, I thought about Don. Nicholson's character was exactly the same. Rules didn't matter. Everything was the Code. When they were carrying Nicholson out at the end, kicking and fighting, that's how I always thought Don would go out. In a ball of fire."

Cherry mostly just keeps going. He would like to slow down, like to stop, as Rose wants him to do, but says he doesn't know how. He hasn't had a vacation in his adult life. He owns a cottage on Wolf Island in Ontario, but he was there for only two days last year. He owns a boat, but it hasn't been in the water in two years. The craziness keeps him too busy.

He sits in the basement den of his modest house in Mississauga, Ontario, a suburb of Toronto. Except for the money he spends on his clothes, he is not an extravagant man. He does have three Lincoln Mark VIs, but all of them are at least ten years old. He says he likes them because they are like him, "a little ostentatious, a little old, but still going." He says he doesn't do much, outside of the work. He sits here a lot, watching hockey games on the giant-screen TV. He has the satellite dish. He can watch a lot of games.

He is eating a tuna fish sandwich. At his feet is his dog. This is a new dog, Baby Blue. The original Blue, the beloved dog, died four years ago. The original Blue was a trusted warrior. Her blue eyes were supposed to be a defect, but Cherry always thought they were a sign of strength. The original Blue was the toughest, meanest, bravest dog a man could find. Cherry doesn't like this new dog very much. He says, "If an intruder came, Baby Blue probably would try to kiss him to death."

The new dog is trying to lick tuna fish from Cherry's plate. He shoos her away.

"This dog," he says. "We took her to the opening of one of the bars. In Oshawa. We're there a little while, and she's all tired. Falling asleep. We had to leave early, take her home."

"Don," Rose says. "The dog was walking on top of the bar. The people were feeding her drinks. Everyone was giving her beer. The dog was drunk."

"You think?" Cherry says.

Damned dog. Where will it all end? The old Blue wouldn't have gotten drunk. The old Blue could hold her liquor.

As Time Runs Out

FROM SPORTS ILLUSTRATED

HE ENTERED the arena with his wife on his arm and a container of holy water from Lourdes in his black leather bag. His back and hips and knees ached. That was the disease, they told him. His ears rang and his stomach turned and his hands and feet were dead. That, they said, was the cure. Each step he took brought a rattle from his bag. Twenty-four tablets of Advil were usually enough to get him through the day.

He braced himself. No doubt someone would approach him this evening, pump his hand and say it. Strangers were always writing it or saying it to him: "We're pulling for you, Vee. You can do it. Nobody thought you had a prayer against Houston in that national championship game in '83, and you pulled that off, right? Keep fighting, Vee. You can do it again."

No. Not in the same breath. Not in the same sentence, not in the same paragraph, not in the same magazine or book could the two be uttered: a basketball opponent and a cancer eating its way through the marrow and bone of his spine. A basketball opponent and death. *No.* In their fear of dying, people didn't make it larger than it was. They shrank it, they trivialized it. Vee versus metastatic adenocarcinoma. Vee versus Phi Slamma Jamma. Go get 'em, baby. Shock the world, Vee.

No. No correlation, baby, he longed to tell them sometimes. *None.*

The cameras, the reporters, the microphones awaited him inside the Civic Center in Tallahassee. A brand-new season. Iowa State at Florida State, 46-year-old Jimmy Valvano's first game back as an ESPN college basketball analyst since he had learned last summer that he most likely had a year to live.

He tried to quicken his pace. His left leg wouldn't let him. Four or five times each day he dabbed his finger in the holy water and made the sign of the cross on his forehead, his chest, his back, his hips and his knees. Then he poured a little more into his palm and rubbed the water deep into his hands and feet.

When he was coach at North Carolina State, Vee used to pause at this point, just as he entered the arena. Having delivered his pre-game talk, he would leave the locker room on the lower level of Reynolds Coliseum in Raleigh, mount the steps that led to the court, and stand on the top one, still unseen by the crowd. For a moment he would not be an actor at the heart of the drama. He would be a spectator absorbing the immensity, the feeling of it all — the band blaring fight songs, the crowd roaring, the cheerleaders tumbling through the air, the players taking turns gliding to the glass for lay-ups. And he would think, God, I am lucky. What do other people do when they go to work? Go to an office, sit at a desk? I get *this!*

Yes, here was Vee's gift, the gift of the select, to be in the swirl and at the very same moment above it, gazing down, assessing it, drinking in all of its absurdity and wonder. It enabled him to be the funniest man and most fascinating postgame lounge act in sports; it enabled him to survive the scandal at North Carolina State that stripped him of his reputation and his job. Even during his most harrowing moments, part of Vee was always saying, "God, in a year this is going to make a great story." Exaggerate this detail just a little, repeat that one phrase four or five times, and it's going to have 'em howling. Even in the darkness after he had been forced to resign, he looked down at himself lying in bed and thought, Boy, that poor son of a bitch, he's really taking a pounding. But he'll be back. Give him time. He'll be fine.

That was what cancer had stolen. The fear and the pain and the grief swallowed a man, robbed him of detachment, riveted him to *himself.* "I can't do it," he said. "I can't separate from myself anymore."

He tightened his grip on the black leather bag and walked under the lights.

*

It flooded through him when he walked onto a basketball court —
the jump shots with crumpled paper cups he took as a little boy
after every high school game his dad coached, the million three-
man weaves, all the sweat and the squeaks and the passion so
white-hot that twice during his career he had rocketed off the
bench to scream . . . and blacked out . . . and five or six times every
season the backside of his suit pants had gone *rrr-iii-p!* He wore
Wolfpack red underwear just in case, but it didn't really matter. A
guy could walk around in his underwear at home; Vee was at
home. Maybe here, for two hours tonight, he could forget.

He looked up and saw a man striding toward him. It was the
Florida State coach, Pat Kennedy, who had been Valvano's assistant at Iona College. Kennedy leaned toward Vee's ear and opened
his mouth to speak. Those who had been in a bar at 1 A.M. when
Vee was making people laugh so hard that they cried, those who
had seen him grab the deejay's microphone at 2 A.M. and climb on
a chair to sing Sinatra, those whose hotel doors he had rapped on
at 3:30 A.M. to talk about life and whose lampshades he had
dented with his head when their eyelids sagged ("Had to do something to wake you up! You weren't listening!") . . . they could not
fathom that this was happening to him. Vee was a man with an
electric cable crackling through his body; he might walk a couple
of dozen laps around an arena after a big win to let off a little hiss,
or wander the streets of a city until dawn after a loss. He was the
kind of guy you wanted to cook dinner for or show your new house
to, because that would make it the all-time greatest dinner, the all-
time best house, terrific, absolutely *terrific* — and Vee *meant* it. And
now Kennedy's mouth was opening just a few inches from Vee's
ear, and there were a thousand thoughts and feelings scratching at
each other to get out — "Every day with you was an exciting day.
Every day you had ten new ideas. Every day you left me with a smile
on my face, saying, 'Boy, that Valvano's something else.' And you
left me thinking I could do more with my life than I'd ever
thought before. Certain people give life to other people. You did
that for me" — but no words would come out of Kennedy's
mouth. Instead he just kissed Vee.

This was what Valvano missed most after his coaching career
ended in April 1990. Nobody kissed a TV analyst, nobody hugged

him, nobody cried on his shoulder. Vee used to astonish the directors who hired him to give those dime-a-dozen, $50-a-pop guest speeches at their summer basketball camps in the Poconos back in the seventies. The directors would look back as they strolled to their offices after introducing him, and they would see a guy in a floppy Beatle haircut pulling a white rat — a *real* white rat, gutted and stuffed by a taxidermist and mounted on a skateboard — toward the microphone and roaring to the kids, "What kind of a greeting is *that?* Look how you're sitting! I come all the way here and what do I get? A coupla hundred crotch shots? I'm supposed to stand up here and give a good speech staring at a coupla hundred sets of jewels? Whadda we have here, a bunch of *big-timers?* I want *rats!* Let's try it again. You only get out of life what you demand! I'm gonna come to the microphone all over again, and this time I want a standing O, and once I get it you can bet I'm going to give you the best damn speech I possibly can!" The camp directors would look back again and see a couple of hundred kids on their feet, cheering wildly. Look back a few minutes later and see them crying. Look again and see them carrying Valvano from basket to basket to cut down the nets and chanting, "VEE! VEE! VEE!" And for the rest of those camps, the directors and counselors would have to peer in every direction each time they opened a door or walked down a path, because Vee had convinced a few hundred kids to leap from behind walls and bushes in front of them, to sacrifice their bodies like True Rats, to shuffle in front of the big-timers and *take the charge!*

He didn't recruit kids to his college program; he swept them there. He walked into a prospect's home, and fifteen minutes later he had rearranged the living room furniture to demonstrate a defense, had Mom overplaying the easy chair, Dad on the lamp, Junior and his sister trapping the coffee table. Where the hell else was the kid going to go to school? In the thirty games Vee coached each season, the hundred speeches he eventually gave each year, the objective was the same: to make people leap, make them laugh, make them cry, make them dream, to *move* people. "Alive!" he would say. "That's what makes me feel *alive!*"

And then one day last spring he was playing golf on a course in the hills overlooking the Mediterranean in the north of Spain. He had weathered the scandal at N.C. State. He had won an ACE for excellence in cable-television sports analysis. He had turned down an offer to coach at Wichita State and signed contract extensions with ABC and ESPN. He had time, finally, for long dinners with his wife, for poetry readings and movies with his 12-, 20- and 23-year-old daughters. He had an assignment to do sideline commentary on a World League football game in Barcelona; he had a tee time on the course just north of the city. "How beautiful it was that day," he would remember. "How happy I was. . . ." And then he felt an ache in his testicles. That's how death comes. A pang in the crotch when a man's standing in the sun gazing across the green hills and the bluest goddam sea in the world, deciding between a three-wood and an iron.

He laughed at all the inevitable aching-testicle jokes; the doctor was almost sure it was just an infection or perhaps referred pain from the lower backache Vee had been feeling. He was still laughing while in the MRI tube last June at Duke University Hospital, joking through the intercom with the nurses about the heavy-metal music they were pumping into his headphones as they scanned his spine to see if he had damaged a disk, when the radiologist glanced at the image appearing on his screen, and suddenly the laughter stopped and the nurses fell silent. And the dread, the sick dread began to spread through his stomach as the radiologist quietly said, "Come with me, Coach." And then: "Let me show you a picture of a healthy spine, Coach. . . . Now look at yours."

The vertebrae in his were black where the others were white. And the dread went up Vee's chest, wrapped around his ribs and his throat, but he squeezed out another joke: "You forgot to use the flash."

No laughter. "Coach, this is just how we see it in the textbook. . . . Coach, I'm ninety percent sure this is cancer."

The world spun, and he asked a dozen questions that couldn't be answered yet, but the look on the radiologist's face said this was bad, very bad. Vee walked into the waiting room and told his wife, Pam, and they held each other and cried and drove home, where his oldest daughter, Nicole, was helping his middle daughter, Jamie, with a Music 100 class project. They were banging on a piano key, beating a wooden spoon against a pot, a pencil against a wine bottle and two candlesticks against each other when the door opened and their dad said, "I've got cancer. I'm going to die. . . . I don't want to die. . . . I'm sorry. . . . I'm *sorry.*"

It was still incomprehensible five months later. His sockets were a little deeper, his olive skin wrapped a little more tightly around his skull, but the thirty-five pounds he had lost made his body seem fit, trim. His hair, against all medical logic, had survived massive chemotherapy. He lived in a land where people vanished when they became terminally ill. Most people who saw him walking through airports, stepping in front of cameras and cracking jokes about his plummeting weight ("Hey, I'm the quickest analyst in the country now — there's not an announcer who can go around me!") assumed his cancer was in remission. It was not. "How you doin', Coach?" they would call.

What could he say? "Hangin' in there," he usually replied. "Hangin' in there."

The crowd at the Civic Center caught sight of him now. The Florida State band rose to its feet, waved a sign — Welcome Back, Baby! — and chanted, "JIMMY VEE! JIMMY VEE! JIMMY VEE! . . ."

It was a Friday night. On Monday morning, as he did every two weeks, he would walk into the basement of the oncology center at Duke and sit with a hundred people who stared into the nothingness, waiting hours for their turns. His name would be called and a nurse would say, "Veins or port?" and he would say, "Port," which meant that his veins had collapsed from being pierced by so many needles, and that the four vials the doctors needed today would have to be drawn from the lump over his left breast, where a plastic access valve had been surgically inserted. He would remove his shirt, and a nurse would swab the lump with disinfectant and squirt it with ethyl chloride to numb it, flush out the tube inserted inside his superior vena cava with saline solution, take his blood and send him back to the waiting room while the lab ran tests on the blood. He would wait another forty-five minutes, murmuring something now and then to Pam or a word of encouragement to nearby patients; then he would go to the office of a doctor who tried to be cheerful but who saw forty cancer patients a day; and then he would be sent to the third floor to lie down again and have Velban, a cell killer, pushed into his veins through the port in the hope that it would kill as many cancer cells as healthy cells. Finally he would limp out clutching Pam for support, his body bent as if beaten with a bat, and you could count on it, somebody would ask him for his autograph, and you could count on it, he would smile wanly and say, "Sure."

". . . JIMMY VEE! JIMMY VEE! JIMMY VEE!" He put the headphones on and turned the sound up so he could hear the producer's cues over the ringing that was always in his ears now, and then he stepped onto the court to tape an introduction to the game. He could feel it now, surging up through the hardwood, into his deadened feet — the thump, thump, thump of basketballs as the two teams pounded through lay-up drills. Everything had a beat, a lovely chaos with an old, familiar rhythm. The players were grinning and slapping five with him, the fans were waving paper and pens at him, the band was blaring the theme song from *Rocky,* the cheerleaders were tumbling through the air, and Vee's right foot was tapping. In one breath he looked into the ESPN camera and told the audience how Iowa State would have to use its speed and *stick the jump shot* to win, whereas Florida State would have to *pound it inside.* In the next breath he turned to the boom mike and the interviewer on his right to answer her question about the cancer consuming his spine, and with the horn section and the backflips and the crowd's roar all around, he fell into that same easy metaphor and delivered it in that same hoarse, hyped voice. "I'm not happy to be *here.* I'm just happy to *be!* Even as we speak the good cells are going after the bad cells. You gotta encourage 'em. Good cells. . . . *Go get 'em!* That's what's going on right now! . . . *It's hoops time! Let's play some hoops!*"

"I'm helpless! I make no decisions! I have no control! I'm totally at the mercy of the disease and the treatment! I'm not a dad! I'm not a husband! I'm a *freak!* I can't do anything! I just lie there and they stick needles into this lump in my chest and pour poison in my body, and I don't believe in it. I'm a *freak!*"

He couldn't cry *that* into a microphone to the million and a half people listening at home and watching in bars, but it was right there, at the back of his tongue, at the base of his brain, welling up and wanting to spill. It did, sometimes. There was no reason to hide it, no reason anymore to hide anything. There were days, now and then, that he passed huddled in his bathrobe in front of the television, flinching from the pain, curling up in sorrow and wondering how in God's name he would summon the strength again to make the quip that would put everyone around him at ease, to tell the world in that hoarse, hyped voice, *You gotta get it into the middle, it's the only way to beat a trap defense!* as if there were a hundred thousand more tomorrows. There were days when Jamie, who had taken off her junior year at N.C. State to help him through this horror, would shout, "Get up! Go talk to your doctor! Go see a priest! Don't just lie there! You've given up! Get up! Yell at somebody! Yell at *me!*"

"Can a doctor or a priest take the cancer out of my body?" he would ask.

"I don't know! I just want you to *do* something! Yell, fight, punch! Even if it's all for nothing. So we can say, 'There's *Dad.*'"

The old Dad, The Charge of the Light Brigade Dad, son of a man who had a booming voice and an ear-to-ear grin and a yellow-pad list of things that Vee's team needed to get right to work on ... but didn't they understand? How could Vee allow himself to hope? If Vee liked a movie, he saw it five times. If Vee liked a song, he transcribed every word, memorized it, sang it twenty times a day and talked his kids into singing it with him a half dozen more times on the way to the beach. Vee couldn't throw half or three quarters of his heart into anything; he had to throw it all. Didn't they know how dangerous it was for a man like him to throw all of his heart into a hope as slender as this? Vee was a dreamer. Vee had no life insurance. A man whose lows were as low as his highs were high couldn't hope too hard, couldn't lean too far, because the next downturn in his condition or the next darting away of his doctor's eyes could send him whirling down a shaft from which he might never escape.

Besides, where were the hooks to hang his hopes on? Doctors couldn't even find the origin of his cancer — they were guessing the lungs, even though he had never smoked more than an occasional cigar. With his kind of cancer, there were no tumors to X-ray, no reliable way to chart the course of the disease. "You'll know when it's getting worse," they told him. "You'll know by the pain." So he would wake up each morning and ask himself the terrifying question: Is there more pain?

Get up! Yell! Fight! Punch! He tried. He refused to put on the gown when he checked into the hospital every sixth week for massive doses of chemotherapy. He refused to take the prescription pain pills. He talked to God out loud. He marched into the salon and ordered them to buzz off all of his hair — *he* would take it off, not the chemotherapy. The same way, in the last minute of a tie game when the other team had the ball, he flouted convention and ordered his players to foul and risk handing the opponents the game-winning free throw — *Vee* wanted the rock at the end, *Vee* wanted the last shot. He refused to sit there, cringing on defense, waiting for fate to happen to him.

But the joke was on him. The hair grew right back and never fell out. Every tactic in this new war came back at him turned upside down. Every stoking of his fever to live increased his horror of death. And he would remember that astonishing flood of emotional letters that dying people had written to him after N.C. State had shocked Houston nine years earlier, people thanking *him* for giving them a reason not to give up, and he would sit there, shaking his head. Could he explain all that during the next time-out? Could he let everyone know that he only had to see his three daughters walk in the house in order to cry now, that a TV commercial showing a dad accepting a bowl of cereal from his little girl, hugging her and saying, "I must be pretty special for you to bring me bran flakes," brings tears to his eyes because they're just so goddam happy and lucky?

Iowa State guard Justus Thigpen's jump shot was descending a good foot in front of the rim, a fine opportunity for Vee to say, as he had with a slow, stupefied shake of his head two days earlier at home, "*Justus Thigpen!* Can you believe it? Who knows how much time I have left, and I've been sitting here poring over *Justus Thigpen's stats* in the Iowa State basketball brochure. I'm sitting here reading, and I quote, that 'Justus Thigpen was twice selected Big Eight Player of the Week' and that 'he scored 11 points at Kansas and 17 points in ISU's overtime win on ESPN versus Colorado.' *What the hell am I doing?* The triviality of it just clobbers me. You get this sick and you say to yourself, 'Sports means nothing,' and that feels terrible. God, I devoted my whole *life* to it."

He might say *that* to a million and a half people. He *could* say that. He was a man who converted feelings to thoughts and thoughts to words with stunning ease — solid to liquid, liquid to gas; it was beautiful and terrible, both. Sometimes he would look at his daughters or his wife and say, "God . . . I'm going to miss you," and it would rip their hearts in half. What were the rules after you had dragged out of the doctor the fact that only a few patients with metastatic adenocarcinoma diagnosed in its late stages, like Vee's, lived more than two years, and most were gone within a year? Did you tell the people you loved all the things that were banging at the walls of your heart, or did you keep them locked inside to save your family the agony of hearing them? Nobody taught you how to do this; what were the rules?

Maybe it was time now for the TV camera to focus on his hands, the left one balled and the right one wrapped around it, desperately trying to squeeze some feeling into it as Bob Sura zinged in a twenty-one-footer and Florida State's lead swelled to 50–31. Perhaps Vee should tell all the viewers and listeners, even if it wasn't what they had tuned in to hear: "I'm being deprived of my senses. I can hardly taste food anymore. I can't hear. I can't feel. My wife will have to button my shirt soon because I won't be able to feel the buttons between my fingers. It's got my feet and my hands and my ears . . . but it doesn't have my mind and my heart and my soul. And it's not *going* to. I'm going to fight this as long as I can. I'm going to keep doing what I love.

"I'm going to have to miss some games because of chemotherapy. I don't think you're going to see John Saunders in the studio saying, '*Live! From room 401 at Duke University Hospital, it's Jimmy Valvano!*' because I'm going to be at the sink throwing up. I don't want to be wheeled to the microphone to do games, but I *will.* I'll keep doing this until my mouth doesn't work, until my brain doesn't function."

Maybe he should tell them what he does some days at home in Cary, North Carolina, how he removes his shoes and walks barefoot in the grass. Just to feel. How he puts his hands around the trunks of the pine trees and closes his eyes. Just to *feel.*

Here was a story he could tell. Goddam it, the Seminoles were up by twenty-one at halftime, let him tell it. It was the one about a twenty-three-year-old coach at Johns Hopkins University who was on a bus ride home from Gettysburg, Pennsylvania, with his players, exuberant over his squad's 3–0 start. A twenty-three-year-old

coach who had plotted his life on an index card: five years, high
school head coach. Five years, small-college head coach. Five years,
university assistant coach. Five years, small-university head coach.
Ten years, big-time university head coach. A twenty-three-year-old
who didn't know he was going to compress the first twenty years of
the plan into thirteen, who didn't realize he was going to have his
dream, live his Pocono camp speech, cut the NCAA title nets at
thirty-seven . . . who didn't know his life might already be half over.
His players called him to the back of the bus. "Why is winning so
important to you?" they asked. "We've never seen anything like it.
You're irrational."

"Because the final score defines you," he said. "You lose; ergo,
you're a loser. You win; ergo, you're a winner."

"No," the players insisted. "The participation is what matters,
the constancy of effort. Trying your very best, regardless of
whether you win or lose — that's what defines you."

It took twenty-three more years of living. It took a rampage in
his office at home after a 39–36 N.C. State loss to Virginia in 1982,
lamp busted, chairs toppled, papers and books shoved everywhere.
It took charging through a locker room door so hard that it
knocked out the team doctor. It took the pre-game talk of his life
and the coaching jewel of his career, the 1983 NCAA championship upset that helped rocket the Final Four onto the level of
the World Series and the Super Bowl. It took a couple of dozen
Christmases when his wife had to buy every gift and decorate every
tree. It took bolting up from the mattress three or four times a
night with his T-shirt soaked with sweat and his teeth rattling from
the fever chills of chemotherapy and the terror of seeing himself
die again and again in his dreams — yes, mostly it took *that* to
know it in his gut, to say it: "They were right. The kids at Johns
Hopkins were *right*. It's effort, not result. It's *trying*. God, what a
great human being I could've been if I'd had this awareness back
then. But how can you tell that to any coach who has a couple kids
and a mortgage and 15,000 people in the stands who judge him
only by wins and losses? Do you know, that 39–36 loss to Virginia
was ten years ago, but I could never let go of that game until I got
sick. Now it doesn't bother me at all.

"But I can't sit here and swear I'd do everything differently. I
wouldn't trade those years. Nobody had more fun than me. How

many people do you know who've had their dream come true? You're looking at one. That was my creative period, my *run,* my burst of energy. . . ." Start his own company, JTV Enterprises? *I can do that.* Write his own newspaper column, his own championship-season book? *I can do that.* Broadcast his own daily radio commentary, his own weekly call-in radio program and local TV show in Raleigh? *I can do that.* Sell the advertising time for his own radio and TV shows? *I can do that.* Commission an artist to paint an NCAA championship-game picture each year and sell the prints to boosters of the school that wins? *I can do that.* Commission a sculptor to produce life-size figures of the greats of sport for teams to showcase outside their stadiums? *I can do that.* Write a cookbook? (He didn't know where the plastic bags for the kitchen trash can were.) *I can do that.* Make 10 Nike speeches, 20 alumni-club speeches, 25 to 50 speeches on the national lecture circuit and a dozen charity speeches a year? *I can do that.* Design and market individualized robes to sports teams that have female journalists in their locker rooms? *I can do that.* Appear on the Carson show, the Letterman show? *I can do that.* Host his own sports talk show on ESPN? *I can do that.* Take on the athletic director's job at N.C. State as well as coach basketball? Are you sure, Vee? *I can do that.*

This was not for glory, not for money. There was none of either in the AD's job, for God's sake. It came from a deeper, wider hunger, an existential tapeworm, a lust to live all the lives he could've lived, would've lived, should've lived, if it weren't for the fact that he had only one. A shake of the fist at Death long before it came knocking, a defiance of the worms.

Pam Valvano: "Girls! Dad's in the living room!"

Daughter: "Which channel?"

Vee: "Live! In person! Downstairs! I'm actually here!"

Home at 1 A.M. Wide-eyed in bed at two, mind still grinding, neurons suspicious, even back then, of sleep. "*Inside! Get the ball inside!*" A daughter standing in the hall in her pajamas, hearing him cry it out in his sleep. Up at 5 A.M. for the two meetings before the breakfast meeting. Blowing out of his campus office at 4 P.M. to catch a plane. Day after day, year after year. "A maniac," he said. "I was an absolute maniac, a terrible husband and father. Everybody in the stands went, 'Awwwwwww, isn't that cute?' when my little girl ran across the court in a cheerleader's outfit and hugged me before every home game, but for 23 years, *I wasn't home.* I figured I'd have 20 years in the big time, who knows, maybe win three national titles, then pack it in at 53 or 54, walk into the house one day, put on a sweater and announce: '*Here I am! Ozzie Nelson's here! I'm yours!*' I always saw myself as becoming the all-time great grandfather. Leave the kids with me? No problem. Crapped his pants? Fine, I'll change him. Vomited? Wonderful, I'll clean him up. I was going to make it up to them, all the time I'd been away." His eyes welled. "God. . . . It sounds so silly now. . . .

"But I didn't feel guilt about it then. My thinking always was, I would make a life so exciting that my wife and kids would be thrilled just to be a part of it. But I remember one Father's Day when I happened to be home, and nobody had planned anything, nobody even mentioned it. How could they have planned anything? I'd probably never been home on Father's Day before. I might've been in Atlanta giving a Father's Day speech or in Chicago receiving a Father of the Year award, but you can bet I wasn't at home on Father's Day. Finally I asked them what we were going to do, and my daughter Jamie said, 'Dad, we spent all our lives being part of your life. When are you going to be part of *ours?*' It hit me like a punch in the stomach.

"But it went on and on, that insatiable desire to conquer the world. I was an arrogant son of a bitch. But it wasn't just arrogance. I kept thinking of those lines from *The Love Song of J. Alfred Prufrock:*

> *And indeed there will be time*
> *To wonder, "Do I dare?" and, "Do I dare?"*
> *Time to turn back and descend the stair,*
> *With a bald spot in the middle of my hair —*
> *(They will say: 'How his hair is growing thin!')*

"I *wanted* to dare. I wasn't afraid to show my bald spot, my vulnerability, by trying new things. I'd go to bed after watching TV on a Saturday night, and my mind would be saying, '*I* should be the host on *Saturday Night Live.* I can do that.' I look back now and I see the truth in the Icarus myth. You know the story about the boy who's so proud of his wings that he flies too close to the sun, and it melts the wax and he falls and dies? What enables us to achieve our greatness contains the seeds of our destruction.

"Every season I had bronchitis, bad colds; twice I had pneumonia. The night we won the NCAA, I was sick as a dog. I was the Mycin Man all season — erythromycin, clindamycin. I wouldn't rest. I'd just pop the antibiotics and keep going. Who knows? Maybe I put my body in a position to get this. I've been reading books about cancer. They say it often occurs if your immune system is lowered, and then you have a trauma. . . ."

Yes, a trauma. To hell with that basketball game; it was going to end just as it began, a Florida State blowout. Here was a man who lay awake every midnight, chewing on mortality — let him talk. Let him wonder out loud if a book published in 1989, and the fifteen months of investigations and media barrage it set off, was his bullet . . . and then try *not* to wonder, try to shut that midnight whisper down and ignore the connection between cancer and personal trauma, because otherwise he would have to blame a few people — a writer, a local managing editor — for this nightmare he was living, and he would have to hate, and hatred and blame were the worst detours a man could take when he was locked in mortal combat to live. "I can't do that," Vee would say. "I've got to fill these days I have left with love and laughter and forgiveness. But I *wonder*. . . ."

January 7, 1989, the first headlines. A book entitled *Personal Fouls*, by Peter Golenbock, was about to appear, accusing Valvano and his staff of fixing grades, hiding drug-test results from authorities, diverting millions of dollars from the alumni club to the players and paying the players off with automobiles. One publishing house rejected the book; another one bought it, and the hammer blows began in earnest, usually starting with the Raleigh *News and Observer* and then ringing throughout the country, banging at the core of who Vee was. He called press conferences, he dug up graduation statistics, he demanded hearings by the North Carolina State Board of Trustees. But the Icarus arc was now at work — his glibness becoming proof, to his critics, of his guile; his gargantuan appetite for life proof of his greed.

The NCAA investigation lasted eight months. In the end the investigators found no million-dollar diversions, no automobiles, no grade-fixing, no hidden drug tests. They found two punishable violations — players had sold complimentary tickets and complimentary sneakers — and the NCAA placed N.C. State on two years'

probation, declaring it ineligible for the 1990 NCAA tournament.
Dave Didion, the lead investigator, wrote Valvano a letter. "I
wanted to let him know that he had cooperated with me more
than any coach I had ever worked with," said Didion, "and that not
everyone thought he was evil. I wanted to let him know that if I
had a son who was a prospect, I would be proud to have him play
for Jim Valvano. He wasn't the smart-ass egomaniac I'd antici-
pated. Yes, the graduation rate of his players was not good . . . but
no one cared to look at the overall graduation rate at N.C. State.
Yes, he probably shouldn't have recruited some of the kids he did.
But if he hadn't, he'd have ended up playing against them and getting his brains beaten out by them, because everybody else wanted
those *same* kids."

Then came the final blow: allegations of point-shaving a few
years earlier that involved former N.C. State forward Charles
Shackleford. No one believed Valvano had knowledge of it, and
nothing would ever be proved, but the hammering had to stop. In
April 1990 he was forced to resign. "The pain of that — having
my mother, my brothers, my wife, my children reading the things
that were written about me," he said. "I felt physical *pain*. There
were things I should've done differently, but I knew I hadn't done
anything *wrong*. The insinuation that I didn't care about the
kids. . . . I *hated* that. To be lumped with coaches who cared only
about winning and nothing about education. . . . I *hated* that. I ma-
jored in English, not P.E. I had two daughters on the dean's list. All
but perhaps two of my players at Johns Hopkins, Bucknell and
Iona graduated. I didn't change. I'll take responsibility, but that's
different from blame. I didn't admit the kids to N.C. State who
didn't graduate — our admissions office did. In hindsight it's easy
to say who shouldn't have been recruited, but who knew before-
hand? Sometimes kids from worse backgrounds, with worse high
school grades, did better than kids from decent homes, with decent grades.

"Maybe I trusted the kids too much. The school wanted me to
force education down their throats, and I wouldn't do it. They
wanted me to say, 'You don't go to class, you don't play. I take away
ball.' What does that tell a kid? That *ball* is more important than
education! My approach was, If you don't study, you pay the consequences. You flunk out. I tried to excite them about learning. I

had Dereck Whittenburg read *King Lear* and then go to the chalk-board and do a pre-game talk on it. I wasn't one of those coaches telling them to learn but never reading a book myself. I *lived* it. They saw me reading Shakespeare on buses. They saw me trying things outside of sports all the time.

"I guess I was unrealistic to think I could change kids. I should've said to them, 'I love you, but I don't trust you yet. You have to do this and this your first two years here, and *then* I'll trust you.' And there's no way around it — I didn't have as much time to give them after I became athletic director. I tried to do too much. They couldn't just walk into my office at any time of the day, like before, and talk. It was a little less each year, especially for the 13th, 14th, 15th players. But each time, the change was impercep-tible to me. It happens without your realizing it.

"And now I'm fighting to live, and the irony of having people think of me as a man who cared only about winning and athlet-ics . . . it overwhelms me. I'm looking for a reason to hope, a reason to *live,* and the only thing that helps me do that is my education, my *mind.* If I survive this, or even if I just wage this battle well, it will be because of what I grasped from reading, from understand-ing the world and my place in it, from learning to ask the right questions and to grasp all the alternative treatments for this dis-ease — from *academia,* not from athletics. People think a sports background helps you fight death. Are you kidding? Athletes and coaches are taught that they're special. You're *nobody* when you're a cancer patient. You're *nobody.*

"I want to help every cancer patient I can now. For some reason, people look to me for hope. I'm feeling half dead, and they're coming up to me in the hospital for *hope.* I don't know if I can han-dle that, but it's the only conceivable good that can come out of this. If the Clinton Administration wants someone to raise money for cancer research, I'm here. If I survive, I'm going to work with cancer patients one-on-one and help them find a way to hang on, like so many people are trying to do for me. *Half a million people* die of cancer every year in America, one out of every four of us will get it, and there's no moral outrage; we *accept* it. I'm all for AIDS funding and research, but how can the government give ten times as much per AIDS patient as per cancer patient? Bar-bra Streisand isn't singing for cancer, Elizabeth Taylor isn't holding a celebrity bash for cancer, and yet every time I go into that cancer building at Duke, it's a packed house! If it means more doctors, more space, more money, we've *got* to get it, because millions of people are going to find out that this is one hell of a way to go."

The basketball game was nearly over now. Valvano's mind and tongue were still flying, the jokes still crackling, but a deep fatigue was coming over his body. He looked across the court and saw his wife speaking to a woman beside her, saw his wife smile. And he thought: It's so good to see her smile, but how many times have I seen her crying lately? What's going to happen to her? Will she be all right? He would take a deep swallow of air the next day as he remembered that moment, that look across the court at her as the coaches shouted and the players panted and the fans roared. "You see, I had it all planned for our twenty-fifth anniversary, last August 6. I was going to give her three gifts: the deed to four acres where she could build her dream house, a big diamond ring, and a nice trip, just the two of us on a beach. She'd lift me up when she heard it and I'd cut the nets, a standing O. . . . *Goddam.* What did she get instead? A sick husband in a hospital bed getting Mitomycin, Cisplatin, and Velban dripped into him. She got to clean me up when I vomited. *That's* love. I'd told her, 'We're going to get old together, Pam.' Probably the nicest thing I'd ever said to her. 'We're going to get old together.'. . . *Goddam.* . . . *Goddam.*"

The game ended, and then he did something he had never done before. He thanked the hundred fans who had gathered to wish him well, said no to the coaches who asked if he would like to go out . . . and went back to his hotel room with his wife. She fell asleep, and he lay there at 1 A.M., alone, hungry for food and wine, hungry for conversation he was missing, and the laughter. He ordered a pizza, stared at the TV, and cried.

He jumped from his seat one day not long ago. The backside of his pants didn't rip — they weren't that tight anymore. A paragraph had jumped into his eyes from a book he was reading. "That is why athletics are important," wrote a British sports writer named Brian Glanville. "They demonstrate the scope of human possibility, which is unlimited. The inconceivable is conceived, and then it is accomplished."

"That's *it!*" cried Vee. "*That's* why we strive! That's the value of sports! All those games, they mean nothing — and they mean *everything!*" His fist clenched. He hadn't poured himself into emptiness for twenty-three years, he hadn't devoured Justus Thigpen's stats for nothing, he hadn't. The people who compared his upset of Houston to his fight against cancer were right!

"It's what I've got to do to stay alive," he said. "I've got to find the unlimited scope of human possibility within myself. I've got to conceive the inconceivable — then accomplish it! My mom's *convinced* I'm going to get better. My mom's always right!"

In early December, when the pain grew so fierce he had to call off a weekend of studio work for ESPN, he had a local shop print up one thousand small cards. He had hundreds of people across the country calling him, writing him, encouraging him, but he needed more. VICTORIES it said on each card. "Valvano's Incredible Cancer Team of Really Important Extraordinary Stars."

"See?" he said. "I'm going to make a *team.* I'm going to give a card to everyone I meet as I go around the country doing games. On the back of each card are the requirements of my players. One, they have to say, 'Jimmy Vee, you will make it.' Two, they have to say it out loud — it's important to verbalize. They can call my office number and, if I'm not there, leave a message on my answering machine: '*Jimmy, don't give up!*' And three, they have to do something to improve their own health, whether it's mental, spiritual or physical.

"My own team — everybody can join. This is it, baby, my ultimate pre-game talk. I *need* this one, *gotta* have it. Gotta have so many people calling my answering machine each day that they can't get through. Gotta have people all over the country opening their windows and shouting it out: 'JIMMY VEEEEEE! DON'T GIVE UP!' "

JOHN ED BRADLEY

Get a Load of Me!

FROM SPORTS ILLUSTRATED

YET ANOTHER fine yellow noon on Marco Island, Florida, and, miracle of miracles, Buster Douglas is already out of bed.

He's wearing what he always seems to wear these days: white canvas boating shoes, loose-fitting gym trunks, a faded striped shirt that never stays tucked in. And he's looking big. Buster's looking like a helium balloon after the gas has been left on too long. About 320 pounds of big, though you'd be hard-pressed to get him to admit that. "I never get on a scale now," he says. "I really don't know what I weigh. I don't care."

At his house by the sea, Buster squeezes into his Porsche 930S Turbo, a convertible, and starts north for Naples, about 16 miles away. Buster has his day planned. First, the tires beneath him need to be rotated. Second, he'll stop by his favorite deli and get something to eat, maybe a submarine, maybe soup. Third . . . well, there really isn't a third, not that he can remember.

Buster paid $125,000 for the car, and, a few restored clunkers notwithstanding, it's easily the sweetest thing on the road. "Do you take American Express?" he asked the car salesman that day in Beverly Hills, California, then promptly handed over a credit card. The Porsche is black except for the places on the doors where Buster had this painted, in purple script: JOKER. You can't miss him as he comes thundering down U.S. 41, the former heavyweight champion of the world hauling ass with the top down, his young dreadlocks looking like the prickly hide of a pineapple. On the stereo the rocker Prince sings in liquid falsetto, providing

Buster with the perfect theme music to guide him through yet another day without much to do.

"Wait'll they get a load of me," Buster says as he weaves through traffic. "Wait'll they get a load of . . . me!"

That's a line from the movie *Batman*. It's something Jack Nicholson said after a mishap — a vat of toxic waste transformed him into a diabolical fiend. Buster's always quoting from the pictures now that at thirty-three he has retired from the fight game and movies have become so important to him. Day in and day out he watches them on his big-screen Mitsubishi, imagining himself a movie star.

Along with *Batman*, Buster likes to quote from *Raging Bull*, the film about boxer Jake La Motta. Buster imitates Robert De Niro imitating Jake La Motta imitating Marlon Brando in another movie, *On the Waterfront*. It gets pretty confusing sometimes. "I coulda been a contender," Buster says. And you don't laugh because it seems to mean something, Buster speaking that line. Also, Buster is giving it his best. His eyebrows dance like snails, and his mouth is a bitter scowl.

By his own estimate Buster has seen *Raging Bull* ten times. He especially likes the scene in which De Niro deposits a bucket of ice down his pants to cool his stubborn passion. Buster's been in that situation himself, having a woman in his room before a big fight and wanting to *be* with her, as they say. She's lying there with a come-hither look on her face, pleading, "Hey, Buzz, come on, baby. Come back to bed." In the movies, as in real life, the fighter does what he shouldn't. Then a few hours later some doctor's waving a penlight in his face, asking how many fingers he's holding up or whether the boxer remembers his name.

For those who have forgotten, James Buster Douglas is the man who beat Mike Tyson in February 1990 — the only person on this planet, in fact, ever to have beaten Tyson as a professional. It happened in Tokyo, and people who were there said it resembled the kicker in another boxing film, Sylvester Stallone's *Rocky*.

There was the undefeated Tyson and his aura of invincibility, and there was Buster Douglas of Columbus, Ohio, and his hard-luck tale. Buster's mother, Lula Pearl, had died just a few weeks earlier; he and his wife, Bertha, were on the outs; and he was battling what felt like the flu. Much of Las Vegas had turned its back

on the bout, the odds against an upset being so high. Buster's
name might've been Bubba, for all anyone cared.

From the outset Buster controlled the fight, keeping Tyson off
balance with practically every piece of action he'd ever learned in
the gym. Buster was well ahead when, in the eighth, Tyson unloaded a nasty right uppercut and dropped him to the canvas. A
long count ensued — a long, long count — but Buster managed
to rise to his feet and continue. He continued to the tenth, when
he himself unloaded on Tyson and knocked him flat on his back.
Buster retreated to a neutral corner, doubting that Tyson would
stay down for long. But then Buster found his arms being lifted up
over his head, saw his friends storming the ring, heard the roar of
the crowd rising to a hysterical pitch.

JUST LIKE IN THE MOVIES, the *Time* magazine headline read.

It was a short reign, Buster's. Having earned his fifteen minutes
of fame, he was widely feted and given the key to at least one city,
and he made the circuit of late-night TV talk shows. He flew
around in a private jet. In Vegas he stayed in a penthouse at the
Mirage and watched incredulously as a man-made volcano erupted
every fifteen minutes or so just outside his window. He met movie
stars and was surprised by how short, how puny most of them were.
And he trained little and indulged much. By fall Buster weighed
260 pounds, some 30 more than he'd carried into the ring against
Tyson.

Then the end came, in October of that same year, right there in
Las Vegas. Evander Holyfield beat him in three rounds of the most
uninspired fisticuffs ever witnessed. Buster hardly put up a fight.
After falling to the canvas, he sat there pawing his face with his
glove, checking for blood, seeming to make no effort to return to
his feet. He was still checking when referee Mills Lane counted
him out. "I don't know if he could have got up," Lane said afterward. "But he sure never tried."

"I thought Buster Douglas was disgraceful tonight," another observer was heard to say. That happened to be Eddie Futch, one of
the most respected trainers around. "In my opinion," Futch continued, "he could have got up in time. But he chose not to do
so. . . . Maybe he had his own reasons."

Buster left the ring as clear-eyed as when he'd entered it. And
then, almost as quickly as he'd been thrust upon the scene, Buster

disappeared. "Fade to black," a script about his life might've read at this point. That or "The end."

No one spoke Buster Douglas's name anymore — except perhaps to use it as an example of how far and how quickly an athlete could fall. And when his victory over Tyson came up, it was no longer called the biggest upset in boxing history. Time had turned it into something else: a fluke. Rather than being credited with beating the best heavyweight since Muhammad Ali, Buster was said to have fought a psychologically impaired man in Tyson, hardly the monster of his previous fights. Tyson's personal problems had beaten him, not Buster Douglas. Or so people said when they could remember his name. Bubba Douglas? Buster Douglas?

Well, it really didn't matter anymore, did it?

Warm days and nights. Strip malls rising from the mangroves. Pretty, suntanned young women in spandex and on rollerblades, cruising along the sidewalks. It's paradise, all right, and just a few more reasons why Buster spends the fall and winter months in southwestern Florida, safe from the rain and snow that hammer his other home, Columbus.

Buster pulls up at a car dealership and tells the service adviser what he wants done. He just remembered the third thing on his list of chores for today: Go to a boating supply store and buy a map, a tackle box, and some artificial lures.

Weather permitting, Buster will be in the Atlantic Ocean a few days from now with Larry Nallie and a couple of other guys, fishing for marlin down near the Keys, along the edge of the Gulf Stream. He and Nallie became friends back in junior high school, and now they're partners — Nallie is Buster's business manager as well as his closest confidant. He oversees the nearly $30 million Buster made as champ. Although this fishing trip will be one of mindless recreation, it's not unusual for Nallie to get in his car and drive all the way down from Columbus to discuss financial matters with Buster.

"Need counseling?" Buster likes to say with a snort of laughter. "Call 1-800-WHEELS. Larry Nallie: the only accountant in America who drives cross-country to give out advice."

In the waiting room of the autohaus Buster lowers himself onto a short leather couch and faces a television tuned to *Headline News.* Riddick Bowe appears on the screen, looking nifty in a double-breasted suit. Bowe won the heavyweight title in November by beating Holyfield, and lately he has been traveling around the globe, presenting himself as either the Goodwill Ambassador, the People's Champ or the Second Coming of Ali. Which identity Bowe will finally settle on is anybody's guess, but already he's succeeded in being Everything Buster Douglas Was Not. Yesterday Bowe met Pope John Paul II, and today the news is all over the airwaves. Bowe gave the pontiff a pair of boxing gloves, as if an old man in a long white robe — and wearing a crucifix around his neck, for heaven's sake! — could possibly use such a gift. But Buster says he likes Bowe just the same. He likes Bowe's style inside as well as outside the ring. It's boxing Buster never liked.

"To me," he says, staring at the TV with his sunglasses on, "it was like playing the lottery. I remember once in Columbus when the lottery was up to 15, 20 million, my mother says, 'You playing the lottery?' And I laughed and said, 'I'm playing the lottery right now. This boxing is the lottery.' And that's really how I saw it — as a way out."

But a way out of what? That is the question. It wasn't as if Buster had to struggle when he was growing up. He lived with his grandmother until he was six, then his parents took charge. His mother was a great lady, a real presence in the home. She worked as a cook at a restaurant, and you could bet there was always a good, hot meal on the table when Buster and his three younger brothers came crashing home at the end of the day. Buster's father, Bill Douglas, had been a professional fighter, and he held steady employment as a boxing instructor for the parks department. True, Bill could be a bit domineering, but he was a father, and he was always there. At least his intentions were good. Some of Buster's friends hadn't enjoyed the privilege of ever being introduced to their dads. Buster didn't grow up in a slum, and he didn't attend troubled inner-city schools, and he didn't run with gangsters.

So a way out of what?

Well, for Buster, a way out of doing anything but what he feels like doing. A way out — to put it exactly right — of having to live his life like everybody else.

"Mr. Douglas. The Porsche is ready."

"Huh?"

"Your car is ready."

Buster gets up off the couch just as a piece about Mike Tyson is coming on TV. At the Indiana Youth Center, where he is serving a six-year sentence for a rape conviction, Tyson is inmate number 922335. He makes 65 cents a day handing out equipment in the prison gym. The news report is about lawyer Alan Dershowitz and his appeal to obtain a new trial for Tyson. Dershowitz's red mustache has the mesmerizing effect of a pocket watch swinging at the end of a chain, but Buster manages to ignore the lawyer and leaves the room, his shoes squeaking musically as he heads outside. The young women in the business office stand up and watch him on his way. It's hard for some people to believe that a man Buster's size was ever anything but big and fat. They have to strain to imagine the streamlined creature lost in that wealth of flesh, the champ hiding inside this terrifically outsized human.

Situated once again behind the wheel of his Porsche, Buster starts for the nearest deli, the hungry ache in his gut serving as a compass. He has decided: He will have the cream of broccoli soup, the turkey sandwich, the chocolate chip cookies. The cookies are high in fat content, but Buster will order the sandwich on wheat bread to compensate for the extra calories.

"Wait'll they get a load of me," he says again, whipping the car into traffic, laughing with his head rocked back.

When Buster goes to a video store, he doesn't rent movies; he buys them brand-new. He takes them home "by the case," as he puts it, and stacks them on top of the television in the den. There must be about twenty stacks on the Mitsubishi now, each about ten, fifteen cassettes deep. From a distance the top of the set looks like the Manhattan skyline. The tapes are high-rise buildings reaching for the stratosphere, a jumbled mess on a small piece of ground. People tell Buster he should build some shelves for his collection. He tells them he likes it the way it is.

Every now and then Buster will disappear into the bedroom and watch a tape of one of his old fights. He likes to be alone during these moments and to let his mind drift to the time depicted on the screen. He doesn't watch the fights he lost, such as his title bid against Tony Tucker, in 1987. Just those against people he beat. When he watches he remembers things he thought he'd forgotten, and sometimes even the old smells return. But invariably,

Bertha comes in to check on him, pushing a crack in the bedroom door: "You O.K., baby?" And that breaks the spell. He's no longer 225 pounds, feeling the heat of lights overhead, hearing the cheers. "You O.K., baby?" And, just like that, Buster Douglas turns back into just another guy with more life behind him than in front. He has never watched the Holyfield fight, mainly because he doesn't have to. "It's all right here," he says, pointing to his head.

And the truth is, you'd need eight months of film for that one because Buster's bout with Holyfield actually began the moment he flattened Tyson and earned the distinction of being called the best heavyweight fighter in the world. It began in Tokyo, if you have to know, before the sweat on Buster's back even had time to dry.

While Buster and friends were just beginning to celebrate inside the ring, promoter Don King was already at war outside, frantically trying to have the decision overturned. There, in the same arena, in a room nearby, King convened with officials from at least two sanctioning bodies and reviewed tapes of the bout, studying the eighth-round knockdown of Buster to determine whether, as King argued, the count of the referee had lagged behind that of the official scorekeeper. Upon emerging two hours later, King called a press conference and declared that "two knockouts took place," the first, by Tyson, naturally nullifying the second.

"Buster Douglas was knocked out," King said to the group, "and the referee did not do his job and panicked. As the promoter of both fighters, I'm only seeking fair play."

King was unsuccessful in reversing the outcome, but he did draw clouds over Buster's victory party. King later said he simply was trying to set the stage for a rematch — a claim he made, curiously enough, in a New York City courtroom some five months into Buster's reign. King and Buster had ended up suing each other. Buster and his manager, John Johnson, charged that King had breached his contract with them by trying to have the result of the Tyson fight overturned, and therefore King had forfeited his right to promote Buster's first title defense. King sued to uphold his promotional rights, and he named as defendants not only Douglas and Johnson but also Mirage owner Steve Wynn, whom King accused of wrongfully interfering with the King–Douglas contract. The dispute was settled shortly after it went to trial. King agreed to assign his promotional rights to the Douglas–Holyfield fight to Wynn. In exchange, Buster's-camp had to pay $4 million to King. Much to Buster's dismay, the person hit hardest by the settlement was the one who had made any future fight possible in the first place: James Buster Douglas. The money to settle would come off the top of his purse for the Holyfield fight, and it wasn't chump change, even if Buster was now the highest-paid athlete in the world.

Buster hated losing the money, but he figured he could live with the agreement. Boxing was a business, after all, and tough hits were to be expected. Had that been his only problem, he might've had an easy time preparing for his fight with Holyfield. But other matters kept getting in the way, and Buster found himself scrambling to resolve them all.

To begin, Buster now was forced to deal with the death of his mother, the person he'd cherished most in this world. He'd long dreamed about the kind of life he'd give Lula Pearl once he became champ. He'd buy her the greatest house around, fly her to exotic cities, dress her in silk and gold and pearls. He'd be the perfect son, since she had been the perfect mother.

In the weeks before he fought Tyson, Buster had been able to endure the pain of Lula's death by force of will alone, but now it struck him just how final the loss was. She wasn't coming back, no matter how hard he wished it weren't so. Some days he could hardly stand it; he wept, he missed her so bad.

And there was another woman whose absence was painful for Buster. He was tired of being separated from Bertha, and he wanted her back. It was easy for a millionaire athlete to get a woman, a beautiful woman, a woman so perfect as to stop your heart. But in Buster's case, none filled the void the way Bertha did. "A mannequin," he called one woman he had dated in the interim. And he gave a word to describe how she made him feel: *empty.*

Also, Buster was growing increasingly unhappy with John Johnson. Their professional relationship dated back to April 7, 1984, Buster's twenty-fourth birthday. Johnson was a former Ohio State football assistant who referred to himself as "a disciple of both Jesus Christ and Woody Hayes, though not necessarily in that order." All along, Johnson had accepted nothing less than complete control over Buster's career — just as the tyrant Hayes had ruled over his Buckeyes. But Buster was the champ now, he was the one who'd stepped in there with Tyson, and he was the one who wanted to make the lion's share of the decisions.

In March 1990, Nallie was hired to work as an accountant for James Buster Douglas Inc., and immediately he and Johnson found themselves disagreeing on how to handle the fighter. Money always seemed to be at issue, and rather than settle arguments peaceably, Johnson and Nallie took to name-calling. Johnson saw Nallie as "selfish, evil and greedy," and Nallie saw Johnson as a "dictator" who sought to control Buster. The bickering was intense and mean and personal, and the back and forth escalated to a point where it seemed Buster heard nothing else.

Nothing else except when certain members of his family complained about not having received their share of his earnings. Everybody, it seemed, wanted a free this or a free that — a free ride, to say it. True, Buster might've won the lottery by beating Tyson, but did that entitle everyone even distantly related to him to take a cut of the proceeds?

Sometimes Buster wished he were a kid again, without a worry — an innocent dreaming about the perfect, trouble-free life that would be his if he became champ. Why hadn't anyone told him that nightmares sometimes came disguised as dreams? A few weeks after the Tyson fight, Buster decided to escape it all, to just up and leave everything behind. Accompanied by his old friend Rodney Rogers, he rented a car and hit the highway. He drove from Ohio to Virginia, glancing back only to check for traffic in his rearview mirror. He and Rogers stopped at restaurants and ordered whatever looked good on the menu. They listened to Sir Mix-A-Lot on the stereo, giving that a break only when they felt like hearing a little Prince. And they talked about the old days until yesterday started to feel like new again.

Buster and Bertha had been separated for several months now, and she'd returned to her hometown of Chesapeake, Virginia, to be with her family. Besides escape, Buster determined that the mission of his trip would be to patch things up with her. He began by buying her a Mercedes-Benz that she didn't even want. She was perfectly content with her little Toyota. But it had made Buster feel good to buy the Mercedes, so she didn't protest much. At one point they went to look at the ocean, and Buster confessed that he wanted to live by the sea. He had this picture of himself with a Cuban cigar in his mouth, guiding a yacht out to where the big fish run. In the vision he was about the size of his father's father, whom everybody called Big Daddy. He was fat and happy, as people say. A real family man, a dedicated father, a committed husband.

It was the future, that picture. And Buster determined to make it come true. He would find his peace.

By the time October rolled around, people outside his camp were starting to see Buster Douglas's future as well, and it wasn't as king of the heavyweight division.

CRITICS QUESTION CHAMPION'S DESIRE read a *New York Times* headline. Bookmakers made Buster the 8-to-5 underdog in the Holyfield fight, and sports writers wrote that he was already a defeated man. It was clear to everyone that being on top had lost its luster for the champ; Buster was even heard to complain that he no longer cared for the taste of Dom Perignon.

"Kind of moldy," he confessed when asked about the pricey French champagne. "I don't drink it anymore."

Buster is starting to worry about the weather. The temperature is perfect, right at seventy degrees. The sun is a warm, beautiful friend in the sky. But the wind won't stop. The wind blows and blows. The Jolly Roger on Buster's fishing boat stands at constant attention. This means the seas are rough; a small craft advisory has been issued. Buster's fishing trip is in jeopardy. If the wind doesn't stop — if God himself doesn't intervene — Buster, won't be able to go out the day after tomorrow. And Buster, who's been counting on this trip, who really needs this trip . . . well, Buster will be heartbroken.

Fraught with worry, he journeys to his favorite video store and cruises the aisles, searching for the right movie to speak to where his head happens to be at the moment. He wants a film with a "star-studded cast," he says. And there's one in particular, a boxing story with Humphrey Bogart, that Buster's been anxious to see for a long time. Buster thinks Bette Davis is in it as well and maybe George C. Scott. He once thought the title was *Kid Galahad,* and he went so far as to have the store order a film by that name. For

days Buster waited patiently for the movie to arrive, and finally the
store called. He got in his car and drove over, but you wouldn't believe what was waiting for him. Elvis Presley! *Kid Galahad* was one
of those sappy Elvis pictures! "Hell, no!" Buster told the clerk. "I
want Bogart." He left feeling totally let down.

"I am not an animal," Buster says, after spotting a cassette of *The
Elephant Man,* a movie about a hideously deformed English fellow
who uttered those same words.

"Wow. For the first time I feel like you can help me. Somebody
understands." Buster has just strolled by the tape of a comedy starring Bill Murray and recalled those lines, which still make him
laugh. They're the same lines Buster once gave an acquaintance
who was asking too many personal questions. The man was ram-
bling on about the pain and suffering fighters are made to endure,
and Buster dropped that on him. For a long time the man sat
there speechless, wondering if maybe he at last had cracked the
enigma that was James Buster Douglas. Finally Buster was forced to
say, "*What About Bob?* happens to be a favorite of mine."

"What about . . . who?"

"It's a movie. You should check it out."

Buster comes to an area marked NEW RELEASES and picks up
Diggstown, a picture starring James Woods and Lou Gossett Jr.,
whom Buster once happened to meet. Gossett is much bigger than
most actors, and that impressed Buster. On the plastic jacket of the
videotape, Gossett is shown leaning against a padded turnbuckle
in the corner of a ring, his arms draped over the ropes. He looks a
lot like Buster did after the Holyfield fight, what with the purple
bruise under his eye. One more blow and Gossett will be down on
his knees, rubbing his face with his glove to check for blood.
Buster decides to buy it.

Up at the front of the store someone has located a Bogart fight
film, *The Harder They Fall.* Buster runs up to look it over. He traces
a finger over the list of players, disheartened to find that Bette
Davis and George C. Scott aren't among them.

"The one I want has a star-studded cast," he says. "I don't think
this is it."

"Rod Steiger's in it," he is told. "He's a star."

"Studded. The one I want is star-*studded.*"

The movie goes for $9.99, and even a multimillionaire like

Buster can't afford to pass up such a deal. He adds the tape to the six or seven others he plans to buy. Only his left hand is free now, and he uses it to flip through the movies in the bargain bin. He's seen most of them and has a comment for each one: "This is —, this is all right. *Little Man Tate* was good, and so was *Mississippi Masala. Frankie and Johnny,* good. But I found the humor in *L.A. Story* a little dry. Oh, this is —, total —. *Alien 3* I got, good. Real good. *The Color Purple,* that's Bertha's favorite. I ask her, 'What do you see in it? You think I'm like Mister, who's always beating everybody up?' She says it's better than *The Godfather,* but I don't know if I agree. You gotta like any picture with gangsters."

Buster is speaking from authority. Last year he played a gangster of sorts in the television crime drama *Street Justice.* It was his only professional acting role ever, and Buster starred as Daggett, an inmate at a maximum-security prison. Buster got so involved in the part that he took it home with him after the taping was finished. He'd walk around the house as if he were hot to pistol-whip someone. "All right, Daggett," Bertha had to tell him a couple of times. "Chill out now."

Funny thing was, Buster found that acting was a lot like boxing. During the shoot you stayed in your hotel room until they called you down, then you went to the set and waited for your cue. In boxing your cue was a bell; in acting it was a director pointing his finger at you and saying, "Action."

After he sheds about a hundred pounds and returns to fighting shape, Buster will give Hollywood another try. He'll get Nallie to call their contacts out there and see what he can line up. Or so Buster says as he walks out of the video store. "I want to be an act-tore!" he bellows into the wind. "I want to be an act-tore!"

The wind. It catches his clothes and whips them tight against him, and he seems to remember something. He gazes off as if at some enemy and murmurs quietly to himself, his words lost in the throes of something you can't even see.

About an hour before his fight with Holyfield, Buster fell asleep on a table in his dressing room. It wasn't a light sleep, either. They'd had to wake him up, for crying out loud! And then he had felt disoriented, displaced. What was he doing here? Why couldn't he just go home?

The walk to the ring — that, too, he remembers as odd. Buster had reached forward and rested his hands on his trainer's shoulders, which was something he had never done before. Always in the past he'd been throwing punches, stretching, trying to get loose. He'd thought it looked cool when a fighter entered the ring resting his gloves on his trainer's shoulders, but it had never worked for him. Why he was doing it now, just before his first title defense and after thirty-five professional fights, Buster couldn't begin to imagine.

It was a little like having an out-of-body experience. "Stop this," he wanted to say. "Hey, everybody, let's just stop this before it begins." He wished a big storm would suddenly blow through and cancel the thing. A hurricane right out there in the Nevada desert would've suited Buster just fine.

He didn't feel like the best heavyweight in the world, the one who'd done a number on Iron Mike. If anything, he felt average. Just another stiff with a pair of red cherries taped to hands with no place to go. Just another . . . corpse!

Something else about that night was peculiar. He could hear what people were saying at ringside — he could actually hear their conversations. Larry Nallie was there in the corner, holding one of Buster's championship belts over his head. "Hey, man, where's *my* belt?" somebody said. Buster turned around, and there was the president of one of the boxing organizations that had sanctioned the bout. The man was unhappy that Nallie was showing off somebody else's belt.

"You're holding up the wrong one," the man said.

Buster gazed out at the crowd, searching for his father. "Help me," he wanted to say. "Help me." A few weeks before, Bill Douglas had come in to work with him, to try to spark something. Bill had introduced Buster to the ring when Buster was just a kid in grade school, and he had worked with Buster during much of his professional career; but before the Holyfield fight Bill hadn't been able to get his son to respond. Buster figured that if anybody knew how he was feeling now, it was his old man. He kept looking out at the faces, whispering to himself, "Where are you, Dad? Where are you?"

He didn't feel like fighting, not Holyfield or anybody else. The bell rang, though, and in that instant there were only two people left in the world. Buster charged out to meet the other one, and unfortunately for him, that man had come to win.

A few days after the fight Buster was only too glad to leave Las Vegas. He had never really felt accepted there, mainly because the town, a Tyson stronghold, had seemed to resent Buster for toppling its hero. Buster hadn't been able to get a haircut without the barber going on about what a great guy Tyson was and what a great tipper. Why, Tyson shed $100 bills like trees shed leaves! Now, after such a poor showing against Holyfield, Buster felt like a pariah. It was too early to return to Columbus and all the well-meaning friends certain to offer their condolences and to make him feel even worse, so he flew to Los Angeles with Larry Nallie and Rodney Rogers.

They rented a car and took rooms at a swank hotel in Beverly Hills. They'd planned to stay only a night or two but ended up camping there a whole week. Since none of them had brought many clothes, they went to a giant shopping center and bought what they needed. Buster would later recognize the place in *Scenes from a Mall,* a Woody Allen–Bette Midler movie. Buster bought a double-breasted purple suit and later wore it to a Halloween party at the Roxy nightclub. He had the Joker's laugh down pat, and now he had the look. "Wait'll they get a load of me," he said time and again that night, apparently failing to register the irony in the statement.

Less than a week earlier, after all, Buster had found himself sitting on a canvas floor, swatting at invisible blood on his face. After his dismal showing, you would have expected to hear something else coming from his mouth. Mea culpa, mea culpa might have been more appropriate.

One afternoon he and his pals were driving through Beverly Hills and passed an exotic-car dealership. In the window a Lamborghini sat high on a display, and it seemed to beckon to Buster, inviting him to stop and give it a test drive. "Bo was just here," a salesman told Buster. He meant Bo Jackson. Buster could hardly fit in the car, and he felt disappointed. He probably would've bought the thing. As he was getting ready to leave, someone called his attention to a Porsche convertible. "I want to sell you this car really bad," the salesman said. "But if you go and kill yourself in it. . . . No, you've got to respect this car."

Buster took it out overnight. He couldn't get over the car's power, the brute force at his disposal. People gawked when he passed them by. He considered the Porsche a present to himself for all his hard work; he was flexing his muscles just this once. Before paying for it, Buster negotiated to have the word JOKER painted on each door.

That was his first major purchase. Another was the five-acre tract of land in Columbus where Buster hopes to establish a multiuse community center for inner-city youth. The enterprise will be his way of giving back to the city that gave so much to him. According to a prospectus Nallie helped to prepare, the center will give Near East Side residents access to recreational sports facilities and health, medical and educational services "in a one-stop-shop setting." Buster plans to hang a portrait of himself in the lobby, on the frame of which will be engraved these words: JAMES BUSTER DOUGLAS, FOUNDING FATHER.

Buster made another major purchase last year when he bought the manse at Marco Island. He didn't want to raise his children in Vegas, so he and Bertha decided to give Florida a look. A chauffeur drove them down in a stretch limousine, another recent purchase of Buster's. The farther south they went, the warmer it got, and this suited Buster fine. As a kid he loved the hard Midwestern winters, but as he got older he grew to despise them. He and Bertha stayed in a fancy rented house, and after only a couple of days they decided that the island suited them just right. Marco was developed twenty-five years ago, and if you get away from the giant hotels along the main beach, it still feels like the secluded fishing village it once was. After all he had been through, Buster welcomed the isolation. Although it looked as if his would be one of the few black families in the area, if not the only one, he thought he could escape there and find the peace that had long eluded him. He and Bertha decided to buy the second house the real estate agent showed them. At $775,000, the 6,400-square-foot mansion looked like a steal, as did the $150,000 boat Buster later bought to dock on the canal out back.

He christened the boat *Lula Pearl* and had an artist paint the name on the hull along with a picture of a shell with a sparkling pearl. Trimmed in teakwood, the boat sleeps six comfortably and is "perfectly seaworthy," as Buster likes to boast.

He seems to mean it wouldn't sink if you took it out in the ocean, and this means a lot to everyone who climbs aboard.

"Sometimes," Buster is saying to a visitor one day — the day, in fact, before his much-anticipated fishing trip — "I feel as if I'm bursting open with joy. My heart, it's so big, man, it wants to just come leaping right out of my chest."

He is standing on the bridge of his boat, gazing out toward the sea. He is a man who will tell you he has everything: a good, kind woman who loves him, two sons and another child on the way, friends galore, a house in Florida and several in Ohio, money in the bank, an honorable reputation. "And yet," he continues, "if you talk to certain people in Columbus they'll tell you I'm depressed. They'll say I've put on weight because I'm down over all that happened, that I'm hiding from the world here. But it isn't true. I'm happy.

"I'm happy!"

He has no desire to ever fight again, he says. Not even $25 million for a Tyson rematch would bring him back. Not even $50 million! "Listen, baby," he says. "I'd love to see ya, but I can't be with ya. Sorry." He laughs, looking toward the water again. "Besides, there're just too many fish for me to catch."

Not long after he says this, the telephone rings, and Bertha calls him inside. A man named Scottie Dingwell is on the line — the same Scottie Dingwell whom Buster hires to captain his boat. "The wind," Dingwell tells him. "It isn't wise to go out. Better cancel and plan for later on."

If they made a movie about Buster Douglas's life, you wouldn't see this part: our hero slamming the phone down, cursing under his breath. "I knew it!" he says to Bertha.

She nods, seeming to agree.

That afternoon Nallie finally arrives from Columbus. He's disappointed about the fishing trip being called off, but nowhere near as upset as Buster, who's taking it hard. To feel better, Buster makes a run to the deli for a couple of sandwiches, then comes back and piddles around the house. Everyone's in the living room watching *I'm Gonna Git You Sucka,* but Buster isn't up for a movie.

It's difficult to watch a comedy when your life calls for a drama, a tragedy, so Buster keeps to himself. He can picture schools of big ones swimming in the ocean now — fish that weigh as much as he does, fish that can give him the most gratifying fight of his life.

Finally, when it's dark, he and Nallie and another friend go out and lounge on the *Lula Pearl*. All the fishing gear is there ready to go; if the outriggers could talk, they'd tell you they're anxious to pull up a record catch. Buster grabs a beer and puts on a CD. It's Bob Marley, singing his Rastafarian heart out.

At three o'clock in the morning Buster will still be here, stranded on a yacht that isn't going anywhere. He'll be thinking about his life past, present and future, and feeling slightly awed by a wind that never ceases to blow.

BUD COLLINS

Boxing Grieves Loss of 5th Street Gym

FROM THE BOSTON GLOBE

MIAMI BEACH— and this is the Ballad of the Sad Classroom:

> *Readin', 'ritin', 'rithmetic*
> *Don't make the grades here,*
> *Prof. Dundee marks "A" if you stick*
> *Jabs in the other guy's ear.*
>
> *Many a two-fisted scholar*
> *Studied for punchin' PhD,*
> *Whether Pep-clever or brawler*
> *None matched poet laureate Ali.*
>
> *But bang the drum slowly,*
> *Toll the mournful count to ten,*
> *Wreckin' ball comin' like Rocky:*
> *Obliteratin'; School's out, Amen.*

It's no fun to contemplate the razing of citadels of learning, the destruction of laboratories, the disappearance of a classroom where the prodigy and valedictorian of the 5th Street Gym, Muhammad Ali, was nurtured, along with numerous other advanced-degree headbreakers.

"Double-tough lifetakers," Sam Silverman used to laud such *cum laude* pugilists.

You stand at the corner of Washington and 5th, South End of

Miami Beach, and only stillness that seems a death rattle drifts from the open second story windows. For forty years the rattle of punching bags emanated from those slits to mingle with sunbeams and traffic din. The place, a big, low-ceilinged room, about 130-by 60, could be called the Harvard of the Sweet Science without overly offending the highly tolerant proprietors, the Dundee Brothers: the dean, Chris, and Professor Angelo (although Harvard may not quite rate as the 5th Street Gym of the fine arts). Chris promoted fights, Angelo tutored the fighters.

Like Harvard, it did attract students from around the globe, a magnet and landmark such as Widener Library. Imagine the Widener being torn down and you can grasp the enormity of the 5th Street Gym's demise. Think of the maestros of manhandling who trained here for their recitals — champions named Sugar Ray (Robinson and Leonard), Willie Pastrano, Carmen Basilio, Luis Rodriguez, Sugar Ramos, Joey Maxim, Jose Napoles, Ralph Dupas . . . too many to recount. And, of course, the titan himself: arrived as Cassius Clay, becoming the greatest of all American athletes — Muhammad Ali.

How can this be, this room gutted and quiet, waiting for the breaking ball to knock the two-story building flatter than Ali did George Foreman early one mysterious morning in Zaire nineteen years ago? "Rumble in the Jungle!" Ali called his reascension to the heavyweight throne.

"You gonna rumble young man!" his witch doctor, Bundini Brown, would screech over and over. And, man, didn't he rumble?

But Ali got old and tired too fast, and so has his study hall which, its owners say, will be more useful destroyed and transformed to an American architectural classic — a parking lot.

"It was falling apart, but I wanted to save it, have it renovated," says the pedagogue of pedagogues, trainer Angelo Dundee. "But the owners, nobody else did. I felt awful when it closed. I offered to bring my fighters back here . . . but . . . no go. Sad. Everybody in the world of boxing knew the 5th Street Gym. It was . . ." He stops, not wanting to be too sentimental about a reformed Chinese restaurant, a place where egg rolls preceded tough eggs as features.

It was what a gym should be — stained and grungy, a seedy parlor for palookas and princes of the science. A shabby ivory tower. You had to climb stairs to reach higher learning. It has ever been thus. The distinguished gyms were stale, aromatic walkups where fresh air was suspect. Stillman's in New York. The New Gardens on Friend Street in Boston. All gone now.

Dundee is a little apologetic about his new "gym-uh-nasium," as the fight set often pronounced such studios. "North of here, in Hollywood, it's in a health club. First floor."

"Too antiseptic, and lowdown," is the verdict of Dr. Ferdie Pacheco, Dundee's friend and Ali's onetime physician.

"No termites," confesses Dundee, who was in Ali's corner from the start. "I'd warn newcomers to 5th Street about the man-eating termites, and that we might go through the floor at any moment," he smiles.

Incomprehensible that the Miami Beach city fathers would allow this historic treasure to vanish. Especially since it's right around the corner from the revived and celebrated neighborhood called the art deco district, roamed by commercials-making camera crews from everywhere. The mayor must be as hardheaded as the stone crabs for which nearby Joe's is renowned.

So the Sad Classroom is going, going . . .

Beau Jack, the 72-year-old ex-lightweight champ, sits amid rubble and ghosts in a corner, keeping a "sad, sad" deathbed vigil until the wreckers arrive. "So many good men here. Now nothing. It's terrible."

It wasn't always sad. The classroom was noisy and electrified by Ali's presence, his confidence and sense of fun. He showed up in 1960, says Dundee. "He said, 'Angelo, get all your bums ready for me. I'll take 'em all on.' He was a great learner.

"He lived in the ghetto in Overtown over in Miami then. Every day he'd run here, over the causeway. Until they got to know him the cops would stop him, suspicious of a young black kid running the bridge. You know how that goes."

He was beautiful in 1964, entertaining visitors to the gym, bragging captivatingly about how he'd whup that big old ugly bear, Sonny Liston, and take the title.

Nobody believed except Ali, Dundee and John Gillooly, the droll Bostonian who columnized for the *Record* and was almost alone in correctly picking the upstart whom he called "Gaseous Cassius."

Liston, the *Record*, Gillooly have departed. Ali has slowed to an elderly pace. And school's out at his classroom.

Weight Bench Warriors

FROM TROPIC MAGAZINE

THERE ARE mirrors on every wall, and in the contorted chrome frames of squat machines, and in the mirrors the faces do not smile. The mouths are grim slashes, surrendering nothing, but the eyes give the game away. Given time, no one can resist. Some sneak furtive peeks; the bolder ones preen and flex, mesmerized by what they see.

I am, of course, in a gym. Around me is the now common populace of the great American workout hall: Men and women, straight and gay, brushing so close, wearing next to nothing as the rock 'n' roll grinds — yet wandering through a world less sexed than sterile. The cool air allows only a faint soapy musk of solitary sweat; no one dares smell bad. It is serious and simple, this business of the Big I; there is but one question, asked with a glance and answered in a body language of inflated arms and shrinking waists: What am I becoming now?

It is not a happy place — and that is logical, since a gym is a self-help manual fleshed to three dimensions — everyone here is looking to get bigger, leaner, slimmer, stronger; everyone is looking to *improve*. They come in all packages, old and young, for reasons ranging from vanity to fear to doctor's orders. But mostly, they are men about my age. I know why we are here.

I speak now not of baby-boom men, those hipsters who have given up the ghost to full-fit jeans and dreams programmed by VH-1, but of this generation under thirty-five, still fighting the good but fruitless fight, lifting weights and running miles and doing aerobics — as if preparing for something, a test, maybe, trying to get strong for a fight that may never come.

We are serious about this, about the way we play. You can sense it under the playground hoops, on the tennis courts and softball fields; fights break out, pickup games become battle. No one is having much fun. This is strange coming from the generation of low expectations; we've always managed to tread water by taking nothing too seriously, ready to puncture with our daily Letterman list any politician/celebrity/ideal that threatens to get too gassy.

And yet, mere games have become a matter of import to us. Everyone seems to have something to prove. This is idiotic on one level, yet makes an odd kind of sense once you consider that working out, playing games, watching games — and watching commercials about working out and playing games and watching games — have made up a good part of this generation's waking life.

For more than a decade, we were told to feel the burn and go for it and just do it, so we got hot and went and did, making sure to buy a new pair of sneakers with each new stage. Competition was the drug of choice. How did the jingle go? Michelob Light — For The Winners! Whoever the marketing genius was, he knew his audience, knew he had to offer something they didn't have.

What they didn't have, ever, was some kind of crisis.

You see, we saw all the bad romantic movies. We read the war poetry. *If I should die think only this of me . . .* We learned of World War I and the Lost Generation and the Great Depression, World War II, Korea, McCarthyism, Cuban Missiles, Vietnam — they came one by one, these national tests that turned boys to men, so regular they seemed to be scheduled.

We were raised on the memories. There were horrible recollections of gassings and blood and poverty, but told with a survivor's secret sense of pride. We knew there was risk, knew we were supposed to feel gratitude for escaping unscathed. So we waited our turn, but quietly. All our lives, we expected this great cathartic moment — bullets whizzing, history witnessed — that would hurl us into adulthood.

It never came. What came was the oil crisis, then the Iran hostage crisis, then seven years of Donald Trump.

Desert Storm? We were already too old. Anyway, it wasn't the same: a remote-control war, lasting weeks, not years.

Recently, the writer William Styron looked back at his service in the Pacific in 1945 and wrote, "It was a war we all believed in and I'd wanted to test my manhood; part of me mourned that I never got near the combat zone."

Part of us mourns the same thing, I think — certainly not the killing or dying, but the feel of taking part in something bigger than oneself, in seeing who we really are in the harsh light of real pressure. It has been said that we are this century's cleanup crew, the generation charged with disposing of the deficit and mending the ozone layer. But you don't get stronger gathering garbage.

Yet, we are the healthiest generation in history. And the most self-contained, if only because no political party, no ism, no national crisis has won our hearts. We were both Reagan Democrats and Clinton Republicans. We are not True Believers. In the end, we always fall back on our bodies, our selves — not just for the purpose of attracting partners or feeling better or living longer, though that, too, is part of this fever of competition — but by default. For lack of anything better, our games became our test.

So everybody is doing something — racquetball, golf, body-building; it is the age of the mini-jock now. Every generation needs a D-Day, or even a Woodstock. Luckily, our pivotal moments are broadcast nightly — a crisis manufactured, but a crisis nonetheless — the World Series, the Super Bowl, the Finals. Every week, a city's pride on the line, won in four quarters, two halves, sudden-death overtime.

It is no coincidence that sports exploded in popularity as the sense of national mission faded.

And so we play, as one era lurches into another. *Newsweek,* anticipating the ascension of the baby boomers in George Bush's departure, devoted a January cover to *The World War II Generation and How It Changed America.* That kind of distinction does not seem to be our fate.

It is hard to change anything while staring at your own image, while running in place.

IRA BERKOW

Walking Away, While He Still Can

FROM THE NEW YORK TIMES

PULLMAN, WASHINGTON — Timm Rosenbach remembers clearly
the beginning of the end because everything was pitch black.

He woke up in a dark room with his head strapped to a table,
still wearing his Phoenix Cardinals uniform and shoulder pads
and hip pads and cleats. He was frightened and alone, not sure if
he was alive or dead. He couldn't move, didn't want to move. He
knew he had been hurt, but didn't know how badly. He thought
about his friend and former college teammate, Mike Utley of the
Lions, who the year before had taken a tumble in a game and been
left paralyzed for life from the chest down.

Then Rosenbach remembered the hit he had taken earlier that
day. Was it minutes ago? Was it hours? Rosenbach, a 6-foot quarterback, was dropping back to pass in the third quarter of the
season opener when he was blindsided by Santana Dodson, the
Tampa Bay Buccaneers' six-foot-five, 270-pound defensive end, in
one of the brutal encounters that is commonplace in a National
Football League game.

Rosenbach remembered only the resounding impact, as if being
leveled by a tank, and then nothing. Until that moment in the
room. And then, just as suddenly, he blacked out again.

This was Sunday, September 6, 1992, in an X-ray room at St.
Joseph's Hospital in Phoenix. Rosenbach was not aware that he
had been taken, unmoving, from the field at Sun Devils Stadium
on a stretcher and rushed to the emergency room. He was not

aware that he had suffered only a severe concussion when his head slammed into the turf.

He would walk and talk normally again, even report back for work two days later, but the grim experience would not leave him. In the following game, he returned to the lineup only to be blind-sided again, this time by Clyde Simmons, Philadelphia's six-foot-six, 280-pound defensive end, on the Cardinals' second series of the game.

"I made sure that the next time I get hit, I don't go head first," Rosenbach recalled, "and I didn't. I went shoulder first." And he suffered a separated shoulder. He was out of action for a month.

After the last game of the season, December 27, 1992, Rosenbach, at age twenty-six, did what some thought was unthinkable: He walked away from professional football and $1.05 million, the salary for the fifth and last year of his $5.3 million contract. He left the field and the money because he had developed fears that he might be crippled if he continued to play and because he began to "despise," as he said, the dehumanizing aspects of football that "can turn you into an animal."

It wasn't always that way. Two years earlier, in 1990, in his second year in the NFL, he took every snap for the Cardinals, all 1,001 of them, throwing for 3,098 yards to rank third in the National Football Conference. He ranked second in the NFL in rushing yardage for a quarterback, behind Randall Cunningham. He threw 16 touchdown passes. He was admired, as one Phoenix sports reporter wrote, because "He was feisty. Gutsy. Combative. Ornery." His coach, Joe Bugel, called him "a throwback," a "gun-slingin' beer-drinkin' tough" in the mold of the late and colorful Bobby Layne.

Last summer, when it became apparent that Rosenbach had made his decision to quit football and return to Washington State University — where he had starred in football and where he was thirty-eight hours short of a bachelor's degree in general studies with an emphasis in psychology — he didn't call the team. His agent, Gary Wichard, did. Rosenbach changed his unlisted phone number so that no one from the Cardinals organization could call to try to talk him out of retiring and no reporter could call and ask why.

Football generally had been fun for Rosenbach in school, and even into the pros — he once relished the contact, proudly looking in the mirror at his bruises as an affirmation of manhood. But he was not prepared, as a 22-year-old right out of college for the hard-edged business of professional football, nor for the debilitating injuries that had sidelined him. And while his associations with a number of his teammates remained close, his view of this odd occupation became deeper, and darker.

There was speculation that Rosenbach had decided to become a professional rodeo rider, since he had participated as a team roper in a half-dozen events. When he married Carrie Serrano in June 1992, at his new 10-acre ranch in Gilbert, Arizona, the ceremony was held outdoors under a sagebrush arch with groom and groomsmen bedecked in black cowboy hats, tuxedo tops, black jeans and black cowboy boots.

"It's all a mystery to me," said Bugel. "I'd like for him to tell me right to my face what the problem is."

"I've seen young guys retire, unretire, but certainly not a player of Timm's stature," said Larry Wilson, the Cardinals' general manager. "This is kind of strange."

But there was more to it than just the bruises of the business. "I thought I was turning into some kind of animal," Rosenbach said in a recent interview. "You go through a week getting yourself up for a game by hating the other team, the other players. You're so mean and hateful, you want to kill somebody. Football's so aggressive. Things get done by force. And then you come home, you're supposed to turn it off? 'Oh, here's your lovin' daddy.' It's not that easy. It was like I was an idiot. I felt programmed. I had become a machine. I became sick of it."

He remembered those "barbaric yawps," as he called them, when breaking from a huddle and the players began screaming like maniacs. "It lightened things up," said Rosenbach, "but it's still a part of the craziness of football. Like screaming at the other team at the top of your lungs all kinds of threats and obscenities."

He remembers his center, Bill Lewis, telling an opposing lineman, "You touch my quarterback and I'll end your career." He remembers players like Refrigerator Perry snarling with his huge face scrunched up inside his tight helmet. And then there was Reggie White: "He is very religious, and he'd hit you a murderous shot and then say, 'God bless you,' as he pulled you off the ground."

Rosenbach also felt the pressures that go with winning, or losing. "I began to despise the whole business of the NFL," he said. When he was injured, he felt that the coaches, particularly head coaches, hardly recognized him. Since he was of no value to them, he was a virtual nonentity. When he was hurt, he wasn't even asked to travel with the team. "They asked, 'How're you feelin'?' But with no feeling," he said. "Their answer to injury is to give you painkiller pills. And the whole concept of medicine is to get you ready to perform — what happens to you down the road is not of any interest to them.

"Team doctors often lose touch with humanity, too. They are working for the team, and love the association. So you hear players on the plane after a game and saying, 'Hey, Doc, give me some Percodan or Percoset or Codeine Tylenol or something else.' When did players become pharmacists?

"And coaches are so absorbed in the X's and O's that they lose any feeling of being a human being. I guess the pressure is so great on them. I feel they viewed me — us — as robots. A mechanism. And if you don't fit the slot you're nothing to them."

One trick of being a professional athlete, he understood, was not to think too much. He had been a kind of daredevil quarterback, enjoying the contact, loving that glazed feeling when you hardly know where you are, even baiting some of the huge opponents like Perry during the heat of a game — "It takes a long time to get all that into motion, doesn't it?"— but when he returned to the lineup in the latter part of last season, things were different.

He couldn't move the way he used to because his knee was wrapped in a brace, and for the first time he felt fear on a football field, the fear of ending up a cripple. He had already missed the entire 1991 season because of a severed ligament incurred in a preseason practice a week before the opener. The injury required reconstructive surgery and rehabilitation and made him question his existence as a pro football player.

The challenge of going against ferocious linemen like Lawrence Taylor and White and Simmons and Perry, which had whetted his competitive appetite, had taken a different turn.

He said there was a lot of fear in the NFL. "Guys don't talk about it," he said, "but they feel it. And when you really know the game, you can spot them. But a lot aren't making the kind of money I did. And when a guy's making, say, $65,000 a year, and this is the only place he can make that kind of money, he's not about to get out."

After the injuries, his confidence, as well as his enthusiasm ebbed noticeably. He was booed. He remembers the discomfort of meeting people and feeling he had to apologize for his performance or the team's losses.

"Timm would come home in these moods," said his wife, Carrie, "and we were newlyweds. I didn't know what the problem was. He'd sit in a dark corner. I thought it was me. I thought, 'Why can't I make him happy?' But then I began to understand all the pressures he was under. And of course the pain. After some games, Timm was so bruised and battered it would take him a half-hour to get out of bed. And sometimes it would take him a half-hour to get off the couch and into bed."

The other side of life in the NFL for Rosenbach was that of "royalty," as he describes it. In those earlier, more relaxed days, he felt pampered, and that it was his due.

"I had a lot of money — more than I ever dreamed — a great apartment, several cars, and wanted for nothing," he said. "I had become pretty arrogant. My neighbors hated me. I lived in an exclusive condominium in my first few years and played my music loud and didn't throw my garbage in the dumpster but left it on the porch.

"I almost never washed my clothes," he said. "When they got dirty, I threw them into the closet and went down to the mall and bought some more. I was young and rich and a professional athlete and I had no sense of reality. Just like most of the rest of the guys I played with."

Rosenbach's late father, Lynn, was a high school football coach and later the assistant athletic director at Washington State. His mother, Rosie, is an interior decorator. His brother, Todd, teaches special education, and his sister, Dana, is a high school teacher.

"When I went back and saw their lives," he said, "saw how they were all doing well on salaries that weren't a million dollars a year, and happy with their lives, I felt embarrassed for myself."

He spoke with Carrie about quitting and giving up that $1 million, as well as the millions that he might earn in football in the coming years.

"I didn't know how he could just give up all that money," said Carrie. "But after a while I understood. He said that if he had to pump gas, he'd do it rather than play football. And it was true."

In Phoenix, he was being called a "no-show," and a "mystery man."

But his agent, Gary Wichard, said: "Timm's an intelligent, sensitive guy, and he has made a decision that he's had it with football. He could have come in for a year and held for extra points and field goals, but that's just not Timm."

"I'm proud of Rosey," said Jim Wahler, a defensive lineman for the Redskins and a former Cardinal teammate of Rosenbach's. "I'm glad he did it. There are not many people in that position to do that. That's a standup thing to walk out on your own terms and not somebody else's. Most guys would like that opportunity."

He still has his ranch in Gilbert, but now lives with Carrie and seven dogs in a small house in an isolated area about eight miles outside of Pullman, Washington. She is a graduate of Arizona State and is in school at Washington State going for a master's degree in agricultural economy. Rosenbach has returned to general studies with a psychology emphasis.

Is he happier? "Yes," he said. "I was getting no enjoyment out of football anymore.

"It's funny, but when I was in school here before I sat in the back of the class and never said a word. Now I'm involved in the classes, and I'm always raising my hand. I'm sure some of the students are saying, 'Why doesn't that old guy just shut up?' "

Rosenbach hardly looks ancient in his sweatshirt and jeans. He still has that broad, boyish look and a cowlick in his short blond hair. And he also hasn't totally given up on football. He says a college game is still one of the exciting spectacles for him. And he still watches pro games on television, remembering the pleasure of the camaraderie of teammates, though he sees the action differently than he once did.

And he still has his memories of playing the game, every morning. His knees, his back, his shoulders, still ache when he wakes up and slowly gets out of bed. When he drives for any distance in his truck, or walks distances when he is out hunting birds, his body hurts.

"And I'm still an alumnus of the NFL, it is still something I'm proud of," he said. "And I guess one day I'll be invited to some of those alumni golf tournaments, and wear an NFL cap and play, if I can stand up."

For Jenkins, Another Tragic Twist in the Road

FROM THE NEW YORK TIMES

GUTHRIE, OKLAHOMA — In the morning, Ferguson Jenkins had noticed that the hose to the large red vacuum cleaner was missing, but he paid little attention to it, never once imagining what terrible use it might be put to.

Then in the late afternoon, around five o'clock, the phone rang in the kitchen of his ranch house here. The date on the calendar on the wall was Tuesday, December 15, 1992, two days after Jenkins's 49th birthday. Jenkins was outside, smoothing the red clay in the driveway with a shovel, when his ranch foreman, Tommy Christian, answered the phone.

"Sheriff Powell!" he called to Jenkins from the doorway.

"Sheriff Powell?" Jenkins recalled thinking. "What can he want?" The last time he had spoken to Doug Powell was two years earlier, after a robbery at the Jenkins ranch.

From the driveway, Jenkins could see that the sun, weak all day, was disappearing behind the hills and two man-made lakes on his 160 acres. It was getting cool as a wind picked up in this isolated area of the plains, about eight and a half miles north of Guthrie, the nearest town, and about 40 miles north of Oklahoma City.

Jenkins was wearing a green windbreaker, green baseball cap, jeans and work boots. This is a working farm, with 8 horses, 52 head of beef cattle and 60 acres of wheat, and Jenkins dresses for it. So did his fiancée Cindy Takieddine, who lived with him, his adopted twelve-year-old son, Raymond, and his three-year-old daughter, Samantha, the child he had with his wife Maryanne, who was seriously injured in a car crash in December 1990. Her death in January 1991 came just four days after the announcement that Fergie, as everyone calls him, had been named to baseball's Hall of Fame.

The election had been the culmination of a 19-year career in the major leagues, mostly with the Chicago Cubs and Texas Rangers, in which Jenkins won 284 games, was a 20-game winner seven times, won the National League Cy Young Award in 1971 and the American League Comeback Player of the Year Award in 1974, and then finally retired in 1983.

Jenkins is a big man. At six feet five inches and 225 pounds, he is about 20 pounds heavier than in his playing days, but he carries his weight well, with a graceful, slope-shouldered walk. Having learned that the sheriff was on the phone, he entered the two-story redwood house, walked past the Christmas tree that Cindy had decorated for three days, took the receiver and was told that the sheriff wanted to see him in Guthrie. Within fifteen minutes, Jenkins arrived in town in his pickup.

"I have some horrible news, Mr. Jenkins," said Sheriff Powell. "And there's no easy way to tell it.

"Cindy Takieddine and Samantha Jenkins were found dead of carbon monoxide poisoning. They were found in a Bronco pickup on a rural road near Perry."

"No, you're wrong, sheriff," said Jenkins. "You're wrong. I'm picking up Samantha at 5:30 at her daycare nursery." He looked at his watch. "In about ten minutes."

"It was a positive I.D., sir. And a note was left."

"Call the daycare center," said Jenkins. "You'll see; Samantha's there."

Powell called the center for Jenkins, and put the call on a speakerphone. Samantha Jenkins was not at the nursery.

"Mr. Jenkins was devastated," recalled Powell. "This was one of the hardest things I've ever had to do as sheriff, or deputy, in Logan County. Mr. Jenkins is highly admired here. He's been a model citizen, and always willing to speak at civic or school or church groups. As famous as he is, that's how down to earth he is. He rode up to Perry with my undersheriff to identify the bodies, about 30 miles. All the way there and all the way back he never said a word."

It was back in Powell's office that he learned that Cindy, a tall, 44-year-old blonde, had stopped at the daycare center and picked up Samantha, whom she had dressed at home that morning in a green party dress with white sash and white stockings and black shiny shoes, saying it was for a Christmas party at the nursery school. But no party was scheduled.

Before Cindy and Samantha left home that day, Jenkins went to town to buy groceries. It was the last he saw them alive. "There were no arguments," recalled Jenkins. "We were civil to each other."

"She didn't look or act no different," said Christian, the foreman.

After picking up Samantha at the daycare center, Cindy would drive to the deserted road. She affixed the vacuum cleaner hose to the exhaust pipe of the Bronco, ran it up through the back window, sealed the window with the duct tape she had taken from home along with the hose and, with the ignition still running, climbed into the back seat and held Samantha in her arms. The coroner's report estimates that this happened around noon.

A few hours later, a pumper on a nearby oil rigging spotted the car with two bodies slumped in the back seat, and he phoned the police.

On the day after Christmas, twelve days after the tragedy, Ferguson Jenkins loaded his pickup truck with unwrapped Christmas presents and returned them in Guthrie to Wal-Mart, Sam's Wholesale Outlet and Anthony's Clothing Store. They included a jogging outfit and sweaters for Cindy. For Samantha, there were Cabbage Patch dolls, a Minnie Mouse towel set, a Beauty and the Beast towel set ("She loved *Beauty and the Beast*," said Jenkins), coloring sets, a large box of crayons, a sweater that had Santa Claus and reindeer and the word "Christmas" across it, and matching socks.

When Jenkins returned home from the stores, his three daughters from his first marriage, to Kathy Jenkins, were in the house. The girls, Kelly, 22, Delores, 21, and Kimberly, 15— all in college or high school — had come down from their home in Chatham, Ontario, where Jenkins was born and raised, to celebrate Christmas with their father, as they did every year. But this year, they had also come to go to the funeral of their three-year-old half-sister.

Jenkins's 86-year-old father, who is in a nursing home in Chatham, had not made the trip for the funeral. "Said he couldn't take it," said Jenkins. It was his father, Ferguson Jenkins Sr., to whom Jenkins dedicated his induction into the Hall of Fame and who sat proudly in attendance in a wheelchair.

Jenkins had told the gathering at Cooperstown: "My father was a semipro ballplayer and he played in the Negro leagues, but he didn't make the major leagues because he was limited by history" — the color barrier in big league baseball that existed until 1947.

"But he has outlived that history," Jenkins continued. "I always told him that anything I do in baseball, I do for the two of us, and so now I feel I'm being inducted into the Hall of Fame with my father."

Jenkins's mother, Delores, has been dead for several years. She had become blind after complications while giving birth to her only child. "I remember she always walked with a white cane and always made sure that my baseball uniform was sparkling clean and my baseball shoes were polished," Jenkins has recalled. "I'm not sure how she knew, but she never let me out of the house to play ball unless I was all in order."

Jenkins grew up playing baseball and hockey and basketball, and was often the lone black in those leagues in Chatham. "I heard 'nigger' a lot," he recalled, "but I was always determined to make people respect my abilities. I always wanted them to say, 'Hey, watch that black guy, he's good.' And I did get into some fights, mostly in hockey, and lost a few teeth. But I came out of it."

He left home after signing a contract with the Philadelphia Phillies when he was eighteen, having just graduated high school, "a tall, skinny kid of 155 pounds," he said. "My father was a cook on shipping lines in the Great Lakes, and my mother was home alone a lot. I've always felt kind of guilty leaving her, but I knew I had to pursue my career."

Three years later, at the end of the 1965 season, he was called up to the Phillies, as a relief pitcher. In his first game, he replaced the veteran Jim Bunning, whom, he recalled, he had badgered for pitching help.

"How do you grip the ball? How do you throw your slider?" Jenkins would ask Bunning. The next season Jenkins was traded to the Cubs, and Leo Durocher made him a starter. Jenkins would learn his craft well while pitching in Wrigley Field, the smallest ballpark in the major leagues.

With the often lackluster Cub teams, he pitched in bad luck. He still shares a record for the most 1–0 losses in a season, five, in 1968, in games against pitchers that included Bob Gibson and Don Drysdale. Still, he won the Cy Young Award in 1971, with a 24–13 record, leading the league in complete games, with 30, innings pitched, 325, and strikeouts, 304. He won 20 games six straight seasons for the Cubs, and then fell to 14–16 in 1973. The Cubs responded by trading him to Texas in a move that stunned him, and much of baseball.

The next year, 1974, Jenkins won 25 games and the American League's Comeback Player of the Year award. Like his former teammate Ernie Banks, he was never on a pennant-winner. He came close, however, during the 1969 season when the Cubs, leading for much of the season, faded in the stretch as the Mets won the National League's East Division, and then the pennant and World Series.

Jenkins was traded to Boston in 1976, traded back to Texas in 1978, released after the 1981 season and then signed as a free agent by the Cubs. He pitched two more seasons and then retired, two months short of his 40th birthday. He caught on as a pitching coach in the Rangers' organization, where he spent several years with their Oklahoma City Class AAA team before being given his release three years ago.

Jenkins was always one of the most gentlemanly of ballplayers, and was thrown out of a game only once, when he threw a few bats onto the field in a pique. "Fergie, I'm sorry," said the umpire. "I'm going to have to ask you to leave." Jenkins had one other incident of greater notoriety. In August 1980 he was arrested in Toronto on a charge of carrying in his luggage small amounts of hashish, marijuana, and cocaine.

He was suspended by baseball Commissioner Bowie Kuhn, but soon was reinstated by an arbitrator who said that Kuhn could not rule on Jenkins before the courts did.

But while Jenkins was found guilty of possession of drugs in December 1980, no police record exists. At sentencing in the Ontario Provincial Court, Judge Jerry Young told Jenkins: "You seem to be a person who has conducted himself in exemplary fashion in the community and in the country, building up an account. This is the time to draw on that account." Judge Young then wiped the slate clean for Jenkins.

It was while he was with the Oklahoma City team that he found that ranch house. He and Maryanne, whom he had met and married while with the Cubs, had loved the house at first sight, he said. Both liked the solitude it afforded, and the beauty of the landscape there. Her son, Raymond, by a previous marriage, was then eight, and his father had died and Jenkins had adopted him. "I call him Fergie usually," said Raymond, a bright, good-natured youth, "unless I want something. Then I call him Dad."

Ray, who had known only cities, had to make adjustments to farm life, and did, getting to learn how to care for and ride horses, and, at paternal urging, to paint posts, too, not always with pleasure.

Adjustments for him, and for Jenkins, would grow increasingly harder when Maryanne was injured in a car accident near their home, and, after a month in intensive care, died of pneumonia. Samantha was then six months old.

When Cindy Takieddine, divorced and working as a secretary in a law office in Los Angeles, read about Jenkins's election to the Hall of Fame, she called the Cubs to try to locate him, to congratulate him. She managed to get his home phone number. She had met him when he was a young player with the Cubs and she was nineteen.

They had struck up a friendship, although Jenkins says it was never a romance, and he hadn't seen her in about fifteen years. When she learned from Jenkins on the phone that his wife had died, she offered to come with a girlfriend to Guthrie on her vacation, and help him any way she could. He accepted.

"They cooked, they took care of the house and they watched over the kids," Jenkins recalled. The girlfriend soon went back home, but Cindy stayed and they fell in love.

Six months ago they became engaged. He said she started feeling pressure from friends about marriage. "It'll happen, just not right away," Jenkins told her. Meanwhile, she was a great mother and, essentially, a great wife, Jenkins said. She traded her white slacks for farm overalls. She was a talented decorator around the house, putting, as the foreman, Christian, called it, "the woman's touch on it, with all them frills and friggles." He added, "And she was always a lady."

Cindy kept the checkbook in order and looked over the endorsements and the personal-appearance schedule for Jenkins, who flew periodically to card shows, fantasy camps and speaking engagements. She grew to be a loving and concerned mother to Raymond and developed a close bond with Samantha. Cindy also seemed to take to farm life, and was active in classes in town, particularly ceramics. She made angels and deer heads and a Santa Claus for Christmas that was placed on the mantel above the fireplace in the living room.

"There were some spats between Fergie and Cindy, sure; what couple doesn't have spats on occasion?" said Lemoyne Hardin, a family friend. "But it was pretty clear that they got along just fine."

A lot of mail came to Jenkins, much of it asking for autographs, and sometimes Cindy would open it up, see that it was from a woman and throw it away. When Jenkins found out, he said that was not right, that it was his personal property. If she wanted to open his mail, he would be happy to do it with her.

Tension seemed to increase when a sports reporter from Cincinnati called the Jenkins home in early December and Cindy answered. He asked whether it was true that Jenkins had accepted a job as a pitching coach in the Cincinnati Reds organization. Cindy had known nothing about it, and it angered her.

"Cindy knew I was talking with front-office people," said Jenkins. "But I hadn't told her about the Reds, hadn't shared it with her. But I hadn't signed the contract. I still have the contract, unsigned." At his kitchen table recently, he took out a briefcase, and two pink contracts, and showed them still unsigned.

"I told her that baseball had been my life, and that I still had a dream of one day being a pitching coach in the major leagues," he said. "But I said nothing is certain yet, I hadn't made any definite decision about baseball. But she was concerned. She said she was nervous about having to spend eight months alone at the ranch, and she wasn't sure how she could manage the place.

"I told her that she could come visit me wherever I was. It appeared I'd be with the Reds' minor league club in Chattanooga and that things would work out. Not to worry. I think that's what troubled her. I think so. I don't know for sure. I never will."

Jenkins sighed. "I sit here and I seem calm," he said. "But my mind is racing 90 miles an hour. The other night I woke up about three in the morning and came down here and just looked around. I said, 'Why? Why? Why did she have to do it? Why if she's unhappy, chop off her life like that? And take the baby with her?' O.K., be angry at me, but don't punish the baby."

After Jenkins had returned the Christmas presents, he remembers "getting short" with his daughters. The suicide and homicide, the Christmas season, all of it was bearing down on him, "smothering me," he said.

"I apologized to my kids," he said. "I told them, 'Your dad's just not having a good day.' They understood, I think. I said to myself, 'Fergie, get a grip.'

"But I knew I needed help, needed to talk to someone. I thought of calling 911. But then I thought about a chaplain I'd met in the hospital where Maryanne had been. I needed answers and I thought a clergyman might know. I called and told him it was urgent. He said to come right over. We talked for about three hours.

"He told me that God will not put more pressure on an individual than he can handle. Well, I don't want any more pressure. I don't want any more grief, any more sorrow. I really don't know how much more I can take. But talking to him was a big help. And I had talked to a priest, too. He told me he thought that Cindy had a chemical imbalance. But I'm going to be going to some support groups now. I think it's important."

Jenkins is a Baptist, and says that despite his agonies he has maintained a belief in God. "People tell me that God has his reasons," he said. "I'm hoping somewhere down the road he lets me know. I certainly can't figure it out."

The suicide note that Cindy left on the front seat of the Bronco provided no answers for him, either, he said. He took out the letter that was written in pen on the back of a lumber-company receipt. It read:

"My last statement. My name is Cindy Backherms Takieddine.

My address is in my purse. Contact Ferguson Jenkins. He can claim the bodies.

"Fergie said opening his mail is a gross invasion of his privacy — truly immoral. But ruining someone's life and telling them to get out the best way they can — that's immoral. I am to leave with what I came with. I was betrayed.

"I cannot leave and go away without Samantha. I love her more than life itself and cannot envision my life without her. She has been my child for almost two years.

"To all those who love me and Boog please forgive me — I had no way out." Boog was Cindy's nickname for Samantha.

"We had been talking," said Jenkins. "We talked a lot. We worked things out a lot. I never wanted her to leave. I never said that. I don't understand what she meant by betrayal. I just don't know. I just don't know. I've got so many questions. And no answers."

Jenkins was now on the white porch overlooking his property, as the sun, on an unseasonably warm day, reflected on the lakes and the cattle that were grazing, and on the horses. "My uncle Coleman said I should blast the house, that it's unlucky," he said. "I even thought of it. But this is my home, where I'm going to stay. And I'm going to have a priest bless it."

Jenkins ran a hand against his graying temple and looked out at the farm that he loves so much. "It's much quieter now with just me and Raymond," he said. "But we're trying to make it, trying to get things done. And I'm trying to be his dad as much as I can."

Jenkins said he still isn't sure about the Reds job, and who will stay with Raymond if he does go. "I still have things to figure out," he said.

Later that evening, in the dark, he drove for dinner into town to a pizza parlor with Raymond. The lights from the pickup truck reflected on the red clay farm road.

Raymond seemed to be doing all right. His father talked now about the computer game Raymond had been promised for Christmas if he did well in school, in the seventh grade. He had produced a 96 average, and received the game. Raymond talked about the computer game and what he wanted to do when he grew up. "Probably mess with computers," he said. Jenkins smiled.

"Oh, Raymond," said Jenkins after a moment, "it's supposed to start getting cold and rainy tomorrow. I think you'll have to take the horses into the barn."

"O.K., Fergie," he said, quietly and respectfully. "I'll remember."

Father and son sat, lost in thought. Jenkins, in his green baseball cap, was silent behind the wheel. The only sound in the night was the rattling of the truck on the road.

MARK KRAM, JR.

The World Is Her Cloister

FROM THE PHILADELPHIA DAILY NEWS

"I remember a saying I once heard: 'God alone is enough. Everything else is not enough.' "
— Shelly Pennefather, in a letter to former Villanova teammate Lynn Tighe

THE DELICATE VOICE on the other end of the telephone line answered: "Monastery of the Poor Clares." While Lynn Tighe knew that the chance of seeing her old teammate, Shelly Pennefather, was slim — that the Poor Clares observed a strict vow of enclosure and seldom saw visitors — Tighe told the Sister who took the call that she just happened to be in Virginia and was wondering . . . umm, would it be possible to stop in and just see Shelly for a second? The Sister placed her on hold. When she came back on the line and said, "Yes," Tighe wondered if the Sister had sensed something dire in her voice. "Like," Tighe said, "I *had* to see her."

What the Poor Clare who answered the phone heard perhaps was just unbridled curiosity. While no one who knew her was surprised when former Villanova basketball All-America Shelly Pennefather entered the convent one and a half years ago, it came as a total shock when she announced that she was entering a Roman Catholic order of cloistered nuns. To Tighe and the other women who teamed up with Pennefather at Villanova and grew exceedingly close to her, the whole idea of a cloister conjured up a host of uncomfortable images: of dark, forbidding walls; of a stern Mother Superior with lips pursed in disapproval; of stoical nuns dressed in threadbare habits that cascaded onto cold stone floors.

None of that turned out to be so. Located deep in the Alexandria suburbs on a street where children cavorted and the trees were just beginning to show the smallest of buds, the place had a tranquil, inviting feel that Tighe found reassuring. While not sure what to expect when Shelly came out — if she had changed — Tighe stood in the visiting room with an odd apprehension when she heard a voice exclaim with laughter: *"What are you doing here?"*

Seated behind a screen and dressed in her habit, Shelly appeared to be the same old Shelly, overflowing with enthusiasm, wit and a curiosity of her own: How were her old Villanova teammates? And her old coach, Harry Perretta? How was he? The two talked and talked, and when their allotted hour was up, it occurred to Tighe how cheerful Shelly seemed. She radiated joy. When Shelly said good-bye and promised to write, Tighe drove back to Philadelphia and found herself looking forward to the letters.

The letters Shelly Pennefather writes from the placid embrace of the cloister are the only window she has on the world. She cannot leave even for an hour. Nor is she allowed to use the phone. She only can sit with a pen and a piece of paper and set down in words her account of the spiritual journey to which she has committed. While her decision to remove herself from the coarse affairs of society struck some of her old teammates as a loss ("Heck," said one, "she would have made a wonderful teacher"), her letters speak not of a loss to our sputtering planet but of a profound gain.

Because Shelly Pennefather is praying for us.

She is praying for us every day.

Dear Friends,

Greetings from behind locked doors. I always figured that at least one of us would be incarcerated, but I never guessed it would be me!

What you are probably interested in, is what I think of it all. Obviously, most of what "goes on" in a cloister takes place in the very heart of each Sister. There are no distractions to take you away from looking at yourself . . . No music, no TV, no movies, or social outings. Just the soul alone with its Creator . . .

I have learned a great deal about myself, and found out that conquering sinfulness and laying aside self-love and pride is an overwhelming task . . . I feel so thankful that I have been called to this vocation. However, I earnestly beg your prayers for me because I am wholly unworthy of such a calling, and often I tire of the effort that is involved in purifying and perfecting yourself . . .

Please pray for me that I may never grow tepid in my search for God . . .

Love,
Shell

The spiritual journey that leads a person from the thrall of twentieth century culture to the door of the cloister is an immense one, and for Shelly Pennefather — who is now called Sister Rose Marie — it occurred gradually. The daughter of an Air Force colonel who did not allow either TV or radio in the house and who each evening convened his wife and seven children for the rosary, Pennefather attended Mass each day while starring in basketball at Villanova, received her "calling" during her three-year pro tenure in Japan and entered the Monastery of the Poor Clares in June 1991 at the age of twenty-five.

To someone who has grown accustomed to circulating in a democratic society — and enjoying, as Pennefather joked in one of her letters, "the pleasures of the palate" — entering the Order of Poor Clares is like stepping back into the thirteenth century. Founded in 1212 when the beautiful and wealthy Clare heard Francis of Assisi preach the splendor of evangelical poverty, the Order of Poor Clares spread out in the world with the sole objective of "praising and glorifying God." According to Mother Mary Francis P.C.C. in her book, *A Right to be Merry*, the Poor Clare is the "spouse of Christ." The Poor Clare is not allowed to leave the cloister except for hospital care and cannot step out from behind the screen to accept visitors.

Still four years removed from taking her final vows, Pennefather is in a one-year phase in her scholarship in which she is not allowed to see even her parents until July. However, in letters to her parents, Perretta, former teammates Tighe, Karen Daly (née Hargadon), Lisa Angelotti, Kathy Miller and Mary Beth Culp, she describes an existence that is steeped in the observance of devout contemplation. While the consensus is that Shelly has become increasingly pious in her letters — that indeed she has evolved in spirit from Shelly to Sister Rose Marie — there still is a part of her that remains a cutup. Example:

"*I was given a wheat biscuit, a couple of nuts, three pieces of cheese and a grapefruit,*" she wrote of her culinary initiation to the Monastery of the Poor Clares. " '*Appetizers,' I thought. I kept waiting for the main meal . . . I am still waiting.*"

For Sister Rose Marie and the twelve other Poor Clares who share the cloister with her, each day begins not with corporeal sustenance but with penance. The chiming of the Matins bells calls the Sisters from sleep at 12:30 A.M. for prayers, during which, as Mother Mary Francis P.C.C. observed in her book, "the anguish and loneliness and fear of those who have never heard of us and whom we have never heard of" are held up in invocation. When this period of solemn adoration is over at 2 A.M., the Poor Clare pads shoeless back to her "cell," as it is called, and dozes off again until the Matins bells summon them back for prayers at 5 A.M. The Poor Clare never sleeps for more than four hours at a stretch, and, as Sister Rose Marie joked in one of her letters: "*I will not report to you my initial feelings of the bell ringer or her bell!*"

The schedule of events that commences with the dawn at the Monastery of the Poor Clares in Alexandria is observed with strict obedience. There is a public Mass in the small chapel at 7 A.M., during which the Sisters sit in the choir shielded behind iron crossbars. Scant helpings of coffee and bread are served when Mass ends, housecleaning and other chores are then done and, at 11:00 A.M., the Sisters are summoned to chant Scriptures and psalms. In a letter describing her indoctrination to the Poor Clare Program, Sister Rose Marie observed: "*There was a dozen or so prayers that needed to be memorized ASAP . . . trying to figure out when to stand or kneel . . . and most devastating to me, [enduring] life without Twix bars.*"

No Twix bars and no beef or chicken are ever allowed. For dinner — which is served at noon — the Poor Clare is provided each day with soup, a vegetable, potato, fruit and what is called a "third portion," which is set out as the principal dish. Upon the conclusion of dinner, prayers are said again, the dishes are cleaned and, at 2 P.M., the Sisters convene for Vespers, the devotional exercise that ushers in the evening. When Vespers are over, there is a small snack, night prayers, and the retiring bell tolls at 8:30. The Poor Clare returns to her "cell." Still clothed in her habit, she arranges herself on her straw mattress and sleeps until, as Sister Rose Marie observed in a letter to Karen Daly:

"Life proceeds with the usual bells."

Dear Harry,

I thought you could use the help of a few angels (see reverse side of Christmas card), so I send them to you in the hopes that at least a few of them can shoot over 50 percent.

How is my beloved old coach? I do not have a single bit of news about how the team is doing, and possibly that is because I am becoming more and more removed from it all . . .

It is kind of amazing to realize that I stopped playing for you five and a half seasons ago. I wonder if I would recognize you as the same coach . . . I think of you often, and enjoy telling stories about you to all the nuns, most of whom have never seen a live basketball game . . .

Things are going well for me, and I am truly very happy . . . Maybe only in heaven will I realize what an immeasurable grace it is to be given a vocation to the religious life.

Love,
Sister Rose Marie

When Shelly Pennefather graduated from high school in upstate New York, she had basketball scholarships to well over two hundred colleges. She was that good. Through junior high in Colorado and four seasons of high school ball in both Denver and Utica, New York, Pennefather did not lose a single game. Not one. It was not until she came to Villanova that she became acquainted with losing, and Perretta still gets a kick out of that. "She was perfect until she came here," he said with a laugh in his cluttered office at Villanova. "I showed her how to lose."

A picture of Shelly from her old days at Villanova occupies a prominent place on the wall, and whenever Perretta looks up at it from his desk, it reminds him how he happened to recruit her. While the consensus seemed to be that she would attend Providence (she has a brother who played for Rick Pitino there), Pennefather came to Villanova for a visit and Perretta found himself immersed in a conversation with her on the Blessed Mother. Quite religious himself ("I pray the rosary every day," Perretta said), the Wildcats' coach remembers that Pennefather showed him the medal of the Virgin Mary that she wore.

"She told me how she believed in the power of prayer," Perretta said. "We had an unusual conversation."

Shelly Pennefather had simply a wonderful career at Villanova.

When she graduated in 1987, she ended up the school's all-time leading scorer for women *and* men with a career total of 2,408 points. She won the coveted Wade Trophy that season as the outstanding senior in America and still holds 21 individual records at Villanova. She also is part of eight team records. Grinning with pride, her father, Mike, observed that "she was the Larry Bird of her sport. She was something else."

Perretta concurred. "I remember she would come in here, sleep for an hour on the sofa, go down, get dressed and score twenty-five," he said. "Like clockwork."

When the chance presented itself in 1987 to play professionally in Japan for the Nippon Express, Pennefather accepted, and the experience there proved to be pivotal. Although she learned how to speak and write Japanese, she was living alone in a foreign culture and had a great deal of time between games to read and think. She seemed to flourish in the solitude. She continued to attend Mass each day and even had a provision included in her $200,000 annual contract: Wherever her team traveled in Japan, special arrangements had to be made for her to observe Mass. Because Japan has only a small percentage of Catholic churches, that sometimes could be quite difficult.

"She had an apartment alone and she began doing some deep spiritual reading," her father said. "She developed a profound interest in the religious life in Japan."

Until Shelly came back from Japan in the fall of 1990 and started working in the summers for Mother Teresa Missionary of Charity in Norristown, Mike Pennefather had no inkling that his daughter planned to become a nun. However, while growing up in places as diverse as Hawaii, Germany, and Australia as her father traveled the world during his twenty-eight years in the Air Force, Shelly was reared in a home that had two passions: sports and the Bible. Forbidding a TV in the house because he considers it a "sewer," Mike Pennefather and his wife, Mary Jane, pointed each of their children to basketball and the church. Mary Jane even had entered a convent herself at one point in her life. (She would not consent to be interviewed for this article.)

"I knew when Sister Rose Marie began working for Mother Teresa that she was starting to look at this seriously," Mike Pennefather said. "I know Mother Teresa had a deep effect on her. Heck, Mother Teresa has had an effect on the whole world."

Said Daly, a former roommate: "We knew when she came back from Japan that she was considering entering the convent, but when we heard the word 'cloister,' we were shocked. We wondered: Are we ever going to see her again?"

Visitors are allowed in the Monastery of the Poor Clares to see Sister Rose Marie only on rare occasions, and that includes her parents. While the Pennefathers have relocated in suburban Virginia and attend Mass in the public chapel each week, contact with their daughter is limited to three sessions each year. Mike Pennefather leaves her a letter each Saturday when he attends Mass, and while Sister Rose Marie is allowed to read her letters during a period each Sunday, she is not allowed to keep them. Nor is she allowed periodicals.

The world on the other side of the cloister door has become a foreign place to Sister Rose Marie. While she told her former teammates before entering the Order of Poor Clares that she had certain apprehensions, that she knew she had a "calling" but, as she told Angelotti, was not sure she could "follow all the rules," she appears to have become accustomed to her surroundings. The only time she has stepped out of the cloister was for a trip to the emergency room when she cut her index finger on a razor blade, and it occurred to her in one of her early letters how odd that seemed.

"*Of course,*" she wrote, "*it had been close to two months since I had seen people walking in shorts, traffic lights and all the usual scenes of a hot summer day. But what was different — and what I had forgotten — was that I would henceforth be treated as religious, not just another human being. This came to my attention as soon as I got to the hospital and the paramedic chirped: 'Hello, Sister!'*"

Dear Mom and Dad Daly,
    I am still trying to recover from the wounding blow that you did not name your firstborn after me — Shelisha Daly has such a melodic ring to it . . .
    Somehow I immensely enjoy imagining my old roomie swamped with bottles, powder, lotions and diapers. It is so much more picturesque than envisioning you with the latest computer, and infinitely more valuable . . .

I am lost in wonder of the richness of our faith and the inexhaustible grace that God holds out for us in the ordinary comings and goings in our daily life. If only we could be made consciously aware of His presence with us at every moment, how different we would speak or act, or more closely monitor what we watch or read. To think that He is the Silent Listener to our every conversation, all our thoughts and words and deeds lay open to Him. In the silence of hidden, monastic life, His presence becomes so very real . . .

Love and Prayers,
Sister Rose Marie

When Villanova held its annual alumni basketball game for its former women players one Saturday at duPont Pavilion, everybody seemed to show up: Lisa Angelotti came from South Jersey; Karen Daly was there with her husband and baby; Mary Beth Culp dropped in and so did some others. Each had with them a dessert or some other dish, and, when the game was over, the women convened at picnic tables that had been set up and ate. Great fun was had, but something just seemed wrong . . . Shelly was not there.

"Not a single day passes that we do not think of her," said Angelotti, who is a nurse. "We miss her."

Said Daly: "We love her."

A whole group of former teammates visited Shelly back in the spring and it was just like old times, despite the habit Shelly wore and the screen that separated them. Shelly was the same old Shelly, brimming with laughter and joy. The hour passed quickly — too quickly — and when it was over, the women piled in the car and headed back to Philadelphia and Sister Rose Marie disappeared back to her quiet world, a world to which her only window is a pen and a piece of paper.

JOHN HEWITT

Home for Pheasants

FROM GRAY'S SPORTING JOURNAL

VICTOR CHARLIE, sharp cookie that he was, could have had one
more that night, if he'd used a good retriever. Then again, if he'd
had a retriever, he'd probably have eaten it with his rice.

I wasn't worried until the third time I woke up. The first time,
and I wasn't awake long, I marveled that one person could have as
much blood in him as the pool I was lying in. The second time,
just coming on to full daylight, the propwash from the helicopter
woke me on the stretcher and I briefly imagined what the healthier survivors of my first squad would be telling the rest of the platoon at supper: "The frigging lieutenant'll do anything to get a
ride on a slick." The lieutenant still hasn't ridden a slick, a then-
new medevac helicopter. When I opened my eyes, the bird squat-
ting over me was yet another antiquated H-34, obsolete since
Korea, but the backbone of the Marine Corps' helicopter fleet.

"Only on point," I cautioned the private who handed the front
of the stretcher to someone in the aircraft. He laughed. He was
new and had a tendency to flip his selector switch to fully automatic at the first muzzle flash, and about the time everyone else
was replacing their first magazine, he was trying to borrow one,
having emptied all of his.

"O.K., lieutenant. We'll tell 'em you're gonna be O.K. We
thought you was dead for half an hour."

The third time I woke up, though, I panicked a little. A large
corpsman with scissors was cutting my boots off.

"Hey, goddamn it! That's my only pair of boots!" I said, trying to
sit up. My sitting up reflex was out of order. The scavenging in-

stinct, stronger in good Marines than the fighting instinct or even
the beer-drinking instinct, had driven me, laid over four days before ever setting foot in Vietnam, to the Okinawa processing depot.
The P.D. was a gold mine. Marines rotating back to The World dis-
embarked there, stripped and discarded their dirty, sweat-soaked
jungle utilities and jungle boots and showered, continuing on in
stateside issue clothing. Having no illusions about being able to find
the highly desirable jungle clothing new in my size once I got in-
country, I selected two pair of each from the discard bins and
washed them twice at the B.O.Q. My radio operator, in rags when I
met him the day I picked up my platoon, and just my size, got my
spare set.

"Relax, lieutenant," the other corpsman said, as he ran his own
scissors up the seam of my shirt-sleeve, "Where you're going, they
don't wear these."

My skipper, the only other Kansan in the company, was waiting
to debrief me in recovery when I woke up the fourth time. "Hewitt,"
he began, "if you had to pay those two neurosurgeons by the hour,
you wouldn't see another paycheck before your next tour. And if
you didn't keep your rifle any cleaner than they said you keep the
inside of your head, it wouldn't work either. So what happened?"

After that, I woke only occasionally. The ward they had me in
was pretty austere and what always woke me up was the attendant
rolling someone else out with the sheet over his face. I had read
about such places in college, in some of the poems Walt Whitman
had written during the Civil War, wards where those expected to
die were put.

Once two doctors in scrubs were looking at the chart at the foot
of my bed, dictating what I guessed was the telegram that the very
sober captain and gunnery sergeant from the hometown reserve
unit delivered — in their class A's, medals and badges, spit-shined
dress oxfords and frame covers — to my parents. A gray-haired
Red Cross lady wrote as one of the doctors spoke:

"Patient remains very critically ill. Condition deteriorating, prog-
nosis poor."

"Put in there," I said, startling all three of them, "put in there I'll
be home for pheasants at Christmas."

The Red Cross woman looked at the older doctor, who cleared

his throat and continued, "Patient claims he will be home for . . .
what?"

"Pheasants."

"Pheasants by Christmas." He shook his head and went on to the
next bed. "Marines," he said.

That was August. My father, Clyde, read Tom the telegram over the
phone. The operative word was pheasants and Tom, my twin who
was stationed at Fort Bragg, put in for a two-week Christmas leave
the next morning.

By Christmas Eve, Clyde and I had both gotten over being glad I
was still alive and were getting considerably concerned over where
our next meal was going to come from.

I executed a U-turn in my seven-year-old Falcon wagon at the
west end of the third small town we'd scouted uselessly for restaurants and cruised back to the highway, peering through the falling
snow at the darkened store fronts.

"Nuts," Clyde said, "I expected this out of Bennington, but this
is *Concordia*. These places all roll up their sidewalks at five o'clock.
Now what're we going to do?"

"Crash Tom's in-laws' Christmas Eve dinner. It's only nineteen
more miles to Belleville."

"Oh, we can't do that."

"Watch us." Pete, five years old and in his prime, woke up when
I stopped at the stop sign to turn onto the highway and raised his
head. As long as someone remembered his Purina, he was not at
the mercy of the vagaries of small-town restaurateurs.

Tom's mother-in-law had cooked extra, just in case, and a card
table was set up to accommodate the two younger kids whom
Clyde and I displaced from the dining room table. Lest there not
be enough roast beef to go around, Clyde and I split the other en-
tree, a cottontail. Judging from the number of number sixes we
encountered, someone needed a little less choke in their rabbit
gun.

The snow-filled north wind that rose in the night, rattling windows and waking both of us as we slept in our sleeping bags on the
parlor floor, drifted many of the east-west roads shut. The pheas-

ants, which had survived the first six weeks of their own baptism of fire, were no more accommodating Christmas Day than the restaurateurs had been the night before. The storm, as we expected, had them bunched up in draws and heavy cover, but even when we found them, they were giving us the slip, running ahead, flushing wild and at unpredictable times. Though we walked the best spots Tom knew, we had only three roosters when I turned the car toward home, just before sundown.

The light was failing when we passed the cemetery crossroads with the dense cedar windbreaks on two sides standing out dark on the white prairie. "If we could only figure a way to outsmart a bunch of these darn things and get in range before they . . . *hey!* Go on! Go on! Go on! Don't slow down! Go clear to the half-mile line before you turn around." Tom had seen a cock run into the ditch opposite the north windbreak.

"Hell's bells, Tom," Clyde said, "You can't get out and hunt here. This is their damn *cemetery*."

"So?" Tom argued. "That's probably what everyone around here thinks. So the birds won't expect us to put the surround on them here. John'll drop you off at the south end of the first windbreak, me at the gate on the east, then park at the other windbreak and walk it west with Pete. I'll run diagonally across to the northwest corner ahead of you two and block them there. They won't hear me in this wind. We know there'll be one in there ahead of John and I got my plug out, just in case."

The two of them exited the car silently at their appointed spots, latching their doors behind them gently. I parked and Pete was on birds before I was across the ditch, his black tail working furiously. Through the screen of cedars I caught glimpses of Tom, 200 yards away, bisecting the graveyard at a dead run, holding his shotgun high as he dodged between dark marble slabs and hurdled the rows of lower markers with names on them that reflected the Czechoslovakian origin of most of the local families. He looked for a moment the way he had looked ten years before, when he'd quarterbacked the seventh-grade football team and he ran the keeper play and broke into the secondary.

By now the birds were probably running, too, from two directions in a three-way race they didn't know they were in, with time

running out for some of the runners faster than any of us suspected. Clyde, like me on the outside of his row of cedars, was out
of my sight. We'd meet at the corner.

It was a good race, of which I wish I could've been there for the
end. Judging from the amount of shooting, Tom did not beat the
pheasants there by much and at the first shot, I was off with Pete at
a run, myself. He'd need the dog.

Tom was still running the last I saw him, disappearing over a terrace in cut milo northwest of the cemetery, with Pete halfway out
to him and closing fast. I stopped and scanned the snow at the corner, which was covered with pheasant tracks. Clyde approached
with his own Model 12 over his shoulder, scowling.

"Man, somebody's going to see us in here and Tom's in-laws will
never hear the end of it. Did he get any?"

"Him and Pete must have at least one cripple on the ground
over the hill. I see a bunch of empties here and one dead one over
yonder. Look at the tail on that rascal."

"Maybe we better scour around, the amount of shooting he did,
there ought to be more'n one dead."

There were three, which, together with the cripple Pete finally
caught up with, was his limit for the day. There were two loaded
shells in the snow, too, where he was trying to reload while he ran.
We retraced his route back through the cemetery, the snow being
less deep than along the cedars, Clyde and I each carrying a pheasant, Tom carrying two.

"Lord's sakes, Tom," Clyde remarked, "You stepped right on
people's graves. You could've at least run in between."

Tom grinned his limit-of-pheasants grin. "Dad," he said, "You
think once you wind up here, you care whether somebody steps on
your grave chasing a pheasant? Pete! No!" Pete had stopped to lift
a leg on a large stone. "That's Diane's Uncle Milan's father's, I
think."

He had shot his gun dry at the corner, seven shots, which was how
many were in each of the three volleys the burial detail from Fort
Riley fired beside the casket being lowered into the open grave
fifty feet north of Uncle Milan's plot, in the ninety-degree heat two
Julys hence, the next time I visited St. Katharine's. It was the last

time I ever wore my dress whites, the only time I ever wore the black nylon mourning band on the sleeve, which had come with the uniform jewelry kit we'd all had to buy at Quantico.

"Here we go," I thought, when the echoes of the rifle shots died away and the bugler began taps, but I and the widow with her arm hooked through mine, also standing at attention, got through even that dry-eyed. What she was thinking about I have no idea, but I was remembering four pheasants and a tiny figure and a black dog, disappearing over a terrace into snow-covered milo next to this cemetery on a dark winter evening.

"You kids done real good," Uncle Milan assured us, tears streaming down his own face, "Just what Tom would've wanted."

I was holding open the door of the funeral parlor limousine for Diane when Terry separated himself from the other mourners and approached. Other than for Tom's wedding three summers earlier, he and Tom and I had never been to western Kansas together outside pheasant season. He started to tell me something, his face wrenched and contorted trying not to cry, but he gave up and all that came out through the tears was, "Goddamnit anyway!" three times.

I returned alone late that evening. Thought maybe they'd need a hand shoveling the dirt back in or something. It was all done already, mounded up against the inevitable settling, tamped down, and I was surprised how red the soil was for Kansas, how remarkably similar in color to the dirt I'd washed out of the boots I'd scavenged on Okinawa. A temporary metal marker was stuck into the ground at the head. "Thomas T. Hewitt," it said, "Captain, U.S. Army. April 21, 1945–July 2, 1970. Killed in Action, RVN."

The sun, setting red behind the terrace, cast shadows of the cedars the length of the cemetery, over the trimmed evergreens, the neat rows of stones and monuments, the vases of flowers here and there beside a stone.

"Be seeing you, Tom," I said. "Get us some birds located."

In the ditch where the first draw north of the cemetery crosses the road, a cock pheasant crowed, as they do in Kansas at sunset. And sunrise.

GEORGE PLIMPTON

Fishing on the FDR

FROM ESQUIRE

Many men go fishing all their lives without knowing that it is not
fish they are after.
— Henry David Thoreau

As you get onto the FDR Drive at Ninety-sixth Street in Manhattan, you can't miss them — maybe six rods, perhaps as many as
fifty on a nice day when the word gets out that the fish are running
in the East River. In the summer the sun umbrellas are set back
among the sidewalk benches, and often there are jury-rigged
sheets and tarps to provide shade or to get under if the sky darkens
and the summer rains come through. It has often struck me that
many of the cars going by within feet of this activity contain people
on their way to the famous fishing grounds of Long Island, maybe
to Montauk to head out for Butter Hole and the big tuna heading
north. One wonders if they give so much as a passing thought to
their minor league brethren on the East River esplanade.

I bicycled up there the other day — a warm summer weekend
morning. I had no idea what to expect. Obviously there are fish in
the river; a news story some years back reported someone dropping a line out of a tenth-story Sutton Place apartment that over-
hangs the water.

It turned out that almost all the fishermen I visited off the
Ninety-sixth Street ramp were Puerto Rican. The radios in the
grass behind them blared out salsa rhythms, barely audible above
the roar of the traffic on the Drive.

The first fisherman I talked to was Urbano Ortiz, an employee at the Metropolitan Hospital behind us, and five years on the river. His wife, Lucy, was with him. Each had a rod out, and also a wire cage baited to catch blue crabs. Urbano filled me in with some practical details — bluefish, striped bass, flounder, eels, of course, were in the river, the fish coming down under the Triborough Bridge and heading for the Lower Bay and the sea. Ortiz's equipment was typical of that found along the esplanade — an 11-foot casting rod, 40-pound test line, a 5-ounce lead sinker, and a hook baited with a slice of bunker that he buys at the Ideal Pet Warehouse at 116th Street and First Avenue. Many of the fishermen use bolts and screws they find in the street for sinkers. The bottom in the basinlike stretch of the river at Ninety-sixth Street claims a lot of rigs. No use being fancy about sinkers!

Attached to most of the rod tips is a little silver bell, which allows the angler to leave the rod leaning against the railing and retire to a camp stool, perhaps to light up a cigar, and bask in the salsa from the boom box until the tinkle of the bell alerts him that something has hit the bait. Lucy remarked that on a windy day you can hear the bells all the way down the long line, false alarms, and that's when you have to keep a closer watch on your rod tip.

I noticed that some of the rods were tied to the railing with a strip of cloth. Ortiz nodded. He said that if a big fish hit, a guy dozing off in his camp chair could lose his entire rig. He'd seen it happen. There were big ones out there. The largest fish he'd brought in was a seventeen-pound striped bass that would have cost him his rig if he hadn't had his rod tied down. He fought that fish for fifteen minutes. I asked how he had managed to haul the fish up the seawall, which drops down about fifteen feet to the water. He said that when he has a truly big fish on the line, he whistles between his teeth and everyone comes running.

"My husband has a whistle you can hear for five miles," his wife said.

"And if you can't whistle between your teeth?"

"You scream," Ortiz said with a smile. "They come and give advice. '*Cógelo suave! Cógelo suave!*' 'Take it easy! Take it easy!' Someone brings a gaff."

He pointed up the river to a man wearing a black T-shirt and a New York Yankees baseball cap. "That's the guy with the gaff. He's had one ever since he lost a real big fish. A good guy to talk to. His name is Carmelo Lugos."

I went over and introduced myself. Lugos told me he had been fishing the area for twenty years. He worked out of two enormous tackle boxes. I noticed a tray of lead sinkers . . . no bolts or screws for him! He had two rods out. After reeling one of them in to check the bait, he leaned back and whipped the line far out into the current. I was astounded by the length of the casts — up to 150 yards out, the splash of the bait and sinker just barely visible.

That morning Lugos had caught one bluefish and lost another. Last year, he told me, he had hooked a striped bass that he fought for forty-five minutes, slowly horsing it in to shallow water at the base of the seawall. He told me the fish was six feet long, like a torpedo, and because hauling it up the wall would have snapped the line, he had no chance of bringing it in short of leaping over the railing and wrestling the fish like an alligator.

I asked Lugos how much he thought the fish weighed. He paused for a moment and guessed maybe eighty, ninety pounds. Quite a fish! — close to the record (if he was to be believed), which is a striped bass caught off Atlantic City by an angler named Albert McReynolds, its weight seventy-eight pounds, eight ounces.

"Hey!" I said. "Anyone along the wall *see* this happen?"

He smiled and told me that he had the fish on early in the morning and the only guy around was a kid about ten years old.

It was a scene to recreate in one's mind — perhaps not of the majesty of *The Old Man and the Sea*, but compelling enough if you thought of the morning traffic going by, oblivious of the drama just yards away, the boy watching, and the man in his New York Yankees cap battling the biggest fish of his life.

"There's nothing you could have done," I said.

He shrugged and pointed to the aluminum gaff about fifteen feet long leaning against a nearby tree. He'd got it soon after he lost the monster striper. If he'd had it that day, well, who knows? If the bass had truly turned out to be a record, it was nice to think that New York's East River (!) would have been listed as the place it had been caught.

"What would you have done with a fish like that?" I asked.

He looked surprised. "Eat it." He said that if a fish was big, like the one he'd lost, he'd have a big family dinner, with his relatives

turning up at the door to share. It didn't seem to bother him that
the fish came from a river known for its sludge, oil slicks, and so
on. It was a question of cleaning them properly. Another fisherman,
overhearing us, said that the best way to prepare an East River fish
was to barbecue it over a charcoal fire so that "the oil drips out." It
was good eating. He told me that the night before, he had given
one of his catch to a homeless man and told him how to cook it.

"Was he pleased?" I asked.

The man shrugged. He said that the homeless man had taken
the fish and disappeared round a corner.

We stood there for a while, looking out over the river. The rod
tips were motionless.

I asked Lugos, "Have you ever seen bodies drift by here?"

"Bodies?" He thought for a moment. "Six or seven."

"Think of that," I said, half to myself. "Just drifting by."

"Last year I see no bodies," he said.

"Things must be getting better in the city."

He hunched his shoulders.

We began talking about the best time to fish. The man who had
given the fish to the homeless man said he liked to stay overnight.
He had a little tent in which to get out of the rain or doze for a
while. The traffic was light, so he could hear the salsa music from
his boom box. He could watch the sun come up over the factories
in Queens. He wasn't adamant. He said anytime was good to fish
the river.

I stayed for a while to see if there was any action. Nothing doing.
A Bertram fishing cruiser went by in the middle of the river. I noticed there were no rods set in the sockets in the stern.

Eventually I said good-bye to the pair and headed for my bicycle.
I pedaled downriver toward the fireboat station near the overhang
of the Gracie Mansion grounds. Where the fireboat station pier
juts out into the river, there is slack water. It is a pleasant place to
fish from — a small grove of trees and a row of park benches. Four
fishermen were working the spot. Indeed, one of them, an elderly
Chinese man, had just hooked a fish. I parked my bicycle and went
over to watch. I could see the fish — about a five-pound striped
bass — as he worked it into shallow water. The fish made a few
darting runs away from the seawall, but it was plainly tired. A second fisherman walked over to assist. He was even older than the

first, a small stooped gentleman in a frayed shirt and a black Lenin cap. Without saying a word he grabbed the Chinese man's line, his intent to horse the fish in and hoist it up the seawall. The Chinese man made mooing sounds of dismay: It was apparent he felt the fish wasn't sufficiently played out, and sure enough, in a spasm of surprise at being hoisted out of its element, the fish flapped off the hook, landed back in the water with a splash, and scurried for the sanctuary of deep water.

The Chinese man seemed surprisingly contained in the face of this ill-advised assistance. Had the pair been younger, he might well have delivered a quick tai chi kick to the one who had lost him his fish, and punted him into the river. Instead, the two silently went back to their fishing — one to rebait his line, the other to a little camp stool where he gloomily contemplated the bell at the tip of his rod.

I climbed aboard my bicycle and headed downriver once again, past the sunbathers on the grass slopes of Carl Schultz Park. Nobody fishing. The river is narrow at this point — squeezed in by Roosevelt Island across the way. It wasn't until Sixty-third Street, below New York Hospital, that I came across a lone fisherman — a surprising sight because of the swiftness of the current at that narrow juncture. He had two rods out, short models because the river runs deep and there is no need to cast for distance. One of the rod butts was set in a tin can. A trim, elderly gentleman, he was wearing a sky-blue pair of bathing trunks into which was tucked a T-shirt. At his waist he was wearing a bright-yellow Walkman. We chatted for a while. His name was Al Bianco. It turned out he was an ex-prizefighter, an ex-lifeguard, and he had fished the river for fifty years or so. He had started out with a bamboo pole, he told me, baited with ten hooks.

I asked if the fishing had worsened over the years. He answered rather crustily that the fishing back when he started was not only better but more varied. He had caught fish he called "Lafayettes," blackfish, robin fish ("they kinda look like airplanes, with big side fins"), sharks, small cod he called "tommies," even freshwater fish ("porgies"), as well as striped bass and bluefish.

"I fished here when the Drive was called Exterior Street, and up at Ninety-sixth Street the river went all the way in to First Avenue."

"I suppose in your time you've seen bodies go by," I remarked.

"You kidding? Of course I've seen bodies go by. Sometimes I see a body, like a guy in a gray suit, go by, and then later, when the tide changes, the guy comes by again. So what. Hey, you know something?" He pulled me close to him as if what he was going to tell me should not be overheard, even though the nearest living thing was a pigeon on the railing. "When they pull those guys out, if they've been in the river for a while, guess what's living in them?"

"What?" I asked.

"Eels, that's what," he whispered huskily. "You lay these guys flat out on the shore, and the eels come out of their mouths! That's right. Their bodies are like apartment houses for eels."

I changed the subject. I asked what music he had been listening to on his Walkman.

"Al Jolson! He's on my cassette." He took the earphones from around his neck to give to me; above the roar of the passing traffic I heard Jolson's voice, thin and cracked: "Give my regards to Broadway . . . Herald Square."

"Hey," the fisherman suddenly exclaimed. "You ever see an eighty-year-old man dance?"

He took the earphones back, and settling them in his ears he began a wild, gyrating dance, his feet crisscrossing in a blur, his arms flailing — as if his nervous system had gone awry. The pigeon, in its alarm, took off straight up from the railing. He sang along with Jolson as he danced — his voice boisterously off-key (". . . Forty-second Street . . ."). He was toothless, his tongue rolled in his mouth. A jogger gave him a wide berth. When he finished off the dance with a splayed-leg leap, he sat down on a bench, not at all winded by his exertions.

"Hey! Hey!" I said. "What do you call that dance — a buck-and-wing?"

"It's everything," he replied. "You ever see so many moves?"

"No," I said truthfully.

"You want to see it again?"

"I'm due home," I said quickly. "Lunch." It was about ten o'clock. I headed for my bicycle.

I live on the river, a few blocks from where we had been talking. From my windows, three flights up, I look out over the Drive at the river, which, of course, is technically a strait — a channel between

Long Island Sound and the Lower Bay at the tip of Manhattan: The tidal flow goes one way in the morning, the other way in the afternoon. My windows are close enough to the water so that Carmelo Lugos, my fisherman friend from the Metropolitan Hospital site, with a running start from the back of my living room and with a little dexterity, could fling his sinker and bait through the window out over the cars below, over the joggers on the river-edge esplanade, and hit the water. The current is strong except when the water is at slack tide: When it is moving, the tugs with their big barges strain at it. I have not seen any bodies float by, but I have seen slabs of ice, Chinese junks, the occasional tire, a few swimmers (on their way around Manhattan), two-man wherries, cigarette boats, and, one time, the aircraft carrier *Benjamin Franklin,* so close to my windows that it seemed a rather gloomy, gray-hued apartment house had materialized over the river.

Now, after a morning with the East River's fishermen, another dimension has been added to my knowledge of the river — a life beneath its roiled surface that I was never conscious of before. I tell my guests, my children, Yes, that schooner is very impressive going by, yessiree, but let me tell you what's moving around there underneath her. . . .

DAVE PARMENTER

Alaska:
The Land Duke Forgot

FROM SURFER MAGAZINE

"ON THE LEFT side of the aircraft there's a great view of the Malaspina Glacier, which is bigger than the state of Rhode Island," came the even, Chuck Yeager–modulated voice of the pilot.

Halfway through our Naugahyde omelets, Brock Little and I looked at each other and chortled. We'd been in Alaska only a short while, and yet we'd run into this Rhode Island comparison a number of times. It had already become a private joke.

Thirty-eight thousand feet below, an impossible landscape scrolled past the portholes; brutal snow-caked mountain ranges hooked across the eastern Gulf of Alaska like a giant mandible of ogre-ish chipped teeth. Massive panes of crevassed rhino-hide ice creaked in glacial strain toward the ocean, some as big as . . . well, Rhode Island.

Alaska is so huge, its features so outsized, that the place borders on science fiction. The currency of measurement is as elephantine as the state itself. Features are constantly scaled to this Rhode Island standard: the glaciers, the mammoth forest tracts, the medicine-ball cabbages from the fertile Matanuska Valley, the manta ray–sized halibut. Rain is measured in feet, wholesale, rather than sissy California inches. Even the name itself is derived from the Aleut native word "Alashka," or "great land." If there is any "greater" or more bizarrely gorgeous land on the globe, George Lucas will have to build it at Industrial Light and Magic.

Surfing Alaska? Surely an oxymoron if ever there was one. A lot of things have drawn people to Alaska in the past: fur, fish, gold, oil, even elbow room. But never surfing. It's not exactly what Duke Kahanamoku had in mind.

People thought we were pulling their leg. Were we for real or just eccentrics on a cavalier whim, like mad flagpole-sitters intent on defining some new parameter in discomfort? We weren't sure ourselves, stepping off the plane into the mid-summer drizzle of Sitka, Alaska. Wrangling bulging Pro-Lites around like hog-tied steer, we drew quite a few quizzical stares.

"Whatcha' got there son, a canoe?" someone wearing a CPO jacket and hip-waders would invariably ask. Maybe we were potential canoe-borne invaders of his favorite trout lake.

"Naw, it's a surfboard."

Now in Alaska, it's a safe bet that if their rejoinder isn't a hearty, "Them's good eatin'!" you'll be of no further interest and can pass on your way without further scrutiny.

Brock Little, Josh Mulcoy, Bob Barbour and myself heaved and dragged our burdens into the terminal, and we felt a hell of a lot better when the entire surfing population of Sitka was there to greet us. Both of them.

Charlie Skultka and his brother-in-law Todd. We all shook hands, piled our gear into Charlie's truck, and within an hour or so were blasting out of Sitka Harbor in a 14-foot aluminum skiff. This was the Alaskan equivalent of driving down to T Street to check the surf: an hour-long Mr. Toad's Wild Ride to one of the innumerable swell-exposed islands that make up the Alexander Archipelago of southeastern Alaska.

The no-wake rule in the harbor gave us plenty of time to take in the city's layout. It's a quaint yet utilitarian harbor town, set on the low terraces beneath snowcapped coastal mountains snaking around Sitka Sound. Spruce trees carpet every square foot in verdant deep-pile, even on nearly vertical angles. Grimy, diesel-sooted fishing trawlers grappled with incoming cruise liners as immaculate and white as a first communion dress. Sea planes were hauled up on slanted docks, guzzling fuel with happy-hour zest.

Once clear of the fish and diesel smell of the inner harbor, we got our first lungfuls of pure Alaskan air. Glacier-chilled and imbued with the Christmas-tree scent of a billion spruce, the air was so rich and pure that it verged on being an intoxicant.

The outer harbor was dappled with dozens of small, craggy islands. Some were sizable enough to have cozy New England–style homes built on them. Others were mere tree-stubbled sea stacks.

Charlie had a dozen marine charts detailing more than 1,000 islands with something like 10,000 to 15,000 miles of potentially surfable coastline. We'd point to a likely looking setup on a chart and yell over the drone of the outboard motor, "What about this point?" Every inquiry was answered with a shrug and, "No one's ever been down there."

Charlie and Todd had worked over a handful of spots that they knew well, bashing out into wild seas in small skiffs, sometimes camping on a deserted beach, trading rainy gray waves in the loneliest surfing real estate on Earth.

Charlie was a Haida, a native Indian in the region. Solidly built and ruggedly handsome, he had a certain Hawaiian bearing, which showed up even more when he surfed. A surfer of modest ability, he rode with a definite Hawaiian regalness — upright and proud — with none of the exaggerated Wilbur Kookmeyer flailings that plague most intermediates.

"A lot of people say our people migrated here from Hawaii," Charlie told us. As if to support this claim, Charlie gave us the story on his first board. A fellow fisherman had found it drifting far out to sea. It was a mossy, water-logged longboard called a "Tiki," a sixties pop-out from southern California. Most likely it drifted up from Hawaii in the northwesterly flowing Japanese current. Charlie scraped the moss from it, dried it out, and repaired the dings with bluish-marine resin. He learned to surf at Sandy Beach in Sitka, the one sliver of swell window actually in town and accessible by car. If there's a twelve-foot swell on the outer waters, Sandy Beach might be three feet and like a good day on Lake Superior.

I told Charlie about the hairball landing we had sweated out at Juneau. Fog kept us circling over aluminum-cleaving peaks for almost an hour until the pilot found a vein of clearness.

"Oh, yeah. Happens all the time. Those glaciers above the city make their own weather," Charlie said. "That ice field is bigger than Rhode Island."

We anchored off a low, spruce-shaggy point on the southern tip of a volcanic island. A black slab of pitted lava tilted into the ocean with that perfect inclination and sweep that sets surfers a'blubbering from Rincon to Raglan. There wasn't much swell, but a few glassy, head-high peelers wrapped around the point, rehearsing their lines for better days.

It resembled a small day at Third Point, Malibu, may it rest in peace. Except Gidget would have some pretty stiff nipples here, and the bears have even less patience with the Vals than Dora did. This was as far away from the teeming mouse hole of surf culture as you could get in America. Well, almost. . . .

Let he who hath understanding reckon the number of the Beast, for he is a California refugee. We hadn't been in the water ten minutes when a guy in an aluminum skiff like ours sidled up to the lineup during a lull. I instantly recognized the phylum and class. The beard, the dog as Man Friday, the vibe.

"I know what this guy ate for breakfast," I thought. "If we were on Highway One, that skiff would be an El Camino."

"You the *Surfer* magazine guys?" asked the guy, whom we'll call "Dick" for a number of reasons mutually agreed upon later.

"Yep," Charlie answered. He seemed to know Dick.

"Which one of you is the writer?" He had those oversize polarized glasses you see on fuddy-duddies timidly pulling out of Leisure World in Buick Le Sabres.

"That'd be me," I said, thinking, Laguna Beach? Santa Cruz? Palos Verdes? He's behind the times; nowadays, you're supposed to hassle the photographer.

"You're not going to tell everyone about this place, are you?" Dick asked. "I've been surfing here for ten years." I looked for the bandanna on the dog. Nope, must have been in the wash.

"Uh . . . that's not the idea. We don't intend to . . ." I trailed off thinking, "This is unfuggingbelievable."

"Thank you," he said with finality and motored off into the channel, leaving us on a shriveling, ever-smaller planet. Even here, on a remote and uninhabited island, one of thousands in the Gulf of Alaska, where one wrong move or fey lash of weather means a mossy skeleton in six months, there is still the stereotypical Californian paranoiac looking over his shoulder to make sure Salt Creek isn't gaining on him, sweating out the fever of Invasion Fear, as if tomorrow we'd have introduced a leprosy of condos and 7-Elevens and parking meters at his personal retreat.

Charlie was pissed. He explained that Dick hadn't wanted us to come here. Dick was a bodyboarder, and, if that wasn't bad enough, he had also written a book about the selfsame island, using personal or native endearments for place-names. Bob and I later read it, a deeply felt and poetic but overwrought Boy and His Dog love letter to the island. Reading between the lines, one could find that smug sanctimony so many refugee Californians assume, as if having the wisdom to turn their backs on Californication grants them the moral high ground and the deed to their personal Walden Pond.

"Sorry, you guys," Charlie said, his eyes clouding over. "Not many people around here like that guy. No offense, but . . . they think he's a typical Californian."

The waves were fun, head-high on the sets, and for a half an hour the sun popped out and baked the shoulders of our wetsuits. I asked Charlie what this wave was like at six feet.

"Actually, this is the first time I've ever surfed this place," he replied.

"What?"

"I don't go backside very good," Charlie offered. "But this place is 'kill.' I'll have to come out here more."

The next day we decided to start fresh and begin exploring the outer coast of this Catalina-size island. There were a lot of places on the charts that looked suspiciously like a Klondike of Rincons, Burleighs and Mundacas. Venturing on such a quest into the open ocean here is not something to be taken lightly. If by definition "adventure" is adversity rightly viewed, then by all rights anytime you take a boat into Alaskan waters, it qualifies as adventure. Or certainly adversity.

Preparing for extended camping in this wilderness is a serious undertaking. Most camping in the lower 48 isn't real camping. There you phone up Ticketron months in advance, and your credit card reserves you a sandbox-size cubicle of "wilderness" that is really more Festival Seating Motel 6 than Communion with Nature.

But this was the real thing. Alaska has a total tidal shoreline of 47,300 miles. Virtually none of it can be reached by car. So it's boats or sea planes. The tidal range can be twelve to eighteen feet.

When the tide goes minus, it leaves a pre-tsunami scree of exposed sand and rock, often stranding your boat one hundred yards from where you want it to be. When you're lost here, man, not even God can find you.

The region of Alaska we were in can get more than 200 inches of rain in a year — Cornwall on steroids. In medieval Cornwall, when the foul weather drove people batty, they invented witchcraft to cope. Here, they just drink. After a week of constant dreary rain, you can imagine the faintly audible gritty sound of whiskey bottles being unscrewed under rain-slashed roofs across town. After September, the tourist trade fizzles, leaving the locals alone with four-hour days and 100 inches of rain.

"How do people cope?" I asked Charlie. Just one week of fog in Morro Bay and I look like Jack Nicholson just before he lost it in *The Shining*.

"Ninety-nine percent of the people drink," he said evenly. "The other one percent are court-ordered not to."

Charlie didn't drink, at least not anymore. Once, flush with $5,000 in cash after a long fishing job, he got so bombed that he woke up in . . . Mazatlan. He couldn't remember how he got there; just woke up in a hotel in tropical Mexico with a hangover that would have toppled a Cape buffalo. He had $2,000 left.

As our strategy gelled, there remained one final obstacle, Mr. Bear. First and foremost, Alaska is bear country. Bears, bear tracks, bear shit and bear lore absolutely pepper the countryside. Every point in Alaska is Charlie Bear's Point. Charlie Bear don't surf, but he can run 35 mph, swim like Mark Spitz, and climb a tree faster than a scalded cat.

Even in the urban areas, according to a newspaper account, bears "ruined by their taste in garbage" hang out at dumps like Insta-Teller muggers.

In the coupon section of the local newspaper, sandwiched between the Renuzit Fragrance Jars and the Hostess Ho-Hos, is a device known as a Bear Bell. For fifty-nine cents (with coupon) you get a cube-shaped bell that affixes to your clothing, the idea being that, when tromping over hill and dale, or taking an old mattress to the dump, you'll clang and peal like a Salvation Army Santa, thus signaling to any marauding bear, "Hey, comin' through."

Surprising a bear in repose (or any pose for that matter) is a pretty one-sided affair, if you're a stickler for all that statistical stuff. Of course, the Bear Bell is the rock-bottom, low-end ticket in bear repellent. It's sensible and field-tested effective; and for about five bucks you can bell yourself, the fam, the mailman, baby Herman, even Rover. But dammit, it's also un-American. It's what Gandhi would have done to ward off bears.

Which is why you should do what 99.999 percent of Alaskans do: purchase a big ol' mofo firearm and cart it everywhere like a fifth limb. This is the preferred linchpin in the Guerrilla War with bears in Alaska.

Not that you'll ever really need your "smokewagon." Chances are you'll never encounter a bear that will interrupt his berry-slurping or wood-shitting to charge you. But at least you can lend a hand in what seems to be a statewide industry of reducing wind resistance on road signs and mailboxes.

Being lower-48 greenhorns in Alaska, we were constantly teased. "Look out for them bears, boys," they'd warn us with a twinkle in their eyes. We'd explain that Bob, Josh and I were from the notorious Red Triangle in central California, and that once a person reconciled the fear of a sudden, fatal attack by a white shark, well, "bearanoia" seemed almost laughable. One wildlife expert, stretching hard for a great sound-byte on a local news show, called the grizzly bear a "terrestrial version of the great white shark." We howled at that. Bears declare their major well in advance, unlike the stealth-torpedo tactics of a white. It's not like a grizzly suddenly rockets upward from some ursine gopher hole and takes your leg in a splintered second.

Although we had ultra-trick Patagonia rain gear, some Rubik's Cube North Face tents, and fourteen cartons of Pop Tarts, we realized it was time to step up and arm ourselves. Brock was elected sergeant-at-arms. He was the most macho and was used to dealing with big, grumpy locals. He was also the only one of us who had any money.

We went shopping for our peace-makin', lead-spittin' bear control at a little shanty perched over the harbor on stilts. It was called Ye Old Rod and Reel (no lie), and the scene inside was familiar to any veteran surf shop patron. Racks of guns, new and used, stood erect in an intentionally phallic way across the showroom. Two grizzled good ol' boys — one easily measuring on the Rhode Island Standard — sporting NRA sideburns and CPO jackets, tried to sell Brock the firearm equivalent of a twelve-foot Brewer gun, when all he really needed was a Becker.

Brock was keen on a 30.30 Winchester. He cocked the lever and checked the "action," the gun version of kicking the tires on a used car. The elder gun nut scoffed.

"That won't stop no bear," he said, sucking on a cigarette like a snorkel, partially obscured in that pall of acrid smoke that most Alaskans live and work in. "What you need is sumthin' like this here seven millimeter." He brandished a huge rifle, a dreadnought with a bore like a garden hose. "This'll stop 'im right in his tracks." Yeah, and uproot the tree behind him. It would also come in handy if you wanted to bore a new cylinder into an engine block.

But Brock was set on the 30.30. Ten minutes later, he left the shop cradling his rifle, beaming proudly. The day's provisioning was over.

"I've got a rifle, some wool socks, rain paints and a sleeping bag. I'm ready," Brock exclaimed with satisfaction, "to go surfing."

No sooner had we packed the boats when the unthinkable happened . . . the weather cleared up. A rogue slab of glacial high pressure nosed into the soupy overcast, and soon we were smack dab in the middle of the best weather of the year.

Alaska has a feminine, brooding beauty. She is a gorgeous and enchanting woman, even cloaked in her chador of rain and gloom. But when the sun comes out and the mountains glow green, you feel singled out and special. Your heart lifts. It's as if you've just passed a beautiful and classy Garbo in a crowd, and she smiles directly at you.

Of course, as soon as the weather turned glorious, the swell hissed flat like a punctured tire. We motored around the far side of the island for half a day, finally making camp near a rivermouth deep in a wide bay, with a melding of forest and foreshore that made Big Sur look like a wilted Disneyland diorama. Three conical Puerto Escondido–style sandbars were scattered about near the rivermouth, teasing us with one-foot replicas of perfect surfing waves.

"You guys should have come in November," Charlie mused.

"Yeah, or we should have brought Rob Machado," I countered, watching a perfect thirteen-inch set peel down a black sand G-land.

The weather stayed great, and the surf flat, so we put on our camping heads. Our setup was idyllic. Salmon were lobbing out of the river as if each gurgling bend were an inexhaustible silo of fresh silver protein. Bob would stand in the icy river for hours, jacking huge dog salmon onto the bank, his voice fairly cracking with emotion: "This is the J-Bay of fishing. . . . It's like some beautiful dream."

The biggest fish caught was one Bob spotted trapped in a large longshore pool, cut off from river and sea by the extreme low tide. Josh, Brock and I chased it through the pool like a greased pig in a rodeo event. Brock finally cornered it, quickly rolled it up the bank, and drilled its head with three lightning-quick North Shore haymakers. Within two hours eight pounds of salmon steaks were grilling over our campfire.

Walking through the forest you could snack on raspberries and blueberries, which grew everywhere, and wash them all down with ice cold, snow-fed river water. On sand banks deeper in the interior, we found the recent tracks of bears and the leftover viscera of salmon lunch. One set had paw prints as big as dinner plates. Charlie extended his rifle overhead to show us the approximate size of that bear. Great. No surf, but at least the bears were double-overhead.

A couple more days of no swell followed, and we started to wonder if perhaps we weren't camped out at Rincon waiting for a big north swell in July.

The weather began to sour one afternoon, with all the evil portent of an approaching winter in a Stephen King story. By nightfall, a gale was upon us. We moved camp into the protection of the forest, and huddled around the fire, grilling the last of the salmon as all hell broke loose out at sea. In Alaska, they don't call the wind Mariah. They call it Cujo.

Brock and I lay in our tent listening to the creaks and groans of the gale-torn forest, waiting for a bear in the Double-Overhead Club to take us like a nylon Bon-Bon. There'd be a horrid ripping of fabric and he'd come and he'd . . .

The tent flap flew open and a dark head poked through. It was

Charlie. "I need some help with the skiff." Charlie had that under-
stated, taciturn manner most Alaskans have, as if constant exposure to the grandeur of their surroundings had stripped them of
all futile adjectives. We geared up, abandoning our warm cocoon
with longing, and followed Charlie's swinging, fluttering lantern
out onto the beach.

The skiff was sunk. Luckily it was sunk right near shore, but regardless, it was well on the way to a more traditional burial. The
millpond anchorage of the previous day was now a heaving, wind-
nagged four-foot shoredump. The skiff was broadside to the waves,
which were breaking directly into the sorry craft. Half a ton of
sand had gathered along the floor, pinning the skiff in the cease-
less shorebreak. And the incoming tide was still two hours from
peaking.

The three of us wrestled the motor off the mount and set about
reclaiming our vessel, scooping water and sand in gut-busting des-
peration, trying to stay a beat ahead of the incoming flushes of
water and sand. Rain slashed through the lantern's wavering
sphere of light at a 45-degree angle. The wind was the bastard off-
spring of a banshee and a chain saw. Waves broke completely over
us as we grappled with the boat. A few times the lantern blew out,
and one of us had to relight it as the other two bailed furiously.

By 2 A.M. we were able to monkey the skiff up out of reach of the
tide. The last of the dry driftwood was thrown onto the fire back
at camp. I put a pot of coffee on, and we squatted near the
flames, steam beginning to waft from our sodden clothes. For
some perverse reason, this moment was the highlight of the trip,
and we all sensed it. "Welcome," Charlie deadpanned, "to the real
Alaska."

One of us said in the morning, and I don't recall who, "Enough
of this boat shit!" We broke camp and limped back to Sitka in the
remnants of the storm. Confused spikes of windswell hammered
our fourteen-foot skiff, and it took most of the day to gain the
calmer waters of Sitka Sound.

The next morning we were on the dawn flight to a place I'll call
Cape Tanis, leaving Charlie and Todd to their lonely sentinel in
Sitka. We'd heard tell of a better swell window a few hundred miles
up the coast. Best of all, the area had dirt roads leading out to

most of the surrounding coastline. The prospect of not having an outboard hangover every day pleased us, as did eliminating the expense of hiring two boats.

Cape Tanis was a small, remote fishing and hunting Mecca, sort of a salmon Tavarua. In August and September the silver salmon head upstream and the few local lodges fill up. The population swells to 900, three times the winter desolation of 300. People in Sitka warned us that people in Cape Tanis weren't too friendly, that they didn't like outsiders, but we found it to be one of the friendliest places any of us had ever been. Every single person waved when passed on the road. It was a habit that came remarkably easy to us veterans of the 405 Freeway. All you had to do was extend the remaining four fingers normally crumpled in the customary Los Angeles freeway greeting.

We stayed at the Happy Bear Lodge, strangers in a strange land. The bar and restaurant were wallpapered with the skins of bear and lynx. Stuffed salmon gaped vacantly from mahogany plaques, and over the kitchen door was what I swear had to be the world's largest taxidermied king crab. Over by the jukebox stood a posthumous member of the Double-Overhead Club, stuffed and mounted in a snarling rictus. A placard at the base read: "Old Rover, shot by Bad Bob Fraker in May 1979. R.I.P."

The hunters and fishermen regarded us with curiosity, but most were so ensnared in the fishing *plak tow* that they didn't even notice us. We were as out of place as a luge team on Nias. But we all had the same spirit, more or less. At the bar I read a magazine called *Alaskan Hunter,* and a passage in the "Taxidermy Tips" column caught my eye:

"Each year as we get out the hunting gear for the first time, there's a feeling of excitement and anticipation as we think of the hunt. Maybe this will be the year we finally get that big one we've been looking for all these years. As we gaze at our living room wall, or think of how we'd feel if our bear or sheep was standing proudly in a public place for all to see, we dream of that moment, when we finally realize our big dream!"

It's obvious we were of a breed. We were brothers.

Force seven winds had whipped up a solid eight-foot swell. We'd heard quite a few fish stories about a left point at Cape Tanis; on the charts it looked too good to be true. We set out in our rented van and drove as far as we could in the general direction of the point. When we could go no farther we got out and hiked through the foliage, Brock on point with the 30.30.

We found ourselves at the terminus of a large bay. A mile seaward was the graceful sweep of a sand-shoal left point, so we hiked along the beach to get a better look. The wind was offshore here, and at the top of the point, thick, lumpy swells staggered around the cape, punch-drunk and slobbering from a beating out to sea. They refracted into the stiff offshore wind, sifting and smoothing into progressively cleaner lines. Halfway down the quarter-mile point certain waves would bend so severely that they actually became thick Trestles-like rights that wound to the beach like spokes around a hub. It was possible to ride a hundred yards or so from the top of the point on a left, and then bank off a swelling hump on the shoulder that in turn swung its energy right for another 50 yards, ultimately depositing you on the sand with burning quads. From there, it was a short jog back to the top of the cape for another circuit.

To the north was a staggering backdrop, as alien and transfixing as a Martian landscape. The Saint Elias Mountains, at 18,000 feet the highest coastal range in the world, soared into the chilled Alaskan sky, crusted with snow and flanked by the ivory shards of some of those "Rhode Island" glaciers.

Having access to roads set us free. After a day or so of scouting, we were able to make surgical strikes at the point and various beachbreaks. On smaller days we hit the beachbreaks at high tide for some thick, wedgy bowls that strongly resembled Hossegor. In one week we got two eight-foot swells. We spent these at the point, surfing five or six hours a day, stopping only for peanut butter sandwiches shared around a roaring bonfire, which we kept stoked between quarter-mile rides down the sand point.

So what was it like to surf Alaska? How different was it than, say, Oregon or Northern California? All I can say is that it wasn't a matter of how the water felt or what wax to bring, or even how your lungs burned running up the point, sucking in volcanic ash from a nearby eruption. I felt something so much bigger than mere . . . surfing.

They call Alaska the "Last Frontier," but it's more than that. It's the last place where America, its true atavistic spirit, exists. It's the America of John Ford, where accountability and self-reliance still mean something. It's not the litigation-snarled America we have today, full of blame-shirkers and moral cowards. If you break down, you don't call the Auto Club. If a bear looms up on the trail ahead, you don't slap an injunction on him or sue the state because you weren't mollycoddled with warning signs every ten yards. And if you get into trouble surfing, you don't flag down the rescue copter or whistle for Darrick Doerner to swim out and save your lily-white helpless ass.

Elephants, rhinos, even spotted owls all have their sanctuaries now. But what of that breed of Americans also so endangered? The wild-eyed misfits who webbed prairie and desert with the ruts of countless wagon wheels, beating the wildest continent on Earth into docility, staying always one step ahead of the preachers and lawyers and bureaucrats. What of them? Maybe they just took a dogleg turn north when they ran out of "West" generations ago. Alaska is their reserve.

Studying my creased and fish-stained chart one night, I happened upon a discovery that made my heart swell with the rhapsody of my forefathers. A 50-mile chunk of coast, some accident of desolation, was inscribed with that rarest and loveliest of all words: "Unsurveyed."

ROGER ANGELL

Swingtime

FROM THE NEW YORKER

COMING UP out of the dugout before his next at-bat in a big game, Reggie Jackson was always accompanied by an invisible entourage: he was the heavyweight champion headed down the aisle for another title defense. The batter's box was his prize ring, and once he'd dug in there — with those gauntleted arms, the squasheddown helmet, the shades and the shoulders — all hearts beat faster. It really didn't matter what came next — a pop-up or a ground ball, a single or a dinger, or one of those tunneling-to-Peru strikeouts that ended with his helmet askew, his massive legs twisted into taffy ropes, and the man lurching and staggering as he fought for balance down there in the center of our shouting — because what he gave us, game after game, throughout a twenty-one-year career, was full value. Now Reggie is headed for Cooperstown, where the customary sweet ceremonies, on August 1, will transform him into the 216th inductee into the Baseball Hall of Fame. By an odd twist, he will be the only player so honored this year: exactly right.

The laurelled plaque will present Reggie in a Yankee cap (his choice), and the bronze lettering will mention his 563 homers, sixth-best on the all-time list (ahead of Mickey Mantle, Jimmie Foxx, Ted Williams, Stan Musial, and Lou Gehrig, among others). A longer space would include his ten World Series home runs and his eleven American League championships (with three different teams) over a fifteen-year span. All that, plus the 2,597 lifetime strikeouts — the most among all comers, the most by a mile.

From first to last, he was excessive; he excelled at excess. He was, as Catfish Hunter said, the hot dog that couldn't be covered by all the mustard in the world. He was the straw that stirred the drink, as he himself said. He talked about "the magnitude of me," and also declared, "I represent the underdog *and* the overdog in our society." One of his autobiographies is dedicated to "my biggest supporter of all — God." His ego, like his swing, took your breath away, but the dazzled, infuriated beat writers and columnists had to concede that it probably arose from the same deeply hidden, unforgiving self-doubt that whipped him to such baseball heights, mostly in the hard late going. He was Mister October: nothing he said could ever take that away.

My own autumnal Reggie-memories require no brushing up by box score or encyclopedia. Among them are two deadly doubles against Tom Seaver in the sixth game of the 1973 World Series, and the home run against Jon Matlack the next day, which helped throw down my Mets and bring the Oakland Athletics the second of three straight World Championships. There was the splendid 1978 melodrama out at Dodger Stadium when young Bob Welch went *mano a mano* with Reggie in an extended, glaring at-bat and then whiffed him to end the game. (How many of the ecstatic Dodger fans there that day, I wonder, still recall Act II, when the same antagonists met once again on the same site, in Game Six, and Reggie took the kid deep on the first pitch, as the Yankees claimed another Series?)

I was also at Yankee Stadium on October 18, 1977, and hold in memory (along with the 56,407 fans there that night) the sound and sight and arc and afterglow of each of Reggie's three successive home runs (in three successive at-bats, against three different Dodger pitchers, and each on the very first pitch), which won the game and the Series, and set him unmistakably on the journey that he will finish upstate on Sunday. He paused for a bit in the box while the third and farthest-hit ball bounced joyfully around in the black-background rows beyond center field, savoring the magnitude of what he had done for himself — but most of all, of course, for us.

At the Wide-Open Open

FROM THE NEW YORKER

"FOR SURE," as tennis players like to say, the four Majors — the four Slams — present major challenges. But for different reasons. At Roland Garros, in Paris, it's the clay. At Wimbledon, in London, it's the grass. At Flinders Park, in Melbourne, it's the heat. And at Flushing Meadow, in New York, it's the crowd. Or it's the New Yorkers. Or it's Flushing Meadow. Or it's just New York.

Witness the baptism of Andrei Medvedev. "I hate the atmosphere," he said, following an arduous first-round win on Court 16. "After one hour I start to be a little bit crazy and after two hours probably I start to cry." You feared, as always, for the emotional health of the hulking, flame-eyed, impossibly candid Ukrainian yokel, just nineteen and seeded eight. Now listen to Andrei two days later, following an arduous second-round win on the Grandstand Court:

Q: How much did the debris bother you that was falling on the court?
A: Who?
Q: The debris, the garbage.
A: It was fun. . . . The people are just crazy. It is nice. They are crazy. They are nice. . . . Since you don't get shot, it is loads of fun. Seriously.

Readers of the *Times*, seeing quotes like these, must have given smiles of typically warped satisfaction. The kid was acclimatizing. He was catching on fast.

Flinders Park has its light and space, its ocean breezes, and Roland Garros has the enchanted glade of the Bois de Boulogne, and Wimbledon, of course, is a version of suburban pastoral. But Flushing Meadow, despite its ambiguous name (half sylvan, half lavatorial), and despite being far away and horrible to get to, is vigorously urban in feel. By road, the journey is merely purgatorial; through the vaults and crypts of the bespattered subway, it is positively Stygian. Mayor Dinkins happens to be a tennis fan, and so every August, at a single snap of his fingers, the control tower at LaGuardia repermutates and the planes no longer bug and buzz the U.S. Open. This is probably a big relief for the planes. Even the Concorde would find Flushing Meadow a little too noisy.

The Stadium Court looks as though it had been hurled together by an unusually corrupt city official and his twenty or thirty cousins in the construction business. Its bunky, rinky, squeaky aluminum seats just go on being heaped on top of each other, up, up, past camera gantries, past Fuji blimp and MetLife blimp, past pulsar and quasar, to the very limits of the known universe. No football field or baseball diamond lies in the lap of this coliseum: only a tennis court, of the usual dimensions. Watching a match from the stadium's crest — up there in the land of ear pop and nosebleed — is like watching a patch of traffic from a skyscraper. On the model of Wimbledon's Court One and Centre Court, Flushing's two main arenas, Grandstand and Stadium, are wedged against each other like a D backed up to an O; the minor courts are grouped around their walls. And at this point all resemblance ends — it disappears with a shriek. Because then there's the crowd.

The 1993 Open will be remembered as the near-seedless Slam — the wide-open Open. When she was told why Natalia Zvereva had retired after three games of their quarter-final (she had flu), Arantxa Sanchez Vicario offered these sisterly words: "I hope she doesn't give it to me." But it was the men who fell victim to bone ache and night sweat, as they monotonously collapsed against lesser players. It *is* like a disease. Once a few big names have disappeared, the remaining seeds watch their sections of the draw opening up and thinning out. Suddenly, they see a clear path to the final. Despite the pre-match pleadings of their coaches and motivators, they start to say to themselves, "There's no way I can lose to this guy" or "If I stay real solid, what's this guy got that can hurt me?" or "Unless he play unbelievable, I go smear this guy for sure."

Out on court, they begin to believe that they can prevail with talent alone, that they can win by virtue of being in a higher class — that the rankings computer will do the job for them. The lesser player senses this nervous lordliness and takes strength from it. He, too, sees that the grid is now sprinkled with rookies and journeymen. The aristocracy is crumbling. It's a revolution. And the stars are out there all afternoon, thinking: Steffi doesn't have to do this. She's back in the locker room after half an hour. Why can't the men's be more like the women's? Why all this pain-in-the-ass "strength in depth"? Across the net, the maniacal nobody is dancing on his toes and busy with his diaphragm breathing. He has dispensed with his original game plan (one of craven retrieval). His shots have become loathsomely inspired.

Stich went down, exasperated, floppy-shouldered Stich, a player whose self-pitying ill-temper becomes so generalized that he even starts shouting at ballboys. Korda went down. Korda looks like a newly hatched chick, but his game is wonderfully vulpine. When *we* play a shot, we have about three possible plans for the ball (crosscourt, down the line, or dinkily short). Korda has thirty-seven possible plans. Such imagination will entail a few early exits. Lendl retired, and Bruguera (evidently helpless on anything but clay) wasn't feeling well, either, though he trudged through his three brief sets. Agassi went down. Much was said about his "conditioning," which is a polite word for his waistline. We were also told that he wasn't "match-tough." On the other hand, he looked pretty tubby (even without his pelt), and was pretty match-soft, at Wimbledon this year, and he still beat Krajicek in three and advanced to the quarters, losing to Sampras 4–6 in the fifth. The truth was that his opponent at the Open, Thomas Enqvist, is already an intimidating player, at nineteen. His forehand is even more high-tech than Marc Rosset's, the grip so Western that it reminds you of the Oriental penholder in Ping-Pong, and it's rounded off with a prodigious windshield-wiper flourish. If these two had met in, say, the fourth round (where, in fact, Enqvist fell, in three, to Sampras), Agassi could have waddled off court with his head held high. And flown proudly back to Las Vegas (rated by him as "the most beautiful city on earth"). In his own jet. *That's* the trouble with Agassi: he is too stratospheric, too spaced out. Do you know how he got going with Barbra? He fell into a reverie after seeing

Prince of Tides and gave her a call. He just did it. He just went for it. That is what can happen when you lose your concentration and your mind strays from tennis.

Next, in the second round, Edberg lost (to Karel Novacek, of the robotically grooved topspin backhand), and Ivanisevic lost (to Carlos Costa and his day-court loops and floaters). Then, in the fourth round, Becker lost. And *Courier* lost (to Cedric Pioline). The consternation caused by this was a tribute to the Courier aura. Jim has disputed five of the last seven Grand Slam finals; no other tennis player, perhaps no other sportsman, is mantled with such psychotic consistency. It all seemed right: the healthy tide crust of sweat on the peak of his cap, the stadium crowd behind him, and, beneath his cuboid sneakers, the most trusted of all Major surfaces — his native cement. And yet there Jim stood, with all his stats going to hell (more errors than winners on that savage forehand), screaming his head off as one of his opponent's mishits took a further wobble on the sideline: 5–7, 7–6, 4–6, 4–6! At this point, the organizers were rehearsing the fake smiles with which they would greet the sponsors on the closing Sunday, welcoming them to a final between Alexander Volkov and Jamie Morgan.

In the meantime, over on the other side of the draw, Pete Sampras was keeping everybody reasonably reassured — the crowd, the cable people and so on, and, above all, the press. Tennis journalists relish a few upsets to help while away the early rounds of a tournament; it's hard news, after all, and gives them a chance to deploy their alliterative skills ("Boris Becker was bounced out of the . . ." "Jim Courier crashed out of the . . ." "Ivan Lendl lurched out of the . . ."). Once the upsets become epidemic, though, a pall of melancholy introspection descends on the laptops and cellphones of the media facilities. Shoulders slump in the media trailers. Appetites wane in the media dining room. This gets us where we breathe. What are we here for? Where are we going? Because it fosters the suspicion, hard to resist at the best of times, that there are no defining gradations up there at the top — that it all comes down to who is *better on the day*. Never mind about game plans, about moving the two-fister wide on the backhand, or mixing it up to deny rhythm to the baseliner. The match will be decided over breakfast in the five-star-hotel room. The winner will be the man who looks up from his bananas and his zinc pills and says "Go for it" or "Just do it" or "Can I count on that, O Lord?" with the greater conviction.

Holding a split of Evian, and wincing from his injuries (you can see the eyes tighten as he runs these little damage checks), the player comes off court and is led into the interview room, there to hold his post-match press conference. He is often halt of step and encumbered by ice packs. After five sets, even the teenager will move with an elderly rigidity. Before him, as in a lecture hall, forty or fifty of the world's top-ranked tennis journalists sit waiting, motley in baggy shorts and pastel polo shirts, their necks looped and noosed with cameras, pens, sunglasses, and I.D. tags. The player's manner will suggest that the press conference is almost always a drag; but it is part of the general P.R. deal (and you get fined for not showing up). If a player has lost, the press conference is a torment, a bureaucratic italicization of his own grief and self-hatred. If he has won, then perhaps it's not a bad way to bask, briefly, before all the stuff with the masseur and the physio.

The players seemed to agree that there was something special about the U.S. Open. "This is the worst Grand Slam," said Andrei Medvedev, like a union spokesman, before he hared off on his personal vendetta about the food. (One recalled Goran Ivanisevic saying last year that if you eat too many hamburgers "you go to hospital forever.") "It's always kind of crazy here," said Courier (who is very mellow and easy now, like a college senior hugely assured of the admiration of his peer group). "The locker rooms are bad. The lounge is very crowded." It was a relief to get away from everything out on the court, Jim said (before his loss); there the only problem you faced was the absence of oxygen: "You can't breathe." "This is the most difficult to win," said Becker, intimidatingly enormous and half an hour late (no apology), part demigod, part lunk. "You have the crowd here, you have the heat here, you have the noise here."

And the crowd loves to hear all that — about the crowd. Jim Courier has been described as a "meat and potatoes" kind of guy. Now, meat and potatoes doesn't normally know that it's meat and potatoes. But Jim is a modern American, and he *knows* he's meat and potatoes. Similarly, the Open crowd knows it's a bad crowd. Born to be bad. And proud of it. It wouldn't want it any other way.

Essentially, although many of the people in the stand wear tennis gear, and some of them even tote tennis rackets, the crowd at the U.S. Open is not a tennis crowd. It is a sports crowd. What they mainly want the match to be is *close.* They are vociferous, bountiful, and jingoistic. They love Americans and brave losers. When they really get behind a player, they are just as likely to goad him to defeat. For instance, they do the get-them-up pre-point slow hand-clap — and *go on* doing it once the point is under way. If a call of "Out" isn't given, they will give it, and *go on* giving it; while their hero gamely continues the rally, laboring to put the injustice out of his mind, the fans keep yelling. "Out! It was Out! The ball was out! *OUT!* OUT! *OUT!*" They *love* an ace: an ace elicits the "Whoo!"s and "Ow!"s and the double-pinkie whistles. Unlike the connoisseurs of Roland Garros, who hate aces, and unlike the fair-play merchants of Wimbledon, who tolerate them, the Open crowd would be happy with a match that consisted of nothing else. The drop shot, on the other hand, is greeted by soft snarls of "*Faggot.*" Yes, it's a macho scene in Flushing Meadow. Correctly, it turns out, though surprising to me, all the commentators referred to the French player Arnaud Boetsch, a conspicuous pretty boy, as "Butch." Whatever the phase of the game, the crowd, when it isn't shouting, spends its time talking and strolling and, above all, eating.

Or, above all, drinking. One afternoon on the Grandstand Court, I sat between two young purists and happily transcribed their commentary as, down below, Todd Martin approached the end of his five-hour loss to Richard Krajicek. It should be said in fond mitigation that these boys had visited the liquor bar and were, I would guess, well into their last half hour before blacking out. "Smoke him, Todd!" "Look at all them cameras and shit. Come on, Todd! Slow down, man!" "He's lost, guy. He's lost." "This is bad, dude." "This guy is sick, man." "He's tired, guy." "Yeah! Nice! He's gonna win, man." "He's losing it, guy." "Who, dude?" "The other guy, man." A paragon of articulate dignity in the interview room, Todd shows no "personality" on court. Where are his code violations? Where are his cycling pants? But the crowd has an excellent reason for getting behind him: he's American. Thus they get to cheer Krajicek's aces *and* his double faults.

The next day, the rain came, if you please. And it would keep on coming. The crowd slow-handclaps the skies until the sun dully glows through the clouds. Then the court fills with court attendants carrying squeegees and towels. Much smug cheering. The Open crowd, you feel, nurses dreams of omnipotence. These people aren't just spectators. They are players, heavy hitters — they are big noises. As the giant blow dryers start up, with their tremendous killer-bee sound effects, the crowd is propitiated by this expenditure of effort, energy, and dollar bills. Then it starts coming down again. The crowd boos the rain.

Five years ago, in Toronto, I played a set with a retired pro who had once hovered around the world's top hundred. It wasn't particularly humiliating: he was Swedish, and very gentle with me. When the set was over (2–6), we sat in the lounge and tried — as Frankenstein might have tried — to construct the perfect tennis player. This was the autumn of 1988. Here's what we came up with. First serve: Becker. Second serve: Edberg, McEnroe. Backhand: Edberg. Forehand: Lendl. Backhand volley: McEnroe, Edberg. Forehand volley: McEnroe. Return of serve: Connors. Mobility: Cash. Touch: McEnroe. Disguise: Mecir. Recently, and again with professional advice, I updated the Tennis Monster for 1993. First serve: Ivanisevic. Second serve: Stich. Backhand: Edberg. Forehand: Courier. Backhand volley: Edberg. Forehand volley: Becker. Return of serve: Agassi, Chang. Mobility: Chang. Touch: Stich. Disguise: Medvedev. As we were finishing up, and marveling at the prowess of our creation, my Swedish friend said suddenly, "We forgot something. It should have Wilander's head." I didn't quite understand. "Wilander's head," he went on. "Wilander goes to night clubs, he stays up till four in the morning. He's just won three Grand Slams. And he's got no shots!"

The world of top-flight tennis these days, with its P.R. burnish, its sponsor marquees, and its courtesy cars (what good is a courtesy car in New York traffic?), exudes the settled, underlit glow of corporate philistinism. True, a devotion to the arts is not a striking feature of sports in general, but you notice this less in team games, like baseball, and less still in herd games, like football. Tennis is a game of individuals, and one in which artistic possibilities are everywhere apparent (as even the humblest hacker knows). Off-court intelligence is respected on the tour; what we might call "soul" is respected also. It is certainly considered a salute to high intellectual distinction when one player says of another, "He [or she] knows there are other things in life than tennis," or, even more reverently, "He [or she] knows there are more important things in life than tennis." Hence Becker's mystique as the philosopher-king of the sport; hence, too, his poor results. Becker is rather too amply aware that life has its non-tennis sections. Becker thinks, Becker broods; but this is no evidence, for example, that Becker reads. Once every couple of years on the circuit, reading gets a mention. As recently as 1991, we learned that Michael Stich liked thrillers. At the Open itself, it was rumored that one of the top women sought diversion, during a rain delay, with Sidney Sheldon's *The Other Side of Midnight*. Andre Agassi lists his favorite author as "Don't have one, I never read books." Probably the only book that regularly gets passed around the locker room is the Bible. The ambient attitude was indirectly summed up at the Open by John McEnroe. During one of his night-match commentaries, he was confronted, on his monitor, by a swooningly numinous shot of the full moon. As one might say, "You see the camera gantry here," Johnny Mac said, simply, "You see the moon here," and got right back to business.

So it is nice to glimpse players who seem to have a big soul, as opposed to a big chest or a big temper. If Goran Prpic has the face (and the game, and the name) of a poet, and if Becker and Ivanisevic and Medvedev have the glittering eyes of thinkers and seekers, then Mats Wilander has the aquiline severity of the essayist. In his copious spare time, of course, Mats isn't an essayist. He's a guitarist (along with Mac and Pat Cash). But Mats is also a player who thought so hard about the game that he renounced it, three years after he came closer, far closer, to winning the full Grand Slam than anyone else since Laver. He took the Australian, the French, and the U.S. Open, and lost in the quarters at Wimbledon, to Miloslav Mecir. It was one of the greatest one-sided matches in the modern era: a three-set orgy of wrong-footing. The dominant image of that match shows Mecir stroking the ball into the corner while Wilander crosses the center of the baseline in the other direction — his run slowing and loosening, his face stretched back in bedraggled acknowledgment.

Mecir quit the game because of an incurable back injury. Wilander quit because he had almost done it all and could never come so close again. In his visit to the Open (part of a limited, local comeback), he wore down the clay-courter Jaime Oncins in the first round, played the match of the tournament in the second (a dynamic small-hours five-setter against Mikael Pernfors), and then met Cedric Pioline in the third. He lost 4–6, 4–6, 4–6. New to the tour, I asserted myself at the press conference (my ambition being to break into the tennis-journalist top fifty by the end of the year) and asked Wilander whether the game had had time to change in the four years he has been away. It had: more and more power. A few big shots, he said, and suddenly your serve is broken. "I don't remember feeling as helpless before as you can these days." Invited to elaborate on his reasons for early retirement, Wilander said that he felt he was playing on "for the wrong reasons." What are the right reasons? Nobody asked. Perhaps nobody knew. But something tells me that Pete Sampras has a good idea.

The women have been getting equal money at the Open for longer than they've been getting it at any other Major. They get equal pay, but they don't get equal space; and their column inches, I suspect, will continue to shrink. A few years ago, it was possible to argue that the women's game was as interesting as the men's (in the women's game there is *time* for artistry). No longer. That poor idiot in Hamburg who stabbed Monica Seles in the back has also, it turns out, eviscerated her sport. The madman's proud dream has been realized: Steffi Graf is back at the top. But at the top of what? The men's tournament here had been a chaos of surprises. With the women, all we had was a trickle of torpid speculation about whom Steffi would thrash in the final. The answer was Helena Sukova, 6–3, 6–3.

With the women, the contest often seems more abstract and internal, more monologue than dialogue. Some rivet the attention: Navratilova's struggle against mortality and time, for example, and Sabatini's struggle against Sabatini. Martina presents you with an enclosed drama, and you strenuously empathize as she leaps and expletes and (as in her loss to Sukova) weeps — in protest at what gravity is doing to her reflexes, her speed, her self-belief. There is

only one Martina Navratilova. But there are two Gabriela Sabati-
nis; and they play against each other, on the near side of the net.
Her only Slam was the Open, in 1990; she won it by serving and
volleying. Now she has let her serve deteriorate to the point where
nobody could expect her to follow it to the net. In the third round,
she faced an opponent called Ginger, with an umpire called
Bunny (under the auspices of a U.S.T.A. president called Bumpy):
surely, against all this, Sabatini could summon some Latin fire. She
beat Ginger Helgeson in three, and then beat the apologetic new-
comer Lindsay Davenport in three, and then lost in three to Steffi
Graf. Gabriela used to be seeded to meet Steffi in the final, having
bageled her way through the draw. Now she meets her in the quarters, having struggled all the way. Her body language used to say,
across the court: "Never mind my pretty face. Check out these
shoulders." Now it says: "Go on. Raise your game. Play the match
of your life against me."

The eeriest encounter of the tournament came in the fourth
round, where Graf met Mary Pierce, the girl who is under physical
threat from her own father — Jim Pierce, that vividly frightening
loose cannon. Their match, when it was done, looked entirely routine on paper: 6–1, 6–0, in forty-odd minutes. But it wasn't like
that. Mary Pierce came out onto the Stadium Court, under livid
lights, with the air of a Brontë heroine: hunted and haunted, also
proud, also theatrical. She then attempted to blast Graf off the
court — no patience, no finesse, just pure power from the baseline. It was like engaging Mike Tyson in debate and deciding, very
early, to dispense with these fine words and ask him out into the
alley. In the twinkling of an eye, Pierce was in post-match mode:
giving a press conference. She said she was stunned. And she
looked it. She had lost her match, but she had also lost her head.
In this swirl of anxiety and exposure, she was being asked to think
about *tennis?* Graf, who has had dad trouble of her own, displayed
the pitilessness of the champion. There is something resembling
contempt, or triumphalism, in the dispatch with which Steffi will
finish a point: her swivel, her erect stride, the unvarying angle of
her gaze. But this is what her concentration looks like, when it's
on. It is just a frictionless desire to hit the next tennis ball.

Mary Pierce had her own bodyguard, but security has been
beefed up everywhere since Hamburg. It never felt necessary at

the Open, where the line judges already remind you of the prison guards in *Cool Hand Luke,* and even the keeper of the net cord wears a helmet lent to him by Darth Vader. Nonetheless, at changeovers two security men step onto the court and stand there, arms folded, staring at the crowd. That's what security people are really good at: staring. They stare week in, week out. Of course, all this world-class staring may deter the odd copycat, but it won't bring Monica back. Now she is fading like a ghost from the rankings. Without her the women labor through an atmosphere of unreality and fraudulence. And nobody is to blame except the man with the knife.

Although the emotional layout would seem to make for few comparisons, one keeps searching for symmetries between the men's game and the women's. As I watched Patrick McEnroe losing to the sprinting, pummeling, and whorfing of Thomas Muster, I glimpsed Mrs. McEnroe in the courtside seats. She is Patrick's mother, but she isn't his coach. You certainly couldn't imagine this smart and saintly soul coming on like Jim Pierce — slapping Patrick around in the parking lot, say, and calling Muster a scumbag and a piece of shit. It is interesting to recall that Jimmy Connors, of all people, used to depend on maternal inspiration: there was that letter from his grandmother which he ridiculously carried around with him. (What *did* it say? That you could do anything if you really wanted it bad enough?) All the women know, or have known, the dangers of familial intensity. But the only man on the tour who can lay a similar claim is Michael Chang.

Chang is the most exciting player alive. This definitely shouldn't be the case, because Chang's game is based on containment and retrieval. Most players caught with their noses over the net will run back for a defensive lob or an underspun lob. None except Chang will run back for a topspin lob (where the ball bites into the surface and accelerates off the bounce). Chang will run back for a *passing shot.* He really seems to believe that he can outspeed a well-struck tennis ball. At Wimbledon this year, I saw Chang cleanly lobbed by David Wheaton. Anyone else would have said, or whispered, "Yup." Chang leaped to the height of the umpire for the smash, missed, landed, turned, and started chasing. He didn't chase far. He stopped and laughed at his own ardor. Hit into the

open court and Chang will run it down. Wrong-foot him and
Chang will readjust like a bumper car. As for the drop shot, Bernd
Karbacher tried a drop shot on Chang during their third-round
match, inadequately reasoning that Chang was at the far corner of
the stadium and wouldn't get there in time. Chang was there to
greet the ball as it bounced. After some relaxed consideration, he
produced a drop shot. Karbacher never moved. Chang won the
French at the age of seventeen. Remember? He outlasted Lendl
(he cramped, he moonballed, he served underhand), and then he
beat Edberg, 6–2 in the fifth. He has not reached a Major final
since. It has been argued that for various Sinocultural reasons (an-
cestor worship, no outside advice, etc.) Chang has stopped growing as a player. The simpler truth may be that he has stopped
growing as a man. If it were illegal for anyone over five feet
eight to play tennis, then Chang would have an embarrassment
of Slams. He wouldn't be number 1. He would be numbers 1
through 10.

For the first two sets of his quarterfinal against Sampras, Chang
gave the impression, as usual, that he was tired of being cooped up
in a tennis court and wanted to go for a refreshing sprint around
the five boroughs. The first set went to the tiebreaker, which
Chang won 7–0. The second set went there, too, and Chang lost
2–7. Then something happened. After Sampras broke for a 2–1
lead in the third, Chang got just one more game: 7–6, 6–7, 1–6,
1–6. The next day, in the tennis community, all was baffled aftershock. There have been displays — by Becker, by Courier — that
have everyone staggering around and murmuring the word "awe-
some." But this was different, as if we had witnessed some radical
innovation — a new kind of shot, a new kind of racket. "It's the
best couple of sets I've ever seen anyone play," said Tim Gullikson.
"This was a guy doing it all," said Tom Gorman. "I tell him, 'Best I
see,' " said Nastase. Chang himself put it most memorably and
feelingly when he said of the last two sets that there were "no plays
on the ball." Sampras said, "I almost couldn't believe the zone I
was in." Of course he couldn't believe it. He had entered that
realm between shadow and substance: the twilight zone. Now Sampras only had to get past the nonbending, nonswiveling Alexander
Volkov and he was World number 1 again, and into the final to
face the mysterious Pioline.

If Cedric Pioline ever strayed into the pages of *Lolita* and dared to give Dolores Haze some practical help with her tennis game, then Humbert Humbert would undoubtedly describe him as "repulsively handsome." His mug shot cries out for an imaginary biography: "Having spent his early years as a slot machine mechanic in Paris's notorious 'Pigalle' district, Cedric moved south, working as an astrologer in Cannes and Saint-Tropez. He now lives with a mature ladyfriend in Cap d'Antibes." In his press conferences, Pioline turned out to be a likable introvert; he has advanced without the help of the French tennis establishment, he uses a fifty-dollar magnesium racket, and he has a young child and an "almost wife." Out on the court, it's not easy to see what he's got that makes him so penetrating — that made Courier retreat so far beyond the baseline. He sticks his chest out, à la Leconte, and jerks his head up on the backhand, and this looks to be his best shot until you realize that it is simply the showiest. In fact, everything is firm, including his nerve, and he tortures you with depth. What we glimpse in Pioline we already see in Sampras — and it looks like the future. A great serve-and-volleyer with tremendous groundstrokes? Or a great baseliner with a tremendous serve and volley? Imagine a backcourt Courier who as he crosses the service line abruptly metamorphoses into Stefan Edberg. It's a terrifying thought, particularly for the specialists.

As the slayer of Courier — and Wilander and Medvedev — Pioline was the right man to dispute the final, even though he couldn't quite make a match of it. He has never won a tournament, and you don't start out on that road at the U.S. Open. So the day was spent adjusting the fit of Sweet Pete's robes and crown. As I silently predicted after Wimbledon, Sampras has even had his tongue fixed. Remember the way it used to loll out after every point, in that childish, willful-forgetful reflex? Well, the tongue people have been called in, and the tongue problem is a problem no longer. But that's the least of it. In our Indenti-kit of the Complete Player, Sampras may already be number 1 in the first three categories, and he is close to number 2 in all the others. Also, he isn't far from having Wilander's head. He is doing it "for the right reasons." Which are? Sampras doesn't care, much, about being World number 1. He doesn't care, much, about winning at Schenectady. He likes the ones that last two weeks and are contested over five sets.

He is moved by winning Grand Slams. It's clear what he wants. The historian and psychologist (and tennis player) Robert Jay Lifton has shown, over a lifetime of inquiry, that this desire powers most human action, good and bad. Sampras wants what we all want. He wants immortality.

JOHN MCPHEE

Arthur Ashe Remembered

FROM THE NEW YORKER

HE ONCE described his life as "a succession of fortunate circumstances." He was in his twenties then. More than half of his life was behind him. His memory of his mother was confined to a single image: in a blue corduroy bathrobe she stood in a doorway looking out on the courts and playing fields surrounding their house, which stood in the center of a Richmond playground. Weakened by illness, she was taken to a hospital that day, and died at the age of twenty-seven. He was six.

It was to be his tragedy, as the world knows, that he would leave his own child when she was six, that his life would be trapped in a medical irony as a result of early heart disease, and death would come to him prematurely, as it had to his mother.

His mother was tall, with long soft hair and a face that was gentle and thin. She read a lot. She read a lot to him. His father said of her, "She was just like Arthur Junior. She never argued. She was quiet, easygoing, kindhearted."

If by legacy her son never argued, he was also schooled, instructed, coached not to argue, and as he moved alone into alien country he fashioned not-arguing into an enigma and turned the enigma into a weapon. When things got tough (as I noted in these pages twenty-four years ago), he had control. Even in very tight moments, other players thought he was toying with them. They rarely knew what he was thinking. They could not tell if he was angry. It was maddening, sometimes, to play against him. Never less than candid, he said that what he liked best about himself on a tennis court was his demeanor: "What it is is controlled cool, in a way. Always have the situation under control, even if losing. Never betray an inward sense of defeat."

And of course he never did — not in the height of his athletic power, not in the statesmanship of the years that followed, and not in the endgame of his existence. If you wished to choose a single image, you would see him standing there in his twenties, his lithe body a braid of cables, his energy without apparent limit, in a court situation indescribably bad, and all he does is put his index finger on the bridge of his glasses and push them back up the bridge of his nose. In the shadow of disaster, he hits out. Faced with a choice between a conservative, percentage return or a one-in-ten flat-out blast, he chooses the blast. In a signature manner, he extends his left arm to point upward at lobs as they fall toward him. His overheads, in fire bursts, put them away. His backhand is, if anything, stronger than his forehand, and his shots from either side for the most part are explosions. In motions graceful and decisive, though, and with reactions as fast as the imagination, he is a master of drop shots, of cat-and-mouse, of miscellaneous dinks and chips and (riskiest of all) the crosscourt half-volley. Other tennis players might be wondering who in his right mind would attempt something like that, but that is how Ashe plays the game: at the tensest moment, he goes for the all but impossible. He is predictably unpredictable. He is unreadable. His ballistic serves move in odd patterns and come off the court in unexpected ways. Behind his impassive face — behind the enigmatic glasses, the lifted chin, the first-mate-on-the-bridge look — there seems to be, even from this distance, a smile.

DAVIS MILLER

The Zen of Muhammad Ali

FROM TROPIC MAGAZINE

December 1989

IN A SUITE on the twenty-fourth floor of the Mirage Hotel, Muhammad Ali is sitting on a small white sofa near full-length windows that overlook much of the east side of Las Vegas. He's wearing a pair of well-pressed dark pin-striped slacks and a white V-neck T-shirt that has a couple of nickel-size holes in it. One hole reveals whorls of thin white hair on the left side of his chest. His waist is very thick; I'd guess he weighs about 265.

"My man," he says, "Glad to see you."

Ali and I go back a long way. I became a serious Ali watcher in January 1964. I was ten years old, the shortest and skinniest and sickliest kid in town. My mother had died unexpectedly only a few months before. Her death hit me hard. I was in and out of hospitals, pumped full of glucose because I refused to eat. At home, I spent nearly every waking moment staring at the TV. I talked occasionally to my father and less to my sister. I was mostly silent.

Ali was still Cassius Clay. He'd just turned twenty-two and he was luminous as he prepared to meet Sonny Liston for the first time.

I remember sitting mesmerized in front of my dad's small black-and-white television as Ali's voice roared from the huge world outside and through the TV's rattling three-inch speaker. "I'm young and handsome and fast and pretty and can't possibly be beat," the voice said. The voice touched radium in me.

I recall standing for hours at a time after that, in front of the full-length mirror in the bathroom, pushing my worm of a left arm out at the reflection, trying feebly to imitate Ali's cobra jab. My dad took an old laundry bag, filled it with rags and hung it from a ceiling beam in the basement. I pushed my fists into that 20-pound marshmallow 200, 500, 1,000 times a day, concentrating on speed: dazzling, crackling speed. I strove to make my hands move quicker than thought (like Ali's), and I tried to spring up on my toes, as I had watched Ali do; I tried to fly like Ali, bouncing around the bag and to my left.

As I grew up, I used Ali as a constant reference in my life. I eloped with a girlfriend and tried to get married at the Ali–Earnie Shavers bout. But by the time I became the district manager of a video store chain in Ali's hometown of Louisville in 1986, I very seldom thought about Ali. He had been a childhood obsession.

I was driving to one of our video stores one day when a friend pointed across the street a quarter of a mile from the store and said, "Muhammad Ali's mom lives there." From then on, I noticed the house whenever I passed by. On the Friday before Easter 1988, I saw a block-long white Winnebago parked out front. The license plate read "THE GREATEST."

I parked, worked up my nerve, knocked. Ali's brother, Rahaman, answered. He smiled — this was something he'd seen hundreds of times. He said, "He's out in the Winnebago. Go knock on the door." When I did, Ali asked me in, did magic tricks, invited me to stay for dinner. Within a half-hour, he pointed at me. "You have a nice face," he said. "I like your face. You're sincere. After thirty years I can tell. I feel it rumbling up from inside of people."

I've seen a lot of Ali since that day. Recently I've written several pieces about him, including one about becoming friends with him. Because of Ali, after nearly ten years of trying, I am finally able to eke out a living as a writer.

Now, at the Mirage, Ali, nearly forty-eight and sick, stands and steps stiffly to the picture windows overlooking Las Vegas. He motions for me to follow. "Look at this place," he says, scarcely louder than a whisper. "This big hotel, this town. It's dust, all dust." His voice is so volumeless that the words seem to be spoken not by Ali, but by a specter standing in his shadow. "Don't none of it mean nothin'. It's all only dust."

We stare down at the sun-bleached town. In the middle distance, just before the edge of the Spring Mountain range, an F-15 touches down at Nellis Air Force Base. "Go up in an airplane," Ali is saying, his voice sounding full of phlegm and ether. "Go high enough and it's like we don't even exist. I've been everywhere in the world, seen everything, had everything a man can have." His tone is not cynical. It is hopeful.

He shuffles awkwardly back to the sofa and drops heavily into his seat. Ali himself believes the Parkinson's syndrome that has shaken his body and thickened his speech was brought on by blows he suffered as he stood his ground and hollered. The doctors say it may not get worse, it probably won't kill him. But it's not likely to get any better. Ali shows no trace of bitterness.

"The only thing that matters is submitting to the will of God," he says. "The only things you've got is what's been given to you."

He gestures for me to join him by patting the cushion to his left. "How you been?" he asks.

"I'm O.K.," I say. "But my dad died a couple months ago."

This surprises the Champ. He turns and looks at me so empathetically you'd think we shared the same parentage. "How old was he?" he asks.

"Only fifty-nine. And I thought he was healthy. He was getting ready to retire and I thought I'd have lots of time with him. He was both my father and my mother."

"How'd he pass?" Ali asks. "A heart attack?"

I nod yes. Ali pats me on the hand. "I know you miss him," he says. "When I first became champ, people used to call me up, messin' with me, tell me my father'd been killed. Used to scare me so bad. Life is so, so short. Bible says it's like a vapor."

He picks up the TV's remote control from the sofa's armrest and tours the channels, stopping on a music network that is playing an older Michael Jackson hit. He turns off the sound; we watch.

"Gandhi," he says, as the Indian spiritual leader's gray ghost-like image flashes onto the screen. "Mother Teresa," a few seconds later. It's obvious Ali feels a kinship with the faces and their deeds. Images matter to Ali. He intones the names as if they were incantatory.

He switches to a segment of a workout show. Young chesty women sweat stylishly in Easter egg–colored leotards. "They call this exercisin'," Ali says. "It's hard not to be tempted by this, unless you got somethin' like I got, somethin' holy."

"Haven't messed around in almost five years. The last time, a friend caught me. Asked, 'Would you do that in front of your mother?' I told him, 'No.' He pointed at me and said, 'You're doin' it in front of your Father, doin' it in front of Allah.' Maaann, that's heavy. Powerful. He scared me. That's when I really began to get serious about livin' for God."

He moves mechanically for the bathroom, and when he gets there, slowly takes a white, starch-crisp shirt from its hanger on the door and slips it on, then struggles a little with the buttons. Without tucking the shirt in his pants, he pulls a royal red tie — pre-knotted, I'm sure, by his wife Lonnie — over his head. He looks at me through the mirror and nods slightly, which I take to mean he'd like my help. In this moment, the most talented athlete of the Twentieth Century looks so eggshell fragile that I find *my* hands shaking a little. I might have imagined performing this service for my dad, had he lived to his seventies. Never for Muhammad Ali.

Ali is so large I have to stand on my toes to reach over and across the huge expanse of his back to slip the tie under his collar. He puts his shirt in his slacks without unsnapping, then tugs on his jacket. Without being asked, I pick a few motes of white lint from the coat's dark surface and help him straighten his tie.

In the elevator he says, "Watch how people react."

When we reach the ground floor, as the doors open he makes an amazingly loud clicking noise by popping his tongue across the roof of his mouth. The sound is immediately repeated from probably 20 feet away. Less than a minute later, Howard Bingham, who has been Ali's personal photographer and best friend for nearly thirty years, appears in the doorway.

We walk from the elevator, Ali in the lead. Bingham follows me. Within seconds, there are more than one hundred people around us, wanting to touch Ali or shake his hand. Cameras appear from women's purses, as do pens and scraps of paper.

"Do the shuffle, Champ," an older man shouts.

Ali hands me his briefcase, gets up on his toes and dances to his left. He tosses a few slow jabs at several male heads, then for a couple of seconds allows his black shiny street dogs to blur into the patented Ali shuffle. The crowd, ever growing, explodes into laughter and applause. A space clears behind him and he uses it, knows it's there without turning to look. He moves toward the right corner of the wide hallway, waving the audience in that direction, then turns to take his briefcase from me. It contains hundreds of yellow and green and blue Muslim pamphlets, personally signed by Ali and predated with today's date. Bingham reappears with a metal folding chair. Ali sits, places the briefcase on his lap and produces an inexpensive pen from the pocket of his jacket.

Two minutes later, there is no way to skirt the throbbing crowd around Ali. There seems to be every bit of 1,000 people in the hallway. A Mirage security guard uses his walkie-talkie to call for reinforcements.

I stand at Ali's right shoulder, against the wall. Bingham is to my left. We're in those exact positions for nearly an hour before I ask Bingham, "Is it always like this?"

Ali's companion-photographer looks basically the way I recall him from the seventies, a little hang-jawed like the old MGM cartoon character Droopy.

"Always," he says.

"Everywhere in the world. Last year, over 200,000 came to see him in Jakarta."

"How long will he do this?" I want to know.

"Until he gets tired. For hours. All day."

Ali gives every waiting person something personal. He talks to almost no one, yet most everyone seems to understand exactly what he means. He signs each person's first name on the Muslim literature and hugs and is hugged by everybody from three-year-old tykes to their eighty-year-old great-grandmamas. He has a radar that is attuned to children. Whenever kids are near, he goes out of his way to pick them up and snuggle and kiss them, sometimes more tenderly than one could imagine their parents doing. The first time I met him, one of the first questions he asked was if I had kids. I now want to know why he connects so to children.

"They're angels in exile," he replies, speaking in the same tone you'd expect from a monk exposing the uninitiated to the mysteries. "Children are so close to God. They haven't had time to separate from Him."

Women and men in line openly weep upon seeing Ali. Many recount stories about his impact on their lives. Some tell of having met him years before. He often pretends to remember. A huge, rough-looking fellow in his mid-forties takes Ali's hand, kisses it, then refuses an autograph. "I don't want anything from you, Champ," he says. His mud-brown eyes are red and swollen. "We've taken too much already."

I have breakfast with Ali the next morning. He's wearing the same suit and tie. This is not a sign of financial need or that he doesn't remember to change clothes. Even when he was fighting and making tens of millions of dollars, he didn't own more than five suits. He has seldom worn jewelry and his watch is a Timex.

I ask why, unlike the old days, everyone everywhere, seems to love him. "Because I'm *baadd*," he clowns, but then holds up his shaking left hand, spreads its fingers and says, "It's because of this. I'm more human now. It's the God in people that connects them to me."

April 1990

On a layover at Miami International Airport, I see an excited crowd gathered in the concourse. I sense Ali before I see him, a head above everyone else signing autographs. People are looking at him with the same sweet sadness they ordinarily reserve for a favorite uncle who has recently suffered a stroke.

He's not surprised to see me. I run into him like this a couple of times a year. He's wearing a black short-sleeved shirt, a pair of black dress slacks. He's carrying about a hundred of his Muslim handouts. His hair needs combing and his face is swollen. He looks exhausted.

Ali trained for many of his fights just twenty minutes from the airport, at the Fifth Street Gym in Miami Beach. In February 1964, he won the heavyweight championship from Sonny Liston in the old Miami Beach Convention Hall. He still comes to Miami once or twice a year to visit his former trainer, Angelo Dundee.

"I'm tired of traveling," he says. "Still travel so much. Fly all over the world."

I ask if he'd like to get a root beer. We walk to a coffee shop. As we enter he spots a woman slumped across a table with her head folded into her arms. Ali takes a seat beside her and asks what's wrong. She looks up and doesn't seem to recognize him, but tells him her purse has been stolen. The woman is short, heavier than she needs to be, wearing a pink warm-up suit. She has graying black hair and deep-set green eyes that bulge as if someone has grabbed her around the neck and squeezed, not real hard, but steadily for many, many years.

She laughs a weary laugh and says, "It had all my money in it. I don't know how I'm going to get home. And how can I tell my husband? He doesn't like me spending so much, anyway."

Ali puts his pamphlets on the table and pulls a tattered brown cowhide wallet from his pants pocket. It has $300 cash in it and an old picture of him with all eight of his kids. Although he's no longer world-class wealthy, he gives the woman $280.

August 1990

The Champ greets me at the door to his mother's house in Louisville, Kentucky. It's very hot today, over 100. Ali is wearing a knife-creased, sky-blue safari suit and a pair of white tennis shoes. His face has lost much of its puffiness; his pecan-colored skin glows in the late summer sun. In this moment, he looks much like the Ali we remember.

"Man, you look good. Are you working out?" I ask.

"Doin' five rounds heavy bag, five speed bag, five shadow-boxin'. Lost over thirty pounds."

I follow him to the kitchen and take a chair at a cream-colored, linoleum-topped table. Cassius Clay Sr.'s stained and yellowed registration card for a 1972 Cadillac is propped between salt-and-pepper shakers. Ali's dad had died only a few months before. I pick up the paper and think about my father's Social Security card sitting on my desk at home.

"How do you feel?" I ask.

"Got more energy. Move better."

Mrs. Clay comes into the room. "Oh, I'm so glad you're here," she says to me. Like her son, Odessa Clay has a pretty, oval-shaped face. She's wearing a yellow paisley dress and she smells of flour. Although she seems tired and a light sweat shines on her forehead and neck, she smiles her fragile smile. "Would you like a glass of root beer?" she asks.

She brings the soda in an old jelly glass. Ali leaves the room to say his midday prayer.

"These days, what does he talk about when it's just you and him?" I ask his mother.

"Oh, he doesn't talk anymore. He's so quiet now, you forget he's in the house. He writes and reads all the time."

Ali returns to the kitchen, still barefoot from his prayers, moving so quietly I can't help believe he's trying not to disturb even the dust beneath his feet. We go downstairs and sit side by side on the sofa. A gold-framed certificate I haven't seen before is hanging crooked above the TV. I get up to see what's on it.

"In Memoriam," it reads, "the Los Angeles County Board of Supervisors extends its deepest sympathy to you in the passing of your beloved father, Cassius Marcellus Clay."

"It was a relief," Ali says before I have a chance to ask. "He was gettin' so old, in so much pain all the time. Talked to him a week before he died. He said he wouldn't see me again. 'I'm tired,' he said. 'Tired of this pacemaker. Don't want it no more.'

"It happens to all of us. It'll happen to me before long, it'll happen to you. We'll close our eyes and won't open them again. I'm preparing myself for the next life. That's what matters now."

A few minutes later, he says, "I'm tired. I need a nap. The heat's botherin' me." The words sound ancient, totemic. "Are you gowna be here when I wake up?" he asks.

"I think I'll go on home," I tell him.

He reaches to hug me, all the time watching my eyes. His body is so thick, his skin cool and moist through the thin shirt. I remember rubbing my dad's back and shoulders in the hospital. Next Wednesday, it'll be exactly one year since he died. Ali's skin smells of earth and of trees. I kiss him on the cheek.

"Be cool and look out for the ladies," he says. It is his standard way of saying good-bye.

April 1991

Ali has been at a gym in Philadelphia, signing autographs for children. He has gained weight again. He's at probably 250, but he looks O.K. and his energy level is pretty good.

As we leave the gym, I slide into the limo and take a seat across from him. An elderly man who looks a little like Ali's dead father appears beside the car. He taps on my window with his left knuckles, startling us. I jump. "Mr. Clay, Mr. Clay," he shouts and offers Ali, who never eats pork, a hot dog.

He is razor-thin, stubble-cheeked and his eyes are yellow with age, cheap wine and a life spent on street corners.

Ali motions me to lower my window. He takes the old guy's hand for a moment. As we leave the curb I ask, "Do you let everybody in?" I've never seen him refuse anyone.

"Don't want to disappoint nobody. But I try to be careful. There's a lot of crazy people out there. And a lot of people who hurt you without meanin' to."

A couple of minutes later, we pull up to a stoplight. To my left, a heavy woman who has no legs or hands is propped against a doorway. She is playing "Amazing Grace" on a harmonica that has been attached to her mouth by a strand of what looks to be plastic clothesline. "We don't know how that lady got here," Ali says. "She might be like you and me." As he says this, his left hand begins to dramatically tremble. It is the same hand from which once slid that great snake-lick of a jab — the most visible phenomenon of his boxing greatness, the very hand with which he won over 230 fights.

Soon Ali closes his eyes, drops into a light sleep, and begins snoring. Watching, I can't help but consider how the young Ali's seemingly endless energy had promised us that he would never get old. And how in many ways he is now older than just about anyone his age.

This is not sad. One of the first things one notices when spending serious time with Ali is that his life is larger than that of anyone you've known. He seems less than fulfilled only when we see him in the smallest ways, when we don't recognize that his affliction and its aura of silence enlarges both his legend and his life. In a way, his silence helps him come off as something of a seer. As his health appears to deteriorate, he is becoming a more spiritual being. He no longer aches with the ambition and the violence of a young god.

I study the shape of his head, watch its almost perfect symmetry. He looks like a sleeping newborn, or a Buddha. Maybe he's some kind of bodhisattva.

Or maybe he's a bit like Chance, the enigmatic gardener in Jerzy Kosinski's novel *Being There* — mysteries swirling through his life that he doesn't cause or doesn't necessarily understand.

*

May 1991

There are around seventy-five people at a Louisville gym. Almost none are boxers. Ali, dressed in a suit and tie, is playfully winging clownish punches at everybody around him. His moves come fairly loose and reasonably fast.

He sees me and nods, then puts both hands beside his head. I get up on my skates and dance to my left, in exactly the style I learned from him twenty-five years before. He opens his eyes fried-egg wide and feigns surprise.

"I could be your daddy," he says, "if I was white."

We pirouette around the old wooden floor for probably 45 seconds, punching a half-foot from each other's chins and bodies. It's the first time in years I've been able to uncoil a little with Ali. I find myself smiling. I feel good.

He points at a young blond amateur heavyweight who looks like a fraternity kid. The Champ motions toward the ring and removes his jacket. I'm sure he must be joking, but he picks up a pair of licorice-colored Everlasts and walks to the ring apron.

He pulls his tie from his neck and the sixteen-ounce sheaths of leather are strapped on his wrists. "Gonna do five rounds," he yells to the people gathering ringside. The volume level of his voice has greatly increased. The sound no longer issues from high in his throat; there is a musky roundness to his words.

In his corner, a second pulls Ali's shirttail from his trousers; the top button remains buttoned. Someone says "Ding," and then it's actually happening — sick old Muhammad Ali is really boxing.

I want to wince with each blow thrown. I feel sweat sliding down the small of my back. Ali doesn't seem able to get on his toes; his balance doesn't look good. He's throwing jabs, but every punch is missing. I believe the frat kid may be holding back to avoid hurting our ailing legend. Abruptly, around a minute into the round, the Champ drops his gloves to his sides, exposing his chin. When his opponent tries to reach him with punches, he pulls his head back and away, just like the Ali we remember, causing the kid to miss by less than an inch.

At the beginning of Round two, Ali's face is animated, focused, serious. The kid comes out hard, apparently wanting to make it a real fight. He thumps Ali with stiff punches to the chin and the chest. Ali covers up.

The kid steps in and Ali stabs him with a well-timed jab, sweet as a bite from the last tangy apple of autumn. Fifteen seconds later, he shivers the college kid's legs with a straight right lead.

At this, Ali backs off. He doesn't want to hurt his student. The kid gets on his bicycle; for a few moments he wears the expression of someone who has just been made aware of his own mortality. Ali continues to box the rest of the round at a level just slightly above the boy's abilities. With twenty seconds left, he zings in a series of eight jabs and a razor of a right, all designed to make only surface contact, but to confirm that he is still Ali.

The old master does three more rounds with less capable students than the frat kid. Then he steps awkwardly from the ring and immediately begins to walk his great-granddaddy walk.

He takes a seat with me on the edge of the ring. "H-H-How did I look?" he asks. He has to repeat the question twice before I understand. Both of his arms are shaking, as is his head. "D-D-Did I surprise you?"

I admit that he did. He chuckles and nods, satisfied.

He pulls on his jacket and takes probably five minutes to knot his tie. We walk from the gym into a thin mist. The sidewalk is empty. A wet and shining blue Chevy pickup with a camper attached to the bed is at the curb. An older black gentleman wearing a straw hat and holding an umbrella is leaning against the truck. Ali walks to the Chevy stiffly, silently and with great dignity. He has a little trouble getting into his seat on the passenger's side. I close his door. He waves to me.

"Be cool," he says. I wait for the rest of his catch phrase. But he surprises me once again. "Remain wise," he says.

February 1993
It is three weeks after Ali's fifty-first birthday. A light snow is falling on the village of Berrien Springs, Michigan. It sparkles on Ali's oak- and maple-lined driveway. My six-year-old son Isaac is with me. He has never met the Champ and I've always wanted him to.

We drive past the small barn where Ali keeps a boxing ring and training bags. We pass several other buildings and look down on the St. Joseph River, which flows slowly, muddily past Ali's 88-acre farm. We pull behind the modest, green-shuttered, white frame house and park beside the brown and beige Rolls-Royce.

Lonnie, the fourth Mrs. Ali, opens the door to the kitchen. She grew up in Louisville across the street from the Cassius Clay Sr. residence. Her mother is Mrs. Clay's best friend. Like Ali's mom, Lonnie is light-skinned, splashed with a galaxy of freckles, and her hair has an aura of redness to it. Lonnie is a private person, shy and gentle but not gullible, and when she laughs, which is often, she sounds kind. Lonnie and Muhammad were married in Louisville in November 1986, shortly after she earned her MBA from UCLA. Lonnie is a thoughtful, guarded speaker, and her reputation in her husband's business affairs is one for shrewdness tempered by a relaxed, understanding nature. Like him, she has a dead-on, yet nonjudgmental, way of looking at you.

Lonnie is carrying Ali's 22-month-old son, Asaad Amin Ali. Asaad's hair is in a top-knot, almost Japanese style. Although he was adopted, his basically flawless countenance and complexion are like his father's, and his skin is an identical glowing copper color. Asaad is large for his age. He has been walking since he was six months old, and Lonnie tells me he weighs more than fifty pounds.

Isaac and I step through the kitchen and into the family room, a large, warmly lighted area with thick wheat-colored carpet, a 46-inch TV, stereo, and a couple of overstuffed couches. To our right, in the far corner, Ali is sitting at a desk, signing pamphlets. He's not wearing a shirt. He's nearly as round as old Buddha himself.

Ali looks at me and nods almost invisibly, then reaches his arms out to my son, who moves slowly, veneratively forward. Ali's arms encircle him. "You'll remember this when you're an old, old man," Ali says, both to me and to my son. As he places Isaac on his knee, Ali nods toward me again. He wants to be certain I don't feel slighted. "Happy birthday, Champ," I say.

Asaad waddles unaccompanied into the room. As Isaac hops down, Ali grabs up his new son, takes him to his face and kisses and holds him to his right cheek with almost unbearable tenderness.

"Didn't get to see the other eight growin' up," he says. "I'm enjoyin' this baby."

"It's good to have something new in your life," I say. "Something that's growing."

"Want to have five more," he tells me. "All races. When I'm seventy-five years old, they'll be twenty."

"Are you serious?" I ask, although this fits perfectly into his pattern — Muhammad Ali the international man, Ali the champion granddaddy of the whole wide world.

"Naw, it's just a dream," he says. "I know it's a dream."

"Sometimes it's good to dream," I tell him, and quote a favorite Ali line from the mid-seventies: "The man without imagination has no wings; he cannot fly."

Ali asks Lonnie to take the baby. He puts a shirt on and turns to Isaac, who is playing with one of Asaad's toy cars. "Stay here. We'll be back," Ali says with respectful authority. He waves for me to follow.

We go outside. The day glows phosphorescently; snow falls in chunks the size of an infant's hands. We enter the garage and climb stairs. He pulls open a door. A space about the size of a master bedroom is piled floor to ceiling with boxes and envelopes and packages. "This is the mail I don't have time to open," he says.

"How long did it take to get this much?" I ask.

"About six months."

I grab the two pieces closest to my foot. The top one is covered with brightly colored stamps. "From Indonesia," the experienced traveler says. I feel a videocassette inside. The other is a thick letter on onionskin paper; the return address is in Kansas.

"Want you to help me," he says. "Feel bad not bein' able to write everybody."

This is in no way an overstatement. Nearly every day, when he is home, Ali invests three to four hours in opening letters and writing replies.

"Want to get a 900 number, where people can call and get a message, where I can talk with them. Want you to find out how to do it."

"If you want, I'll help," I say. I know he's sincere. I also know Ali has always been able to make money. A 900 number with his voice as the payoff could make lots. But when I think of Ali calling each day to change his message to his fans, I feel a twinge. There's something I've been wanting to ask him.

"Last year, at the twentieth anniversary dinner of the first Frazier fight, you got up to speak and ended up talking for probably ten minutes. You didn't slur or stammer, your volume was fine, you were funny, your timing was good."

He was terrific. And I've seen it on several occasions over the past couple of years, always when there are no TV cameras on him. "How do you do that?" I want to know.

He doesn't tell me. I doubt he knows. Instead, he immediately falls into his old prefight voice.

"This is Muhammad Ali, the greatest of all times. I did what I set out to do. Whupped Sonny Liston, whupped Joe Frazier, George Foreman, whupped the United States draft board . . ."

After thirty seconds or so, he stops and rubs his left hand across his face in the way I do when I've just woken from a night's sleep.

"See wh-wh-wha you can find out," he asks. His voice gurgles like the river behind his property.

As we leave the garage, headed for the house, Lonnie and Asaad and Isaac meet us halfway. "Asaad wanted to go with you, Muhammad," Lonnie says. She hands the child to him and looks at his feet. He's wearing a pair of slick-soled shiny leather uppers. "Don't you dare drop that baby," she says. Her tone is wifely, concerned, but not patronizing. She goes back to the house.

With Ali and Asaad in the lead, we trudge around the driveway. Soon, Ali's son decides he wants down. Ali lowers him to the ground, holding his left hand, and tries to get him to walk. Asaad turns to look at Isaac; he intends to play. I ask Isaac to take Asaad's right hand so he'll go with his daddy. My boy does so in a way that replicates Ali's gentleness. I stay a few feet behind, watching the three of them shuffle along at a toddler's pace. For many minutes, Ali, Asaad and Isaac plod back and forth in a chain through the snow. The only sounds are those of wind in the bare branches of trees and of Ali's scuffling feet and, in the distance, of water tumbling over rocks. Just before we go back inside, I reach to brush the melting snow from the children's hair and shoulders, and from Ali's.

Isaac and I stay at the farm for two days. The Great Man plays with my son for hour upon hour, doing magic tricks, telling ghost stories, chasing him around the house, hiding behind furniture, jumping out to tickle him. When he isn't entertaining Isaac or talking with me, he's often asleep and snoring.

As we're leaving for our long drive home, Ali walks us to the car and closes our doors. It's still snowing, but there is little accumulation. Just enough to make the asphalt slippery. Like Lonnie I'm concerned that Muhammad might fall. There's a video camera in the back seat. When I'm certain that Ali's balance is O.K., I grab it and push the power button.

Ali sees the camera and opens Isaac's door, snatching my son up and holding him at face level.

"This is the next champion," he says. "This man will win the crown in 2020. Look at the face. 2020. Just think about it: I will be the manager. I'll be ninety-three. And we will be the greatest of *that* day, the greatest of *that* time."

Ali places my laughing son back in his seat and points at the lens.

"Watch my feet," he says in his thick slow voice, then turns his back and takes about ten shuffling steps. Looking over his left shoulder, he raises his arms perpendicular to his sides. Then, although he sometimes has trouble walking even on dry land, he seems to levitate about three inches off the ground. The winter light is tawny.

"This is Muhammad Ali in Berrien Springs, Michigan," he says. "Today is the eighth of February 1993. Ain't nobody else like me. Joe Louis, Ray Robinson, they just boxers. I'm the biggest thing that ever happened in sports. I ain't boastin'; it's just the way it is. From Adam until now, I am the greatest in the recorded history of mankind," he says to the camera, and to the world.

As we pull out of the driveway, Isaac is sitting all the way in the back of the car, staring out the rear window. I ask my son if he is crying. He nods yes. I ask him why. "He's so cool, I didn't think anybody could be that cool. I just wish he wasn't sick."

I tell him that it's all right. And I honestly think it is. Even more than all right, Ali's life has been exactly what it was intended to be. Ali himself believes this and it is why he so seldom seems frustrated by his health. He will occasionally lament about what he could be doing if he were healthy, but most of the time, when asked about his malady, he says, "God gives people trials. This is my trial. It's His way of keepin' me humble."

The following week, I go to Isaac's school to talk with his class about our visit to the farm. I ask the first-graders how many of them have heard of Muhammad Ali; all twenty-three raise their hands. After I speak for a few minutes and answer questions, Isaac reads an Ali story he has written. We then play a videotape that includes highlights from the Champ's career, as well as the levitation scene we'd filmed at the farm.

At the end of class everybody, including the girls, leaps around the room, throwing punches at everybody else. For days thereafter, my son tells me, he reminds his classmates that they have seen a man named Muhammad Ali who can actually fly.

Shoot the Moon

FROM THE NEW YORKER

WHITE MEN IN suits follow Felipe Lopez everywhere he goes. Felipe lives in Mott Haven, in the South Bronx. He is a junior at Rice High School, which is on the corner of 124th Street and Lenox Avenue, in Harlem, and he plays guard for the school basketball team, the Rice Raiders. The white men are ubiquitous. They rarely miss one of Felipe's games or tournaments. They have absolute recall of his best minutes of play. They are authorities on his physical condition. They admire his feet, which are big and pontoon-shaped, and his wrists, which have a loose, silky motion. Not long ago, I sat with the white men at a game between Rice and All Hallows High School. My halftime entertainment was listening to a debate between two of them — a college scout and a Westchester contractor who is a high school basketball fan — about whether Felipe had grown a half-inch over Christmas break. "I know this kid," the scout said as the second half started. "A half inch is not something I would miss." The white men believe that Felipe is the best high school basketball player in the country. They often compare him to Michael Jordan, and are betting he will become one of the greatest basketball players to emerge from New York City since Kareem Abdul-Jabbar. This conjecture provides them with suspended, savory excitement and a happy premonition. Following Felipe is like hanging around with someone you think is going to win the lottery someday.

At the moment, Felipe is six feet five. He would like to be six feet seven. His shoes are size twelve. He buys his pants at big-and-tall-men stores. His ears, which are small and high-set, look exaggeratedly tiny, because he keeps his hair shaved close to his skull. He has blackish-brown eyes and a big, vivid tongue — I know this only because his tongue sometimes sticks out when he is playing hard, and against his skin, which is very dark, it looks like a pink pennant. His voice is slurry; all his words have round edges. He is as skinny as a bean pole, and has long shins and thin forearms and sharp, chiseled knees. His hands are gigantic. Walking down the street, he gets a lot of looks because of his height, but he is certainly not a horse of a kid — not one of those man-size boys who fleshed out in fifth grade and whose adult forms are in place by the time they're thirteen. He is all outline: he doesn't look like a stretched-out average-size person — he looks like a sketch of a huge person which hasn't yet been colored in.

On the court, Felipe's body seems unusually well organized. His movements are quick and liquid. I have seen him sail horizontally through thin air. High school players are often rough and lumbering, and they mostly shoot flatfooted, but Felipe has an elegant, buoyant game. He floats around the edge of the court and then springs on the ball and sprints away. When he moves toward the basket, it looks as if he were speed skating, and then, suddenly, he rises in the air, lingers, and shoots. His shot is smooth and lovely, with a loopy arc. Currently, he averages twenty-six points and nine rebounds per game, and he is within striking distance of the all-time high school scoring record for New York State. He has great court vision, soft hands, a brisk three-point shot, and the speed to take the ball inside and low. He is usually the fastest man in the fast break. He can handle the ball like a point guard, and he beats bigger players defensively, because of his swiftness and his body control. When he is not on a court, though, the way he walks is complicated and sloppy. He seems to walk this way on purpose, to make light of his size and disguise his grace.

Before I met Felipe, people told me I would find him cuddly. Everything I knew about him — that he is a *boy*, that he is a *teenage* boy, that he is a six-foot-five teenage-boy *jock* — made this pretty hard to believe, but it turns out to be true. He is actually the sweetest person I know. At some point during our time together, it occurred to me that he could be a great basketball hustler, because he seems naïve and eager — the ideal personality for attracting competitive big shots on the basketball court. It happens that he is not the least bit of a hustler. But he is also not nearly as naïve and eager as he appears. He once told me that he likes to make people think of him as a clown, because then they will never accuse him of being a snob. He also said that he likes to be friendly to everyone, so that no one will realize he's figuring out whom he can trust.

Felipe spoke no English at all when he moved to New York from the Dominican Republic, four years ago, but he quickly picked up certain phrases, including "crash the boards," "he's bugging out," "get the hell out of the paint," and "oh, my goodness." Now he speaks English comfortably, with a rich Dominican accent — the words tumble and click together, like stones being tossed in a polisher. "Oh, my goodness" remains his favorite phrase. It is a utility expression that reveals his modesty, his manners, his ingenuousness, and his usual state of mind, which is one of pleasant and guileless surprise at the remarkable nature of his life. I have heard him use it to comment on the expectation that he will someday be a rich and famous player in the NBA, and on the fact that he was recently offered half a million dollars by people from Spain to put aside his homework and come play in their league, and on the fact that he is already considered a seminal national export by citizens of the Dominican Republic, who are counting on him to be the first Dominican in the NBA, and on the fact that he is growing so fast that he once failed to recognize his own pants. Sometimes he will use the phrase in circumstances where his teammates and friends might be inclined to say something more dynamic. One night this winter, I was sitting around at school with Felipe and his teammates, watching a videotape of old Michael Jordan highlights. The tape had been edited for maximum excitement, and most of the boys on the team were responding with more and more baroque constructions of foul language. At one point, Jordan was shown leaping past the Celtics center Robert Parish, and someone said, "Yo, feature that, bro! He's busting the Chief's face."

"Busting his fucking face," another one said.

"Busting his goddam big-ass face."

"He's got it going on. Now Jordan's going to bust his foul-loving big-ass mama's-boy dope black ass."

On the tape, Jordan slammed the ball through the hoop and Parish crumpled to the floor. While the other boys were applauding and swearing, Felipe moved closer to the television and then said, admiringly, "Oh, my goodness."

Felipe's life is unusually well populated. He is very close to his family. He is named Luis Felipe, after his father. His older brother Anthony is one of the managers of the Rice High School team. Anthony is a square-shouldered, avid man of twenty-five who played amateur basketball in the Dominican Republic and in New York until his ankle was badly injured in a car accident. Until last month, when he was laid off, he worked at a Manhattan printshop and had a boss who appreciated basketball and tolerated the time Anthony spent with the team. Anthony is rarely away from Felipe's side, and when he is there he is usually peppering him with directions and commentary in a hybrid of Spanish and English: *"Felipe, mal, muy mal! Cómo estás* you go so aggressive to a lay-up?" A couple of times a month, Anthony makes the rounds of Felipe's teachers to see if his B average is holding up. "If he's not doing well, then I go back and let my people know," Anthony says. "It's nice, it's beautiful to be a superstar, but if he doesn't work hard he doesn't play." Once, Felipe's father forbade him to travel to a tournament because he had neglected to wash the dishes. This made Felipe cry, but in hindsight he is philosophical about it. "He was right," he says. "I didn't do my dishes." Felipe is also close to Lou De-Mello, his coach at Rice, and to Dave Jones, his coach with the Gauchos, a basketball organization in the Bronx which he plays for during the summer, and to Louis d'Almeida, the founder of the Gauchos. Felipe says he sometimes gets basketball advice from his mother, Carmen, and from Maura Beattie, a teacher at Rice who tutors him in English. Neither of them plays. "You know what, though?" Felipe says. "They know something." His primary hobby is sleeping, but his other pastime is talking on the phone for hours to his girlfriend, who is an American, a resident of Brooklyn, and a basketball fan.

Sometimes his life seems overpopulated. He has so far received four crates of letters from college coaches and recruiters pitching woo at him. Some make seductive mention of the large seating capacities of their arenas. Basketball-camp directors call regularly, saying that they would like Felipe Lopez to be in attendance. Officials of Puerto Rico's summer basketball league have requested

the honor of his presence this summer. There are corporate marketing executives who would very much like to be his friends. Not
everyone crowding into his life wishes him well. There are people
who might wittingly or unwittingly mislead him. Felipe has been
warned by his father, for example, never to have sex without a condom, because some girls who pretend to like him might really
have appraised him as a lucrative paternity suit. Last year, Felipe
and another player were invited to appear in a Nintendo television
commercial, and the commercial nearly cost them their college
athletic eligibility, because no one had warned them that accepting money for a commercial was against NCAA regulations. There
are people who are jealous of Felipe. There are coaches whose
hearts he has broken, because they're not at one of the colleges
Felipe is interested in — Florida State, Syracuse, St. John's, Seton
Hall, North Carolina, Georgia Tech, UCLA, Indiana, Arizona,
Ohio State, and Kansas. There are coaches who put aside all other
strategy except Keep Felipe Lopez Away from the Ball. Some opponents will go out of their way to play him hard. There are kids
on his own team who have bitter moments about Felipe. And there
are contrarians, who would like to get in early on a backlash and
look clairvoyant and hype-resistant by declaring him, at only eighteen and only a junior in high school, already overrated. His response to all this is to be nice to everyone. I have never seen him
angry, or even peeved, but when he isn't playing well his entire
body droops and he looks completely downcast. It is an alarming
sight, because he looks so hollowed out anyway.

"Wait till this kid gets a body," Coach DeMello likes to say. During practice, DeMello will sometimes jump up and down in front
of Felipe and yell, "Felipe! Make yourself *big!*" The best insult I
ever heard DeMello hurl at Felipe was during a practice one afternoon when Felipe was playing lazily. DeMello strode onto the
court, looked up at Felipe, and said acidly, "You're six-five, but
you're trapping like you're *five-eleven*." Anthony Lopez can hardly
wait until Felipe gets a body, so sometimes during the off-season
he will take him to the steep stairway at the 155th Street subway
station, in the Bronx, and make him run up and down the hundred and thirty steps a few times to try to speed the process along.
Felipe is less than crazy about this exercise, although he appreci-
ates the advantages that more bulk might give him: "When I first

came here, I could tell the guys were looking at me and thinking, Who is this skinny kid? Then they would say, 'Hey, let's' — excuse my language — 'bust his ass.' "

Felipe's body is an unfinished piece of work. It gets people thinking. Tom Konchalski, a basketball scout who follows high schools in the Northeast, suggested recently that if Felipe ever wanted to give up basketball he could be a world-class sprinter. Coach DeMello said to me once that, much as he hated to admit it, he thought Felipe had the perfect pitcher's body. Felipe's mother told me that even though Felipe is now a fast-break expert, she thought he should sharpen his ability to penetrate to the basket and go for the big finish — say, a windmill slam dunk. I once asked her whose style of play she wanted Felipe to emulate, and she pointed to a picture of Michael Jordan and said, in Spanish, "If he would eat more, he could be like the man who jumps."

Felipe's father, who played amateur baseball in the Dominican Republic, thought he saw in his son the outlines of a first baseman, and steered Felipe toward baseball when he was little. But Felipe was hit in the nose by a wild throw, and decided that, in spite of its popularity in the Dominican Republic and the success Dominican ballplayers have had in the United States, baseball was not his game. Maura Beattie, his English tutor, is an excellent tennis player, and one day, just for fun, she took Felipe with her to the courts. She was curious to see if someone with Felipe's build and abilities could master a racket sport. He beat her. It was the first time he'd held a tennis racket in his life. Another time, the two of them went to play miniature golf in Rockaway, and Felipe, who had never held a putter before, made a hole in one. Some of this prowess can be attributed to tremendous physical coordination and the biomechanical advantages of being tall and thin and limber. Felipe Lopez is certainly a born athlete. But he may also be one of those rarer cases — a person who is just born lucky, whose whole life seems an effortless conveyance of dreams, and to whom other people's dreams adhere. This aura of fortune is so powerful that it is easy to forget that for the time being, and for a while longer, Felipe Lopez is still just an immigrant teenager who lives in a scary neighborhood in the South Bronx and goes to high school in Harlem, where bad things happen every day.

Currently, there are 518,000 male high school basketball players in the United States. Of these, only 19,000 will end up on college teams — not even 4 percent. Less than 1 percent will play for Division One colleges — the most competitive. The present NBA roster has 367 players and each year only forty or fifty new players are drafted. What these numbers forebode is disappointment for many high school basketball players. That disappointment is disproportionate among black teenagers. A recent survey of high school students by Northeastern University's Center for the Study of Sport in Society reported that 59 percent of black teenage athletes thought they would continue to play on a college team, compared with 39 percent of white teenagers. Only 16 percent of the white athletes expected that they would play for the pros; 43 percent of the blacks expected that they would, and nearly half of all the kids said they thought it would be easier for black males to become professional basketball players than to become lawyers or doctors. Scouts have told me that everyone on the Rice team will probably be able to get a free college education by playing basketball, and so far all the players have received recruiting letters from several schools. The scouts have also said that it will require uncommonly hard work for any of the boys on the team other than Felipe to ascend to the NBA.

Every so often, scouts' forecasts are wrong. Some phenomenal high school players get injured or lazy or fat or drug-addled or bored, or simply level off and then vanish from the sport, and, by the same token, a player of no particular reputation will once in a while emerge from out of nowhere and succeed. That was the case with the NBA All-Stars Karl Malone and Charles Barkley, who both played through high school in obscurity; but most other NBA players were standouts starting in their early teens. Most people who follow high school basketball teams that are filled with kids from poor families and rough neighborhoods encourage the kids to put basketball in perspective, to view it not as a catapult into some fabulous, famous life but as something practical — a way to get out, to get an education, to learn the way around a different, better world. The simple fact that only one in a million people in this country will ever play for the NBA is often pointed out to the kids, but that still doesn't seem to stop them from dreaming.

Being told that you might be that one person in a million would deform many people's characters, but it has not made Felipe cynical or overly interested in himself. In fact, his blitheness can be almost unnerving. One evening when we were together, I watched him walk past a drug deal on 125th Street and step off the curb into traffic, and then he whiled away an hour in a fast-food restaurant where several ragged, hostile people repeatedly pestered him for change. He hates getting hurt on the court, but out in the world he is not very careful with himself. When you are around him, you can't help feeling that he is a boy whose body is a savings account, and it is one that is uninsured. But being around him is also to be transported by his nonchalant confidence about luck — namely, that it happens because it happens, and that it will happen for Felipe, because things are meant to go his way. This winter, he and the Rice Raiders were in Las Vegas playing in a tournament. One evening, a few of them went into a casino and attached themselves to the slot machines. Felipe's first quarter won him a hundred quarters. Everyone told him to stop while he was ahead, but he continued. "I wanted to play," he says. "I thought, I had nothing before I started, now I have something, so I might as well play. So I put some more quarters in, and — oh, my goodness! — I won twelve hundred more quarters. What can I say?"

At three o'clock one afternoon this winter, I went over to the high school to watch Felipe and the Rice team practice. I hadn't met Felipe before that afternoon, but I had heard a lot about him from friends who follow high school basketball. As it happens, Felipe's reputation often precedes him. Before he moved to this country, he was living in Santiago, in the Dominican Republic. The Lopez family had been leaving the Dominican Republic in installments for thirty years. A grandmother had moved to New York in the sixties, followed by Felipe's father in 1982, and then, in 1986, by his mother and Anthony. For three years, Felipe stayed in the Dominican Republic with another older brother, Anderson, and his sister, Sayonara. At age eight, he started playing basketball in provincial leagues, sometimes being bumped up to older age groups because he was so good. He already had a following. "I would hear from a lot of Dominicans about how good he was getting," Anthony says now. "It made me curious. When I left him in the Dominican Re-

public, he was just a little kid who I would boss around. He was
my — you know, my delivery guy." When more visas were obtained, in 1989, Felipe and Sayonara moved to New York. Anthony
took Felipe to a playground near the family's apartment and chal-
lenged him one-on-one, decided that the rumors were true, and
then took him to try out for the Gauchos. Lou d'Almeida says that
people were already talking about Felipe by then. Many high
school coaches had intelligence on Felipe by the time he started
school. Lou DeMello first saw him in a citywide tournament for ju-
nior-high players. Felipe was in the Midget Division. "He looked
like a man among boys," DeMello says now. "If I could have, I
would have taken him then and started him *then* on the Rice Varsity. I swear to God. At the time, he was in eighth grade."

Rice High School is a small all-boys Catholic school, which was
founded in 1938 and is run by the Congregation of Christian
Brothers. It is the only Catholic high school still open in Harlem.
Currently, it has about four hundred students. Tuition is two thousand dollars a year, which many of the students can afford only
with the help of scholarship money from private sponsors, including some basketball fans. At school, students have to wear a tie,
real trousers, and real shoes, not sneakers. There is also a prohibi-
tion against beepers. The school is in a chunky brick building with
a tiny, blind entrance on 124th Street, close to some Chinese lun-
cheonettes, some crack dealers, and some windswept vacant tene-
ments. A lot of unregulated commerce is conducted on the sidewalks nearby, and last year a business dispute in an alley across
from the school was resolved with semiautomatic weapons, but the
building itself emanates gravity and calm. Inside, it is frayed but
sturdy and pleasant. There is an elevator, but it often isn't working;
the gym, which occupies most of the top two floors of the school, is
essentially a sixth-floor walkup. The basketball court is only 55 feet
long instead of the usual 94, and the walls are less than a foot away
from the sidelines. It would qualify as regulation-size in Lilliput.
Rice has to play its games in a borrowed gym — usually the Gauchos' facility, in the Bronx.

At the time Coach DeMello first heard about Felipe Lopez,
the Rice Raiders had a win-loss record of eight and thirteen, tattered ten-year-old uniforms, and an inferiority complex. Catholic
League basketball in New York City is a particularly bad place for

any of these. Since the early eighties, the Catholic schools in New York have had ferocious rivalries, fancy shoes and uniforms from friendly sporting goods companies, and most of the best players in the city. College teams and the NBA are loaded with New York City Catholic League alumni: Jamal Mashburn, now at Kentucky, attended Cardinal Hayes; the Nets' Kenny Anderson and the Houston Rockets' Kenny Smith went to Archbishop Molloy; the Pacers' Malik Sealy, Syracuse's Adrian Autry, and North Carolina's Brian Reese all went to St. Nicholas of Tolentine; the Pistons' Olden Polynice attended All Hallows; Chris Mullin, of Golden State, went to Xaverian; Mark Jackson, now of the Clippers, went to Bishop Loughlin. Rice had won the city Catholic-school championship in 1966 and proceeded to become steadily undistinguished over the next few decades. Four years ago, Lou DeMello took over as head coach. First, he persuaded Nike — and later Reebok and Converse — to donate shoes and uniforms to the team. Then he started scouting Midget Division players who might have a future at Rice. The Gaucho coaches have a cordial relationship with DeMello and began pointing players like Felipe his way. Last year, the Rice Raiders reached the finals of the city championship. This year, they are ranked in the top twenty high schools nationally — the first time they have been ranked there for twenty-seven years.

Coach DeMello is short and trim, and has bright eyes and a big mustache and an air of uncommon intensity, like someone who is just about to sneeze. His usual attire consists of nylon warmup suits that are very generously sized. The first time I saw him in street clothes, he looked as if someone had let his air out. He speaks with a New York accent, but in fact he was born in Brazil, and played soccer there. His motivational specialty is the crisp reprobation wrapped around a sweet hint of redemptive possibility — stick before carrot. When addressing the team, he is prone to mantra-like repetitions of his maxims, as in "Listen up. Listen up. I want you to go with your body. Go with your body. Go with your body. I want you to keep your foot in the paint. Your foot in the paint. Your foot in the paint. In the paint. And put the ball on the floor. The ball on the floor. On the floor."

This particular afternoon, Coach DeMello was especially hypnotic. The team was getting ready for its first out-of-town tournament of the year, the Charm City/Big Apple Challenge, in Baltimore, which would be played in the Baltimore Arena and televised on a cable channel. The Raiders would be facing Baltimore Southern High School, one of the best teams in the area. When I arrived at the Rice gym, the Raiders had been scrimmaging for an hour. Now, during a break, Coach DeMello was chanting strategy. "You guys are in a funk," he said. Someone dropped the ball, and it made an elastic *poing!* sound and rolled to the wall. "Gerald, hold the ball," DeMello went on. He clasped his hands behind his back. "Hold the ball. O.K. You guys are in a funk. You got to get your head in the game. Your head in the game. We're going up against a serious team in Baltimore. They do a hell of a job on help. A hell of a job. A. Hell. Of. A. Job. We need leaders on the floor. Leaders on the floor. All we want to do is contain. Contain. Contain. So you better hit the boards. Hit the boards. The boards."

Everyone nodded. The Rice Raiders are Felipe, Reggie Freeman, Yves Jean, Gerald Cox, Melvin McKey, Scientific Mapp, Gary Saunders, Gil Eagan, Kojo Lockhart, Rodney Jones, Robert Johnson, and Jamal Livingston. Melvin, the point guard, is usually called Ziggy. Jamal, the center, is known as Stretch. Gerald, who also plays center, is known as G-Money. Scientific, the reserve point guard, is known as Science. All of them are known, familiarly, as B, which is short for "bro," which is short for "brother." During practice, they are solemn and focused. During a game, they are ardent and intense, as if their lives depended on it. Before and after each game, they stand in a circle, make a stack of their right hands, and shout, "One, two, three, Rice! Four, five, six, family!"

Most of the Raiders live in the Bronx or upper Manhattan. Once, after a game, I rode in the van with an assistant coach as he dropped the team members off at their homes. A few of them lived in plain, solid-looking housing projects and some in walkups that, at least from the outside, looked bleak. No one lived in a very nice building. Some of the kids have families that come to all their games and monitor their schoolwork; some have families that have fallen apart. Six of the twelve live with only their mothers. Ziggy lives with his uncle, and the five others have a mother and a father at home. Each of them has at least one person somewhere in his life who arranges to send him to attend a disciplined and serious-minded parochial school. Sometimes it's not a parent; the Gauchos, for instance, send a number of basketball players to school.

The coaches and teachers I met at Rice are white. Most of the teachers are Catholic brothers. The basketball team is all black, and not one of its members is Catholic, although Gary told me once that he was thinking of converting, because "being Catholic seems like a pretty cool thing." There is currently a debate in the Catholic Church about financing schools that used to have Catholic students from the surrounding parish but are now largely black and non-Catholic, their purpose having shifted, along with neighborhood demographics, from one of service to the Church to one of contribution to the inner city. The debate may also have a flip side. I had heard that for a time one player's father, a devout Muslim, was unhappy that his son was being coached by a white man. But Coach DeMello resisted being drawn into an argument about something no one on the team ever paid attention to, and the crisis eventually passed. I didn't think of race very often while I spent time with the team. I thought more about winning and losing, and about how your life could be transformed from one to the other if you happened to be good at a game.

The seniors on the team are Yves Jean, Gerald Cox, and Reggie Freeman. Yves has signed a letter of intent to go to Pitt-Johnstown, which is a Division Two school; Gerald and Reggie are going to the University of South Carolina and the University of Texas, respectively, which are both in Division One. Yves grew up in Lake Placid. He was more fluent in ice fishing than in basketball when he moved to New York, but he is big and strong and has learned the game well enough, even as a second language. Usually, he looks pleasantly amazed when he makes a successful play. Gerald and Reggie are handsome, graceful players who would have been bigger stars this year if it weren't for Felipe. Gerald is dimpled and droll and flirtatious. Reggie has a long, smooth poker face and consummate cool. At times, he looks rigid with submerged disappointment. I remember Coach DeMello's telling me that when Reggie was a sophomore he was waiting patiently for Jerry McCullough, then the senior star, to leave for college, so that at last he would be the team's main man. Then Felipe came. Reggie and Felipe now have a polite rapport that fits together like latticework over their rivalry.

The team is a changeable entity. Some of the kids have bounced

on and off the squad because of their grades. One of the players
has had recurring legal problems. The girlfriend of another one
had a baby last year, and because of that he missed so much school
that for some time he wasn't allowed to play on the team. When I
first started hanging around with the Raiders, Rodney Jones wasn't
on the roster, having had discipline problems and some academic
troubles. Sometimes the boys get sick of each other. They practice
together almost every day for several hours; they travel together
to games and tournaments, which can sometimes last as long as
two weeks; and they see each other all day in classrooms, at the
Gaucho gym, and on the street. Usually, they have an easy camaraderie. During the other times, as soon as they are done with practice they quickly head their own ways.

"Are you guys listening to me? Are you listening?" DeMello was
saying. He was now joined by Bobby Gonzalez, an assistant coach,
who was nodding and murmuring "Uh-huh" after everything he
said. Gonzalez handed DeMello a basketball. DeMello curled it to
his left side, and then held his right hand up, one finger in the air,
as if he were checking wind direction. "One more thing. One
more thing. If there's one player you guys want to be looking up to
right now, I'll tell you who it is."

"Uh-huh," Bobby Gonzalez said.

"That guy is Reggie Freeman. Reggie Freeman." No expression
crossed Reggie's face. Felipe, who was standing on the other side
of the circle, flexed his neck, rotated his shoulders, and then stood
still, a peaceful expression on his face. "Reggie is the most unselfish player here. He is the most unselfish. I want you to remember that. He's grown a lot. That's who you should be looking at.
O.K."

"Uh-huh."

DeMello bounced the ball hard, signaling the end of practice.
The boys circled and counted: "One, two, three, Rice! Four, five,
six, family!" They straggled out of the gym, talking in small groups.

"I never been to Baltimore."

"Let me ask you something. You think Larry Bird's a millionaire?"

"Larry Bird? I don't know. A millionaire. Magic's a millionaire."

"Magic's a millionaire, and he didn't have fifty-nine cents to buy himself a little hat and now he's going to die. The man's stupid."

"I don't know if Larry Bird's a millionaire. I do know he's never been to Harlem, and he's never done the Electric Slide."

Felipe on his development as a player:

"Back in my country, I was just a little guy. I tried to dunk, but I couldn't. I tried and I tried. Then, one day, I dunked. Oh, my goodness. Three months later, I was dunking everything, every way — with two hands, backwards, backwards with two hands. I can do a three-sixty dunk. It's easy. You know, you jump up backwards with the ball and then spin around while you're in the air — and *pow!* I'm working all the time on my game. If Coach DeMello says he wants me to work on my ball handling, then I just work at it, work at it, work at it, until it's right. In basketball, you always are working, even on the things you already know.

"When I come to this country, I was real quiet, because I didn't speak any English, so all I did was dunk. On the court, playing, I had to learn the words for the plays, but you don't have to talk, so I was O.K. My coach used his hands to tell me what to do, and then I learned the English words for it. There aren't too many Spanish kids at school. I know a lot of kids, though. I meet kids from all over the country at tournaments and at summer camps. If you do something good, then you start meeting people, even if you don't want to. Sometimes it's bouncing in my head that people are talking about me, saying good things, and that some people are talking about me and saying bad things, saying, like, 'Oh, he thinks he's all that,' but that's life. That's life. I don't like when it's bouncing in my head, but I just do what I'm supposed to do. I'm quick. I broke the record for the fifty-yard dash when I was in junior high school — I did it in five point two seconds, when the record was five point five seconds. I also got the long-jump record. It feels natural when I do these things. In basketball, I like to handle the ball and make the decisions. I can play the big people, because of my quickness. But I got to concentrate or the ball will go away from me. At basketball camp, I'm always the craziest guy — people always are walking around saying, 'Hey, who's that Dominican clown?' But on the court I don't do any fooling around. I got to show what I got.

"In life, I don't worry about myself. My brother will run defense for me. I got my family. Some kids here, I see them do drugs, messing around, wasting everything, and I see the druggies out on the street, and I just, I don't know, I don't understand it. That's not for me. I got a close family, and I got to think about my family, and if I can do something that will be good for my whole family, then I got to do it. I think about my country a lot — I want to go there so bad. In Santiago, everyone knows about me and wants to see me play now. If I'm successful, the way everyone talks about that, I'd like a big house there in Santiago, where I could go for a month or two each year and just relax."

After practice, Felipe and I walked down 125th Street in a cold rain. First, he bought new headphones for his tape player from a Ghanaian street peddler, and then we stopped at Kentucky Fried Chicken to eat a pre-dinner dinner before heading home. He was dressed in his school clothes — a multicolored striped shirt, a purple-and-blue flowered tie, and pleated, topstitched baggy black cotton pants — and had on a Negro League baseball cap, which he was wearing sideways and at a jaunty angle. In his book bag were some new black Reebok Pump basketball shoes; everyone on the team had been given a pair for the Baltimore tournament. Felipe was in a relaxed mood. He has traveled to and played in big tournaments so often that he now takes them in stride. He has become something of a tournament connoisseur. One of his favorite places in the world is southern France, where he played last spring with the Gauchos. He liked the weather and the countryside and the fact that by the end of the tour French villagers were crowding into the gyms and chanting his name. This particular evening, he was also feeling pleased that he had finished most of the homework he needed to do before leaving for Baltimore, which consisted of writing an essay for American history on *Brown* v. *Board of Education* and the Fifteenth Amendment, preparing an annotated periodic table of the elements, and writing two poems for his Spanish class.

One of his poems was called "Los Dientes de Mi Abuela," which translates as "The Teeth of My Grandmother." Sitting in Kentucky Fried Chicken, he read it to me: " '*Conservando la naturaleza se ve en aquella mesa los dientes de mi abuela, que los tenía guardados para Navidad.*' " He looked up from his notebook and gestured with a chicken wing. "This is about an old grandmother who is saving her special teeth for Christmas. In my country, it's funny, old people will go around without their teeth. So in the poem the grandmother is saving the teeth for Christmas, when she'll be eating a big dinner. The teeth are brilliant and shiny. Then she gets impatient and uses them to eat a turkey at Thanksgiving — *'GRRRT . . . suena la mordida de la abuela al pavo.'*" The other poem Felipe had written was about a man about to enter prison or some other gloomy passage in his life. It is called "La Primera y Última Vez . . ." As he began reading it, an argument broke out in front of the restaurant between a middle-aged woman in a cream-colored suit and two little boys who were there on their own. First, the boys were just sassy, and then they began yelling that the woman was a crack addict. She balled up a napkin and threw it at them, shouting, "Why don't you respect your elders? What are you doing out at night all alone? Why don't you get your asses home and watch television or read a fucking book?" Felipe kept reciting his poem, raising his voice over the commotion. When he finished, he said, "It's a sadder poem than the one about the grandmother. I like writing poems. In school, I like to write if it's in Spanish, and I like to draw, and I like math. I'm good at math. I like numbers. How do I write the poems? I don't know how. They just come to me."

Done with dinner, we went back out onto 125th Street and caught a cab up to Felipe's apartment. The apartment was in a brick walkup, on a block with half a playground, a bodega, some unclaimed auto parts, and the depopulated stillness of urban decay. Walking up the four flights to the apartment, we passed an unchaperoned German shepherd napping in the vestibule, a stack of discarded Chinese menus, and someone's garbage, which had toppled over in a doorway. Felipe took the stairs three at a time. He used to dribble up and down the staircase until the neighbors complained that it was driving them crazy. For that reason and many others, the Lopezes were looking forward to moving as soon as they possibly could. Ironically, Felipe has been discouraged from playing in Puerto Rico this summer, on the ground that the basketball league there has a reputation for attracting prostitutes and drug use, when the fact is that spending the summer in Puerto Rico would help him get out of a neighborhood that attracts prostitutes and drug use.

One reason I decided to go home with Felipe was that I thought it might reveal something I hadn't yet seen in him — impatience or embarrassment at living a very humble life when he has been assured that such a rich and celebrated one is virtually in his grasp. That turned out to be not at all the case. In fact, Felipe loves to have people come over to his apartment. That night, he had invited Coach DeMello and his tutor, Maura Beattie, to drop by. When we arrived, they were already there. So were Mrs. Lopez; Felipe's brother Anderson, who moved to this country last year; Anderson's girlfriend, Nancy; Anthony; and Felipe's father. Felipe's sister, Sayonara, was expected as soon as she was through with a meeting at church. The Lopezes are an exceptionally good-looking and unusually large-scale family. Felipe's father, a construction laborer, is broad-chested, dignified, and well over six feet tall. His mother, Carmen, who works in the Garment District, is leggy and vigorous. She competed in track and volleyball as a girl in the Dominican Republic. That night, she was wearing a long flowered dress and black Reeboks. In the Dominican Republic, the Lopezes had a middle-class life. In this country, that life did not change so much as compress. All its hallmarks — Luis's exacting discipline, Carmen's piety, the children's sense of honor and obligation — came over intact, and then intensified in contrast to the disorder of the neighborhood they found themselves in.

The Lopez apartment was a warren of tiny dark rooms. One wall in the living room was covered with plaques Felipe had won — among them the *Parade* All-American High School Boys Award, the Five-Star Basketball Camp Most Promising Player, and the Ben Wilson Memorial Award for Most Valuable Player at ABCD Basketball Camp — and one corner of the room was filled by an old broken television set with what looked like a hundred basketball trophies on top. There was also a new television set, a videocassette recorder, a shelving unit, a huge sofa, a huge easy chair, a huge coffee table, some pretty folk-craft decorations from the Dominican Republic, some occasional tables, big billowy curtains, several floor lamps, and a life-size freestanding cardboard cutout of Michael Jordan. It was an exuberant-looking place. It was also possibly the most crowded place I'd ever been in. The television was tuned to a Spanish soap opera when we walked in, and Maura Beattie and Coach DeMello were sitting beside it, ignoring the show and eating pizza. The Michael Jordan cutout was propped up behind DeMello, blocking the back door. Anderson and Nancy were squeezed together on the couch looking at one of Felipe's scrapbooks, and Anthony was pacing around the room and talking to his father, who was reclined in the easy chair. Felipe said hello to his mother and they chatted for a minute in Spanish, and then she led him to a seat at the kitchen table and set a stockpot in front of him that was filled with chicken stew. There seemed to be a lot of people coming and going, and the conversation perked along:

DeMello: "I'll never forget when Anthony brought Felipe to Rice. He couldn't speak a word of English. I thought, How on earth is this kid going to take the entrance exams? Maura, do you remember that?"

Ms. Beattie: "I'm a math teacher. I'm not an English tutor. But I figured this would be something interesting to do. I didn't want the Lopezes to realize I wasn't really a tutor."

Anthony, walking through the kitchen: "Felipe, are you ready for tomorrow? You got your books with you? You planning to play?"

Nancy, translating for Carmen Lopez: "She says Felipe would rather play than eat. Otherwise, he don't give her no torment."

DeMello: "You should see the tape of the commercial Felipe and Robert Johnson did for Nintendo. They had a lot of fun, a lot of fun. Someone gave them bad advice, though, and it almost cost Felipe his eligibility. He turned down the money, and the commercial has to stop playing when he gets into college."

Ms. Beattie: "You want more pizza? Should we get more pizza? Felipe, would you eat more? He doesn't eat. I don't think he eats."

Nancy: "Would you look at this, all these trophies! Felipe, you got all these trophies?"

Anderson, to Nancy: "One of those is mine. Yeah, really. Nancy, look in the middle of the table and you'll find mine."

Anthony: "Everything everybody tells you is so beautiful — you know, be on TV, score thirty points, be the MVP, have the fame, all right — but you got to pay attention. There are a lot of rules. The NCAA rule is that no coaches can talk to him while he's a junior. They're willing, they're dying to talk to him, but that's not going to happen. When he's ready, we'll meet and talk and see. I had these dreams to be a great player, and I had my ankle broken, so it was all over for me. Felipe is my chance to see it happen for someone in my family, but it's going to happen the right way."

Felipe, coming in from the kitchen with Sayonara, just back from church: "Mommy, hey, Mommy, didn't I grow all these inches over here? One day, remember, I went to my closet and found these little pants and I said, 'Mommy, whose pants are these?' They were only this big — just little short pants — and she said, 'Felipe, those are your pants!' I couldn't believe it! I couldn't believe I ever wore those pants! I just looked at them and thought, Oh, my goodness."

DeMello: "Hey, Felipe, are you ready for tomorrow? Because anyone who isn't ready with their homework done, Brother is going to hear about it, and we're not going to be going to any other tournaments. Are you ready?"

Felipe: "DeMello, I got one thing I got to do tomorrow. I got to type my essay."

Sayonara: "Felipe, I think you're better at basketball than at typing."

Nancy, translating for Carmen Lopez: "She says he has to do the essay. She says they're so proud of him, and with the help of God he'll go to the top, he'll be a great dunker. That's what she imagines for him in five years. For now, though, they don't soup him up. He has to do right. They still walk to Felipe — they're not running."

We drove to Baltimore the next night in a car rented by the tournament sponsors and a beat-up van used by the school. The tournament sponsors were also providing rooms for the whole team in a posh hotel downtown. The following day, after breakfast, the Raiders went for a pregame practice. The Baltimore Arena is big and windy, and it had a depressing effect on the team. They ran some bumbling fastbreak drills and then had shooting practice for forty-five minutes, banging the balls against the rim. The clanking sound floated up and away into the empty stands. Coach DeMello called them together toward the end of practice. "I don't know where you guys are," he said. "I don't know where you are. You got to get your heads here by tonight. By. Tonight. This team, this

team is going to give us something. They've got number 53, he's a
beef, he's six-five. Six. Five. And there's a fast point guard. He
looks really young, he's probably a sophomore, but he does a hell
of a job on help. They don't gamble. They get a lot of shots off.
They help and recover." Pause. "Help and recover. Help and recover. And, Felipe, I saw you start to drop your head because you
missed some shots. I don't want to see that. I want to see you lift
your head and go on. All right, let's head out. I want everybody to
relax and be dressed and in my room at 6 P.M., understand? Understand? O.K. O.K."

The arena is near Inner Harbor, a fancy shopping development
in downtown Baltimore, so everybody walked over there to get
some pizza and kill time. Twelve tall black boys, wearing bright yel-
low-and-green warmups, the pants hanging low and almost sliding
off their hips, made for a sight that was probably not usual at Inner
Harbor. Shoppers were executing pick-and-rolls to avoid them. In
the mall, there were dozens of nice stores open, but the boys
seemed reluctant to go into them. We ended up in a sporting
goods shop that specialized in clothes and accessories with college-
and professional-team logos. Felipe disappeared down one of the
rows. Kojo posted up in front of a rack of jackets, took two down,
looked at the price tags, and then put them back. Reggie and Gerald found hats featuring their future colleges. "Yo, I like this one,"
Gerald said. "It's fly, but what I really want is a fitted Carolina hat.
They only have the unfitted kind."

Reggie glanced at him and then said, "Why don't you wait till
you get to Carolina, man? They going to have everything you want,
man, just *wait.*"

"I don't want to wait." Gerald put on an unfitted hat — the kind
with an adjustable strap across the back — and flipped the brim
back. Gary Saunders came over and looked at him. Gary is a sophomore. An air of peace or woe seems to form a bumper around
him. Some people think he will eventually be as good as Felipe, or
even better. He pulled Gerald's brim and then rocked back on his
heels and said, sadly, "I wish I had a hat head. I can't wear a hat. I
look dumb in a hat." Felipe walked by, wearing three hats, with
each brim pointing in a different direction. He was smiling like a
madman. He admired himself in the mirror and then took the

hats off. "I've had enough," he said to no one in particular. "Now I'm going to my room."

Some things at the tournament did not bode well. For instance, the program listed the team as "Rice, Bronx, N.Y." instead of placing the school in Manhattan. Also, Jamal Livingston had decided to shave his head during the afternoon, and the razor broke after he had finished only one hemisphere. The resulting raggedy hairdo made him look like a crazy person. He was so unhappy about it that he told Coach DeMello he wouldn't play, but Science finally persuaded him, saying, "Stretch, you look cool, man. You're down with the heavy-metal crowd now." The Raiders got their first look at the Southern players as they warmed up. They were big kids, and they looked meaty, heavy-footed, and mean. Damon Cason, the point guard DeMello had warned the Raiders about, had powerful shoulders and a taut body and a merciless look on his face. Beside him, Felipe looked wispy and hipless. Warming up, he was silent and unsmiling. The fans were loud and found much to amuse them. When Jamal stepped onto the court, they began chanting "*Hair*cut! *Hair*cut! *Hair*cut!" and then switched to a chant of "Rice-A-Roni!" and then back to "*Hair*cut!" every time Jamal took a shot.

The game begins, and in the opening moments I focus only on Felipe. Rice wins the tap, but Southern scores nine quick points and looks ready to score more. Three Southern players are guarding Felipe. They struggle after him on the fast breaks, but he slips by and, still skimming along, makes a driving lay-up from the right. Then a fast-break lay-up, off a snappy pass from Ziggy. Then, thirty-two seconds later, a driving lay-up from the left side. The guards are looking flustered and clumsy. Felipe gets a rebound, passes to Reggie, gets the ball back, and then suddenly he drifts upward, over the court, over the other boys, toward the basket, legs scissored, wrists cocked, head tilted, and in that instant he looks totally serene. Right before he dunks the ball, I have the sensation that the arena is silent, but, of course, it isn't; it's just that as soon as he slams the ball down there is a crack of applause and laughter, which makes the instant preceding it seem, by contrast, like a vacuum of sound, a little quiet hole in space.

The final score is Rice 64, Southern 42. Leaving the floor, Felipe is greeted by some of the white men, who have come down to Baltimore to watch his game. One of them comments on how well he played and wants to know what he did all afternoon to prepare. Felipe is mopping his face with a towel. He folds it up and then says, "Oh, my goodness, I didn't do much of anything. I sat in my room and watched 'Popeye' on television and listened to merengue music. I just felt good today."

The last time I spent with the team was the night before they were to leave on a trip to two tournaments — the Iolani Classic, in Honolulu, and the Holiday Prep Classic, in Las Vegas. The flight to Hawaii was so early that Coach DeMello decided to have the boys sleep at the school. After practice, they spent a few hours doing homework and then ordered in pizzas. Reggie had brought a big radio from home and set it up under a crucifix on the second floor, tuned to a station playing corny soul ballads. Coach DeMello had set up a video player and lent the team his NBA highlight tapes. "You guys going to keep it together up here?" he said. "Let's keep it together up here."

One of them yelled out, "Hey, Coach, I got to ask you something. Are there any girls in Hawaii our age?"

Someone told Reggie to turn off the radio, because the music was awful.

Reggie said, "Bro, you bugging."

"It's stupid, man. Find something better."

"Get your own radio, bro. Then you can be the d.j."

"Reggie Freeman's got a problem."

"Hey, Gary, where'd you get that shirt?"

"Macy's."

"Macy's! What, you rich or something?"

"Put on the tape. I want to see Bird and Magic play."

"Bird's a white guy."

Gerald turned on the video player and put in the tape.

"Bird could be a purple guy, bro. He's got a game."

"Here's Magic. This is the gospel, B, so you better listen up."

They sat in rapt attention, replaying some of the better sections and reciting the play-by-play along with the announcer, Marv Albert. After a few minutes, I realized that Felipe wasn't sitting with us, so I wandered down the hall, looking for him. Except for the vestibule where the boys were camping, the school was still and empty. I went upstairs to the gym. One window was broken, and a shaft of light from outside was shooting in. Someone's jersey was looped over the back of a chair in the corner, and it flapped in the night breeze. I walked from one end of the court to the other. My footsteps sounded rubbery and loud on the hardwood. After a moment, I heard a grinding in the hallway, so I walked back across the court and out to the hall. The elevator door opened, and there was Felipe, his shirttail hanging down, his hat on backward, his hand on the controls.

"Were you looking for me?"

"I was."

"I don't want to hang with the guys." He started to let the door slide shut, then pushed it open and leaned against it, grinning. "I just want to fool around. I don't want anyone to find me. I know what I got to do when we get to Hawaii. I just want to go up and down tonight."

Early the next morning, they left for Hawaii. They had a luau for Christmas, won three out of four games, flew to Las Vegas, ate too much casino food, again won three out of four games, and won a lot of quarters in the slot machines. The blustery, bright day they got back to New York, they celebrated Felipe Lopez's eighteenth birthday.

The rest of the season was a breeze until February, when Gil, Jamal, Kojo, and Rodney were taken off the team on account of bad grades. Still, going into the city Catholic-school championship, the Raiders had a record of nineteen and four. They then played St. Francis and won, 72–54, to get to the quarterfinals, and then beat Molloy, 46–36, to advance to the next round. On a cold night last week, they played Monsignor McClancy and lost in the last few minutes, 39–36, and so their season came to a close. The white men were following Felipe in every game. He had been playing so well and so steadily for the last few months that it now was as if some mystery had lifted off him and he was already inhabiting the next part of his life, in which he gets on with the business of making the most of his talent and polishing his game. In the meantime, the white men started taking note of a few young comers, like Gary Saunders, and also some skinny wisp of a kid at Alexander Burger Junior High. He's only an eighth-grader, but he already dunks. They think he's worth watching. What they say is that he might be another Felipe someday.

CHARLES P. PIERCE

The Magic Act

FROM GQ

AT THE CORNER of Washington and Ionia streets, in the city of Lansing, Michigan, there was a grand old movie house called the Gladmer Theater. Growing up on Middle Street, in a small auto-boom frame house, temple of the tiny dreams, you lived in a world that extended north as far as the freeway and south as far as the Oldsmobile plant. But slip off to the side, down Logan to Washington and into the Gladmer, and the world seemed to crack open. There in the dark, you could curl up in the balcony's deep shadows and feel the place come alive in bursts of golden wonder. You could tuck in at noon and stay the whole day. Early seventies movies — Godzilla taking down Osaka, and the new black cinema of the day. Richard Roundtree and Billy Dee. Jim Brown and Ron O'Neal, *Superfly* so very sharp. You'd be sharp, too, if Curtis Mayfield did your music. New stars but the same old dreams. They were selling the old Hollywood there, and if you bought it, you bought it right down to your bones. Life as performance. Performance as life. Walk into the Gladmer and your life didn't dead-end at the Oldsmobile plant anymore.

Earvin Johnson, Jr., would save up the money he earned cleaning yards and shoveling snow and helping Earvin senior on the garbage truck. He'd buy his ticket and stay all day, walking blinking out into the summer twilight or wide-eyed into the winter gloom. "They didn't kick you out until five o'clock," he recalls today. "You could stay and watch the movie two or three times. But those were the times, man. And that was why I wanted to meet these people, to get to know them." He bought the old Hollywood dream, not knowing that it was a dream straight out of movies that had played the Gladmer long before he was born. Old musicals and Tinseltown melodrama. Kid, some day, all this will be yours.

According to popular belief, Magic Johnson was created when a sports writer named Fred Stabley thought that Earvin Johnson, Jr., wasn't a sufficiently respectful nom de hoop for the effervescent young player at Everett High School. Truth be told, though, Magic Johnson was born on those afternoons long ago when Earvin Johnson, Jr., tucked himself into the balcony shadows and watched his dreams explode like skyrockets around him. It is the essential dichotomy of his life. It will one day be the essential dichotomy of his death.

"I wanted to be a part of that," he muses. "There was Earvin, but it was Magic who wanted to be a part of that Hollywood life. Magic is the side where you go to Hollywood and live that Hollywood life and so forth." They were not compatible, Earvin and Magic. Not even in the same person. Where Earvin was eager to be loved, Magic throve on adulation, which is not the same thing at all. Earvin was the happy one, the joyful child who had worked so hard to be the conciliator within his family when his mother threw herself into a new and unyielding religion, the teenager who had made the best of being bused to the predominantly white Everett High, far across town. Magic did the premieres and the clubs. He hung with Eddie and Arsenio, and he signed autographs for the pretty people who came to the Forum to see the Los Angeles Lakers play.

They were coming for him. That was the marvel of it. There were thirties-style Hollywood parties, but with the heedless edge of eighties consumption. There were fine women and more than enough opportunities, and Magic Johnson was one of the biggest stars in town. "I'm living a dream," he remembers. "I'm from Lansing, Michigan. I mean, here I am in Hollywood, and so I was living not just for myself but for a lot of my friends back home, 'cause I would always tell them, man, I met Ali. I met Stallone. I met, you know, Richard Pryor. I know Eddie. I would always call back, and they were living through me. Man, I'd tell my friends that so-and-so talked to me. I said, 'Wow!' They would run over and ask me for my autograph. That's what shocked me the most. I was in awe of the movie stars sitting on the court."

In his mind, Earvin watched it all unfold before him as though
he were at once the audience and the actor, as though he were still
in the Gladmer, still curled up there deep in the balcony shadows,
an odd and lingering distance now come between himself and the
movie that his life had become. The movie rolled through the five
NBA titles with the Lakers in the 1980s, picking up supporting
characters along the way: Larry Bird; teammates like Kareem Abdul-
Jabbar and James Worthy; such sudden, intense rivals as Michael
Jordan. Eddie. Arsenio. Luther Vandross, singing just for him. It
was as though Magic were another John Shaft, another Superfly.
Performance as life. Life as performance. Earvin watched as his
life was hijacked by its own public creation.

"Don't call me Magic," Johnson once told a woman. "Only people who don't know me call me Magic. People who really know me
call me Earvin."

It could not go on, this bow-tight interplay between two incom-
patible personas. Earvin could not function credibly as a kind of
free-floating alibi for Magic's lifestyle, and Magic was not willing to
submit to Earvin's control. The knowledge that the other existed
made each of them insecure. In basketball, for example, it was
Magic who threw the blind passes and orchestrated Showtime, that
resolutely L.A. phenomenon that owed far more to the Village
People than it did to James Naismith. But Earvin was the solid
player, schooled so truly in his own unique fundamentals that he
could see the game three or four moves ahead. Earvin was serious.
Earvin had goals. Earvin was going to be a businessman — a ty-
coon, really. In a town full of players, Earvin was going to be respected as a Player.

There was a terrible pulling and hauling, an awful straining beneath the shallow artifice of celebrity, and an unstated demand
that Earvin be taken more seriously than he could be within the
glittery caul that was Magic's life. They could function within the
context of the NBA and within the context of pure fame. But they
were not prepared, either of them, to work together in the consuming crisis of their lives.

It is a vast story now, sliding inexorably toward the epic. When
Johnson announced on November 7, 1991, that he had con-
tracted the human immunodeficiency virus, the apparent cause of
AIDS, he first let Magic do the talking. It was an up performance.

He even spoke vaguely of beating the disease, which is plainly impossible. "BELIEVE IN MAGIC," said the T-shirts. And at the start, it seemed that it might work. Society appeared to suspend briefly the malicious notion that there are guilty and innocent victims of this disease. When it was rumored that the various companies whose products Johnson endorsed were considering dropping him from their commercials, the ensuing public outcry seemed like a benediction.

Society has allowed itself its AIDS saints — Elizabeth Glaser, say. Or the late Ryan White. But both of them had contracted HIV in a socially acceptable manner: to wit, accidentally, through tainted blood products. Since Johnson openly admitted that he'd become infected through unprotected sexual congress, the early, positive reaction to his announcement suggested that he would be the AIDS saint who could eliminate this final stigma. He would be more than merely an example. His life with the virus would be his witness, his public testimony. Performance as life, and life as performance.

Forgotten for the moment was not only the long history of how the world reacts during times of plague but also the recent, sorry history of how the world has reacted to this particular one. Forgotten was the fact that the lives of saints are not the rosy, sanitized versions that make it into the prayer books and onto the movie screen. Saints are terribly inconvenient. They often make trouble. They often make people look very foolish. After all, Ryan White first became famous because some people in Indiana tried to keep him from going to school. Nevertheless, it was contended that Magic's inimitable persona would be enough to crack open the formidable collusion between unreasoning fear and moralistic stupidity that had attended this epidemic. So loud and universal was this contention that a number of uncomfortable personal truths were swept aside — most notably, that his attitude toward women caused him to treat them as (at best) a disposable commodity.

The performance closed quickly. Magic went on *The Arsenio Hall Show,* and he was loudly applauded for declaring himself "far from being a homosexual." Gay activists threw that back in his face, and a dying AIDS patient named Derek Hodel read him off at a meeting of the national AIDS commission in January 1992. Johnson was learning on the fly about the ambiguities of the disease he had contracted. He did a kids' show about AIDS for Nickelodeon, a gentle, Earvin-like show that was very well received. He played in last year's NBA All-Star Game, and his smile on the victory stand remains the enduring image from last summer's Olympics.

What remained plain, however, was the fact that he never understood the public ramifications of his condition. "It's funny," he says. "I didn't know what was going to happen. I didn't know how people were going to react. I didn't know until you actually got into it and really saw how the other people would respond, until you saw how other people were treated who had the virus, or who already had AIDS." It was out there, however, waiting for him, the human reflex that was born on the day Genghis Khan introduced the flea-bitten rats of East Asia to those of the Balkans. A decade later, a third of Europe was dead, and the survivors were blaming the Jews and burning them alive in their synagogues.

Not quite a year after his upbeat press conference, there was another one, and Johnson wasn't even there. He is gone from the game for good now, his comeback aborted by those same forces that the public witness of his life was supposed to eliminate. Players spoke openly of being afraid to guard him closely, even though they are at far greater risk of dying every time they climb on the team plane. There were renewed rumors about how he had acquired the virus. He wrote an autobiography, in which he discussed his baroque extracurricular sex life, and then undertook a huge publicity tour, on which it seemed he was defending himself against charges of bisexuality by pleading satyriasis.

The woman to whom he had once said "Only people who don't know me call me Magic" was suing him for $2 million, alleging that it was Johnson who'd passed the virus on to her. That Johnson did not attend his second retirement is not surprising. The comeback had been a performance by Magic, a headlong dive for the spotlight, and it had become plain that Magic now scared people. Too many of them had been living Magic's life themselves — still are, truth be told — and they didn't need him out there as the great golem of antibody roulette. That would be just too frightening. So Magic wasn't wanted anymore, and Earvin had the good sense to stay home.

"It would have been good, but not great," he says of his attempt to return to play. "Because if I was Magic Johnson, it would've

been great, see? That's the difference. To show that somebody
with HIV could not just play, because I can play. I can go back now
and play. But I'm talking about somebody that did it and did it the
way it's supposed to be done. To be Magic Johnson, the guy that I
was. You know, he's a lot. He's a lot of roles in one."

There is a *gravitas* to him, pure Earvin-ness, and there is much
more substance than perhaps even he has ever allowed. The smiles
do not come as quick and as easily as they do on television when
Oprah is billing and cooing and asking to see new pictures of the
baby. Blue notes ring behind his words. "I lost the fun of it," he
says. "Fun makes me be Magic Johnson, the enthusiasm. That's a
big part of my game, and then that was taken away. I couldn't use
all my energy to play the game because I was using it all to explain
myself." He cannot be Magic the way he was, but he also cannot be
Earvin, either, because Magic gave Earvin a fatal disease. Magic will
want to go to heaven while Earvin does the time in hell. It cannot
work anymore.

Ultimately, he asked for too much and for too little. He wanted
his normal life back, but his normal life is performance, and performance is life, and there was no part left for him. He forfeited
the only role that was left for him to play, AIDS saint, because
saints — even real ones — need constituencies as much as politi-
cians do.

In *Making Saints,* journalist Kenneth Woodward chides the
Catholic Church because, in choosing its saints, the Church forces
itself "to exclude . . . any evidence of human failure; in doing so,
[they] omit what is truly exemplary in the life of a saint — the
struggle between virtue and vice or, in a wider scope, between
grace and nature." The real world is even less forgiving. Magic
Johnson has not been what the world wanted him to be, and the
world cannot seem to accept Earvin Johnson, Jr., for who he is.
Our grace and his nature have gone to war.

> "He who dies of epidemic disease is a martyr. When you learn that an
> epidemic disease exists in a country, do not go there; but if it breaks out
> in a country where you are, do not leave."
> — Muslim proverb

*

According to Thucydides, a plague fell upon the Athenian Army during the first Peloponnesian War. Soldiers refused to bury the infected bodies of their comrades, and as the conventional religion of the day failed to provide either an explanation or relief, the men turned from the priests of the gods and sought intercession themselves, or else they turned away from the gods entirely. They ran riot, engaging in all manner of sensual excess. The living gave themselves up for dead. "Already a far heavier sentence . . . was hanging over a man's head," the historian reports. "Before that fell, why should he not take a little pleasure?"

Boccaccio writes that during the height of the Black Death in Europe, fathers would abandon their sons. Jews were suspected of poisoning the wells. In 1878, when yellow fever broke out in Memphis, people caught fleeing the city were hanged on sight by the hysterical residents of the surrounding towns. Today, there are undertakers who refuse to bury those whom AIDS has killed, and the disease has been variously described as God's (or nature's) revenge against the carnal and the wicked. When Earvin Johnson announced that he was HIV-positive, he was stepping into the middle of the inglorious history of human intolerance.

Of course, at the time, he knew less about the history than he knew even about his disease. By his own admission, he went through the eighties unconcerned about AIDS. "I thought it was a homosexual thing," he recalls. "It wasn't even close to my mind. We knew it was out there, but I never thought it could affect me. In the circles I was around, it was oblivion." Considering that those circles came to encompass the Hollywood show-business community, which was hit hard in the early stages of the epidemic, this is a formidable bit of denial, but not an uncommon one.

His professional success, however, was immediate and remarkable. It is now beyond cliché to say that Johnson (along with Bird) helped resuscitate professional basketball, which nearly drowned in the late seventies, due to public apathy and a spate of nasty drug scandals. When Johnson entered the game, in 1979, he was a fresh and vibrant presence. In Johnson's Lakers debut, Abdul-Jabbar won the game with a lordly hook shot, only to be seized in an ungainly embrace by the enthusiastic rookie guard. Pictures of the moment show the cool and elegant center looking quite amused, as though someone had just handed him a mackerel. What Johnson did for Abdul-Jabbar, he did for the Lakers and, ultimately, for the entire NBA. Competitively, his Lakers and Bird's Celtics were a matchup for the ages, and one that providentially took place in two large television markets. Moreover, before anyone else did, he saw the genius in the NBA's attempt to market itself as a league — as a single entertainment entity. This succeeded wonderfully; the NBA was able to sell a largely black sport to a largely white audience, even during a decade in which racial relations worsened. Magic Johnson became a crossover hit.

By the time he got to the NBA, he had set the corporate class as his goal; he claimed to idolize Michael Ovitz, Hollywood's king fixer, and now he employs him. Johnson himself has always sought to make things work, to cast the movie of his own life. In 1981, when he engineered the dismissal of Lakers Coach Paul Westhead — a good move, as it turns out, since it resulted in the hiring of Pat Riley — he was simply firing the director in order to get the story to come out right. He had learned quickly and well.

As the Lakers prospered, Magic became one of the town's most vivid performers. Academy Award winners paid him court. He'd made it at last. His life was performance, and performance was his life. Magic Johnson was the next best thing to a movie star.

The good life was a perquisite of his new station. At first, liberated L.A. amazed him. "I mean, you had women with no panties. Women with women," he recalls. However, he soon lost whatever inhibitions he had brought with him, or (more likely) he simply parked them with Earvin and let Magic be Magic. The Lakers became notorious around the NBA, the Forum coming to be known as the league's primary pleasure palace. Games at the Forum were glamorous affairs, forty-one Hollywood premieres a season. Lakers officials noted how often the same women's names appeared on the list of complimentary tickets left by the players. In 1990, forward James Worthy was caught in a police sting operation while attempting to solicit two women from a Houston escort service.

By all accounts, Johnson was central to everything that went on. He helped entertain visiting players, showing the rookies the (you should pardon the expression) lay of the land. In his recently published autobiography, *My Life*, he claims that he once had sex in an elevator, another time in a boardroom, and he has also confessed to *ménages à trois, quatre,* and *six*. At one point, sources say, the Lakers became so alarmed at Johnson's sexual escapades that the team asked the league to step in. Through it all, though, he maintained his relationship with Earleatha "Cookie" Kelly, whom he had met in college, at Michigan State, and whom he eventually married, in September 1991.

He veers between caution and candor while discussing all of this. For example, he claims never to have slept all night with any woman except Cookie, as though that mitigates whatever guilt he may feel. He also seems to excuse promiscuity on the basis of good conversation.

"I think when you talk about [having] a lot of women, people think that's all you're doing," he says. "I wasn't, like, numbers, like a Wilt Chamberlain and thousands of women or whatever. It wasn't even close to that. People don't realize that I was *friends* with these women, not that I just went out and picked one up and that was it. See, I talked to them because I wanted to know what's up here and, see, people are not getting that, so I guess they think it's one night here and one night there and that was it, and it wasn't like that at all.

"When it was time for them to go . . . because I'm a man, I couldn't sleep with any of them. I couldn't sleep with nobody but Cookie. So I said, you know, 'You got to go,' because I was, like, I didn't trust them, you know? So they was, like, 'Oh, you kicking me out?' I said, 'Yeah, you know I told you that before.' So they didn't understand." It's almost as if Magic picked up the women and left Earvin to do the explaining afterward. Later, when he was touring to support his book, he was roundly criticized for revealing as much as he did.

When Johnson announced his HIV status, in November 1991, the NBA shook briefly in its success. There is still that sub-rosa fear that white America responds unwillingly to a largely black sport and that any scandal would bring that odious dynamic back into play. Uncontrolled black male sexuality is one of this culture's most durable racist myths. Indeed, it was the psychological underpinning of the whole system of segregation. The NBA and its new corporate pilot fish wanted no part of a sex scandal to rival the drug scandals of the late seventies.

Hence, the league was relieved when Johnson seemed to be

granted a conditional public pardon, contingent upon his properly performing the bestowed role of AIDS saint. That lasted all
the way through the Dream Team summer of 1992. Public opinion
began to turn only last August, when Johnson started dropping
broad hints that he would like to return to the Lakers full-time.
But there were whispers throughout the league, and for the first
time, Johnson felt himself losing a part of his most basic constituency: the players.

On October 12, columnist Dave Kindred wrote in the *Sporting
News* that if Johnson planned to return to active NBA competition,
he should "tell the whole truth about how he acquired the AIDS
virus," intimating that Johnson could have become infected during unprotected gay sex, an accusation Johnson has repeatedly denied. The charge was the first overt indication that there were
people in the NBA who found Johnson's return unsettling. It
began a media frenzy, and the publicity tour for his book, including a graphic interview on ABC's *Primetime Live,* only fanned the
flames.

Meanwhile, Phoenix Suns President Jerry Colangelo spoke out
about the alleged risks that Johnson posed to his players. Utah Jazz
star Karl Malone, an Olympic teammate of Johnson's, expressed
similar concerns to the *New York Times.* Oddly enough, a controversy
that began with the opinion that "the odds" were against Johnson's
having attained the HIV virus through heterosexual sex had evolved
into one that assumed as credible the even-longer odds that he
could somehow pass the virus along to another player during a
game. In the Lakers' last 1992 exhibition game, in Chapel Hill,
North Carolina, Johnson, playing badly, scratched his arm, and the
photograph of Lakers trainer Gary Vitti bandaging the barely visible wound flashed all over the country. Clearly, Johnson's position
had become untenable. On November 2, he retired again.

Perhaps Johnson thought he could finesse it. Perhaps he thought
Magic could smile and wave and somehow beat the collective fear
that has risen up in the face of epidemic disease over the past
2,500 years. But he was an uneasy saint. People could relate to
Elizabeth Glaser, as a mother struck by vicious happenstance. They
now looked at Johnson and saw somebody who took sexual risks,
especially when he came out and told them just how blatant those

risks had been. That was too threatening, particularly if you're out there yourself. He *had* to be gay, because then straight folks could feel less threatened by their condom-less Saturday nights. Besides, he'd performed well at the Olympics, and the sick are not generally loved until they become pitiable.

"People are real strange animals," Lakers General Manager Jerry West muses. "Everyone has great compassion for people, until it cuts into their livelihood. I think it's a shame because this could've been a remarkable story. If it would've progressed in a normal way, I think it would've quieted a lot of people's fears."

Caught between the hysteria that attends any epidemic and his admitted flouting of sexual convention, Johnson had come to a place where his diplomatic skills were of no use, a place where he could not broker a peace even between Earvin, who needed to be loved, and Magic, who needed to be adored. There was a conflict in the plot to which there was no resolution. He had violated the old Muslim proverb. He had left the country of the epidemic, and he was out there all alone.

They have known each other for years. That's what her friends say. She met Earvin Johnson when they were both students at Michigan State. For some reason, friends say, she was able to touch Earvin when all anybody else wanted was to be touched by Magic. She got married to someone else, had a daughter and then got divorced. In March 1990, she says, she was in the Palladium club in Los Angeles, and she saw him again. On June 22, she alleges in her suit, they made love at her apartment. She says that she asked him about using a condom. She says he declined to use one.

A year later, she discovered that she was HIV-positive. She says she spoke with Johnson by phone in July 1991. She says she wrote him a letter about it on August 29, 1991. She says she found him on September 12 of that year playing basketball with his friends at Jenison Fieldhouse on the Michigan State campus. She says he didn't believe her, that he was too healthy to have AIDS. Finally, last October, she sued him for $2 million.

Among other things, the suit alleges that Johnson knew that he was HIV-positive seventeen months before he admitted it publicly. If her facts are correct, that makes him more than simply oversexed. It makes him willfully reckless. In the dichotomy of his life, it would be the final triumph of Magic over Earvin. It would make him a villain. Johnson will not comment on the lawsuit, saying only that "they have no case, so they have to attack my character."

The woman in question — a 31-year-old health-office worker — is being advised by one Armstrong Williams, a close friend and a conservative Washington, D.C., media specialist whose business partner is Stedman Graham, Oprah Winfrey's fiancé. Theodore Swift, the plaintiff's Lansing attorney, refers all calls to Williams, who was Clarence Thomas's press officer when Thomas was the head of the Equal Employment Opportunity Commission. During the stormy hearings before the Senate Judiciary Committee, Williams worked the halls, drawing for reporters a portrait of Anita Hill as a frustrated and bitter ex-employee.

Williams is shell-mouthed on the whole affair, declining to comment for the record. He has been busy, however. A source familiar with the case insists that it was Williams who orchestrated the steady stream of leaks about the case to Frank Deford of *Newsweek*. Ever since the first story about the suit appeared, Johnson's lawyers have charged that the plaintiff was promiscuous herself and that Johnson may have contracted the virus from her. "I don't know why they have to say that publicly," says attorney Swift. "I haven't been running around calling him a whoremonger." However, since Johnson's defense will undoubtedly involve impugning the plaintiff's character, there is no little irony in the fact that it will be Armstrong Williams's job to keep Earvin Johnson from doing to his client what Williams worked so hard to do to Anita Hill.

Once a portion of the text of the August 1991 letter appeared in *Newsweek*, last November, it became plain that the woman's allegations contradicted not only Johnson's claims at his original retirement press conference but also his autobiography, in which he writes "Of the women I talked to, nobody has tested positive . . . thank God for that." Further, if the woman's story is true, then the past two years of Johnson's life are open to serious revisionism, and his moral claim to leadership on the issue of AIDS education becomes perilously threadbare. In addition, the revelation of the lawsuit prompted inquiries into whether, married or not, Johnson is still carrying on, something that would sink his public image entirely and forever. Last November, the *National Enquirer* ran a purported account of Johnson's weekend trip to Las Vegas to see the heavyweight championship fight between Evander Holyfield and Riddick Bowe, during which, the tabloid alleges, Johnson propositioned anything that moved, except, possibly, the white tigers at the Mirage.

"That whole Vegas thing is a farce," Johnson says. "I can't do anything about it. If they want to follow me, they will. I know the truth of it."

He says he has broken the habit of promiscuity. "Gradually, you take yourself out, and that's what's happened to me," he says. "You're gradually taking yourself out of the club-type atmosphere where all the single people are who want to meet people. And I think it's made it easier to me that I'm not playing.

"As a man, you know, you're always going to say 'There's a beautiful woman.' Now, if a guy says that he can't see a beautiful woman, that's lying. Let's be up-front about it. There's nothing wrong with saying 'That's a beautiful woman.' What's wrong is acting on it." That is clearly Earvin talking, but it was Magic who went alone to Vegas, which is not exactly taking oneself out of that atmosphere he's talking about. See Magic at ringside, smiling in the spotlight, adored if not loved, and you think of Thucydides and his Athenians, who got drunk on their own private religions because they didn't have anything to lose, and even the gods had given up.

He has an office in Century City, not far from the one Ronald Reagan keeps. He goes there after he works out. There is remarkable bulk to him, so much so that one of his friends wonders "Do you really think he knows what he's in for? I don't. We see him all big and strong, but what happens when he gets sick? What will we see, and will we even want to?" In a sense, then, he is buying time, building a kind of public monument to himself while he is still strong enough to do so. Over the course of his career with the Lakers, more than 150,000 people died of AIDS in the United States. He says he's not afraid that one day he will die a very public death.

"If you're truthful with yourself, you can sleep good," he says. "You don't have to worry about anything or any skeletons in [the] closet. I'm not worried about any of that stuff. I've never been a worrier, you know? If something's going to happen, it's going to happen, you know? I keep praying at night, then everything'll be all right. If I eat right. If I get enough sleep. Everything's going to be all right because people can live with this for twelve, fourteen, fifteen, years. So I'm thinking, Why can't it be like this for fifteen years?"

He can look out from his office into the hills above Hollywood. There are a hundred things that could've happened. He could've got cancer, and nobody would care how or why. He could've been drafted by Indiana or Cleveland. "I'd be married for years," he says, "with a lot of children." But he bought Hollywood long ago, bought it in his bones and in his soul, and Hollywood delivered. Tonight, he will go on television with his friend Arsenio, and they will laugh and joke and there will be warm applause and a serenade in his ear from saxophonist Kenny G., and it will be a long way from Lansing, Michigan, and the little road that dead-ends at the Oldsmobile plant. He will be back there in a week, home for Thanksgiving and for a book-signing that will be more restrained than the one at the Manhattan bookstore where a woman screamed "Magic!" and fainted backward into an aisle marked "FANTASY."

No, the people will line up, all decorous and stolid, Christmas carols ringing out of the walls behind them. The signing will be at a suburban bookstore, just up the block from an eightplex movie house that is not a theater, not by a damn sight. "I'm just glad to be home," he will tell the local press, who love him. "Here, I'm just Earvin, you know?" Downtown, the stores are shuttered, the great blank-staring bones of the auto industry. There is a little public park where the Gladmer Theater was. It is a cold and empty place, and it has no stories to tell.

She's No Jockette

FROM THE NEW YORK TIMES MAGAZINE

OUTSIDE IT HAD been madness, everyone screaming her name. Then Julie Krone, having just crossed the finish line at Belmont Park aboard a 13-to-1 long shot named Colonial Affair, came in to the small room beneath the grandstand to meet the press. There was a moment's holy hush; maybe even, among the old-timers, a quiver of spiritual dislocation. This sprout, after all; this squirt, this squiggle who looked as if she should be home eating Twinkies, not steering 1,200 pounds of horse down the homestretch at 40 miles an hour: on this June day she had become the first woman to win the 125-year-old Belmont Stakes and the first ever to win any of the Triple Crown races (the Kentucky Derby, the Preakness, the Belmont).

You would have had to be well beyond the reach of the news media not to know that her triumph had been marred by the fate of Prairie Bayou, the favorite who had fractured a leg and had to be destroyed. Still, there had been twelve horses left and a mile to go; Krone had ridden the winner home by two and a quarter lengths.

Now, some creative thinker was asking how it felt to be the first woman blah blah blah. Krone, who had been wired and elated, said carefully: "I don't think the question needs to be genderized. It would feel great to anyone. But whether you're a girl or a boy or a Martian, you still have to go out and prove yourself again every day."

The air around Julie Krone resonates with first-woman this and best-woman that, and on some bittersweet level she resents it.

Let us be beyond gender, she says. But we are not, and these firsts and bests matter. She has fought hard to achieve them in a business that has never, even in its best moments, been an equal-opportunity employer of women.

Krone is the winningest female jockey in the history of racing. She has earned purses exceeding $52 million (the jockey takes ten percent), a figure no other woman has remotely approached. Beyond gender, she is among the country's top ten jockeys, ranking third in races won this year and sixth in total earnings. She has won the leading-jockey title at major tracks, including Monmouth, Gulfstream and Belmont; at Saratoga, in 1991, she lost by just one race. But another season looms at Saratoga, which opens Wednesday.

Julie Krone is 4 feet 10 1/2 inches tall and weighs 100 pounds. I used to think that all jockeys were this small. In fact, the average is 5 feet 3 to 4 inches tall and there are jockeys of 5 feet 9 and 10; you see them around the barns, bags of bones forever struggling to keep off the weight.

At thirty (her birthday was yesterday), and from not too far across the room, Krone looks like a child. Her voice is a prepubescent chirp; her hair tamps down like the hair of children playing hard in summer; her hands are small, the fingers tenderly pouched in what appears to be baby fat. All this is deception. The little pouches are pure callus, and both pinkies — which look primed for tea — are bent from old breaks, one from punching out a kid who hassled her in school.

The Maryland horse trainer Ben Perkins, Jr., recalls his first encounter with those hands, at his barn in Atlantic City in 1981: "This cute little girl, looks about ten, comes up to me and squeaks, 'Hi!' " his own voice going falsetto, " 'I'm Julie Krone! I'm a jockey!' and takes my hand and *brings me to my knees.* Well, we let her ride, and she rides like a god." His eyes go misty, contemplating nirvana. "The perfect thing," he says, "would be this little small person who would just sit on the horse's back and go along for the ride, just to keep the horse out of trouble. That was Julie."

The fledgling Krone mangled hands to show trainers she was strong enough to ride their horses. She would not suffer being called jockette. She got into astonishing scraps with jockeys she accused of dirty riding, including one wide-screen fracas in which a

jockey whipped her during a race, she punched him at the weigh-
in, he shoved her into a swimming pool and she smacked him with
a lawn chair. They were both fined.

Now her handshake has taken on the lapidary gloss that comes
with self-validation. "I'm gonna be the greatest jock in the world,"
she wrote in her diary at age fifteen. Though she says those were
the thoughts of childhood, and racing may be too fluid to sustain a
"greatest" jockey, nothing she has done since suggests that her ambition has waned.

Pondering the currents of communication that seem to flow between Krone and genus Equus, her friend and colleague Richard
Migliore said recently: "Julie is an extremely patient rider. She just
sits there with a long hold [loose rein], not moving much, and the
horses respond. I could ride like that till the cows come home and
I wouldn't get that result. I am an aggressive rider. I pick up the
horse's head and hold the reins taut. I make the demand. Julie
does not demand. She asks the question and gets the result."

On the track, the colors of her silks blurred in the traffic and the
flying dirt, Krone is still recognizable to the tutored eye by her
style: the reins held loose, almost loopy, rather than clutched up
high on the horse's neck; the hands in motion, the body quite still,
hunkered down like a little comma. Her style is often compared to
that of Bill Shoemaker, who rode for forty-one years, to age fifty-
eight, and still holds the all-time record of 8,833 winners. Shoemaker himself says he is flattered by the comparison.

"It's a sixth-sense thing," he said recently from the barn at Hollywood Park, California, where he trains horses. "You're communi-
cating with the horse through the reins, and he can tell that you
like him, and he likes you, and you both know it. I think you're
born with that. Not all jockeys have it. Julie does."

Trainers are forever talking about her hands. "Good hands,"
they say solemnly, "magic hands." Horses want to ride for Julie,
they say. They talk about her *move,* the way she holds back, holds
back, holds back, and then, coming into the top of the stretch,
makes her move.

Critics say, though none for attribution, that this late move is the
only move Krone has. They say that she lacks versatility, that she
tends to hug the rail and thus gets stuck in heavy traffic coming to
the top of the stretch, where the horses clump up. They say and

they say and they say, but it is hard to hear them above the happily anguished howls of bettors screaming, "*Now,* Julie!," as she nears the quarter pole.

Krone herself says she is tired of this business about the hands, and maybe even means it. I told her one day that every trainer I met described her with the same two words. "Oh, yeah," she said. "Magic hands, magic hands."

No. Relax and communicate, as in "Julie relaxes horses" and "Julie communicates with horses." She liked this better than the hands: "That's a real nice compliment, isn't it?"

"Well, to relax a horse, you find out what he wants. In the post parade, I like to pick up his head and get him to stop, stand there and look around and look out over the grandstand, and think . . ." moving along now, as jockeys do, on a fine anthropomorphic riff, ". . . and then I'll see how he likes to pull. Does he like to keep pulling or have you let him go? Does he like your hands on or off his neck; which will make him less nervous? And all this you can tell by feel, by what he does with his weight and his head and his mouth, so that, by the end of the post parade, I know what he likes."

"But listen," she said, "hands don't win races. What wins races is to ride horses that are fast and competitive."

It is the old circularity: You cannot get fast horses until you win races and you cannot win races until you get fast horses. Since she won the Belmont Stakes, owners and trainers have been offering her plenty of speed. But pre-Belmont, the vital difference between Krone and other good riders who have not been given good mounts had been her ability to sell herself as well as her horsemanship.

A noted turf writer told me: "Julie is very politically savvy. A big jockey will usually exercise a big horse for a big race. But she is always there early, working the horses, and then she'll give the trainers and owners a move-by-move report. Some jockeys don't like her much. They say everything she does is political; they say she's a prima donna. Would they say it if she was a he? Who knows? Who cares? All I know is, she wins."

On a particular day this spring, late in the Gulfstream season, Julie Krone had not been winning at all. Nothing but place money, which is small money, 22 percent of the purse (with 10 percent of that going to the jockey), against 60 percent for a winner; and, as her agent, Larry Cooper, who is known as Snake for reasons lost in the mists of time and discretion, said, "Nobody ever remembers who came in second."

The day before had been terrific. She had won two early races and then, as she had paraded around the paddock, someone had yelled, "Hey, Julie, why don't you give somebody else a chance?" She had laughed, they had all laughed, and then, of course, she had gone out and won again.

But on this luckless day, when she appeared in the paddock before the last race, a small man in a neon-blue sport coat called: "Hey, Julie, you can't ride. Go back to New York!" Krone half-grinned and yelled over her shoulder, "The one day I don't win, and you're yelling at me!"

It played wonderfully. The paddock-fence crowd loved it. Krone rode out to the track and the heckler said: "I'm crazy about her. But I lost a thousand bucks on her today, so I was mad."

The day had started early on the backside. Since 4 A.M., workers had been mucking out the stalls and preparing for morning workouts. By six o'clock, as the aromas of horse and hay rose with the sun, the exercisers were leading the horses out to the track. Randy Schulhofer, a trainer and son of the Hall of Fame trainer Scotty Schulhofer, had arrived at five o'clock and was waiting for Krone to come exercise one of his horses. At seven he was still waiting. I asked when she usually arrived. "Any time she wants," he said. "Spoiled. Got rich too fast." But he said it amiably. They are friends, and she has been riding for the Schulhofers since long before their Belmont victory with Colonial Affair.

Snake Cooper soon appeared in his Jaguar (the agent gets twenty-five percent of the jockey's take), switched to a golf cart and went bopping around the barns, networking. Krone, who is usually early but had eased up that morning, arrived in her Mitsubishi 3000 GTSL. She exchanged big hellos all over, then rode Schulhofer's horse onto the track and breezed off. Among those watching closely was the Texas trainer Carl Nafzger.

"To be a great jockey," he said, "you need five traits: riding ability, physical strength, mental soundness, a great immune system and class. That's the big unknown, class. You get a rodeo cowboy riding bull number 22 with $200 added money in some little bitty fair in Lamesa, Texas, and then you take that same cowboy riding for $10,000 in Cheyenne, and boom! He can't ride. The Joe Montanas, who can deliver when the pressure's on — that's class. That's Julie."

After the workout, she sat down with the Daily Racing Form, which is jockey homework.

I had said that I marveled how, amid the crushing flanks and hooves, amid memories of mishaps and the contingencies of more (Krone has suffered a badly broken arm, a severe back injury and countless lesser injuries), riders could concentrate on the job at hand.

"And I marvel," she had said, "at how accountants can sit and concentrate on a tax form. Anyway, what happens in a race is deeper than concentration. I'll study the Form and see that the gray horse cuts out all the time. Then, when I see him I'm not thinking, 'Oh, yeah, that's the horse that cuts out.' I just instinctively go around him. You read the Form and you store these things and you go race."

As she pored over columns of past performances, William Mott, the lead trainer at the meet, rode by. "My favorite trainer!" she cried, and ran after him. "Everyone's favorite trainer," Snake Cooper said.

"She's good at public relations, isn't she?" I asked Cooper.

"The best — better than I am," he said, dispensing largess.

The agent's main job is to sell trainers on his client, and Cooper, who is forty-four, has a considerable background in sales. "I was in bingo for a while," he says. "Then I was in home improvements. Then I had a couple of retail operations — discount drugs, jewelry. But I didn't like retail so I sold them. Then I was hanging around the track a lot and a trainer said, 'You like the track so much, why not become a jockey's agent?' So I did."

He has represented Krone, by all accounts brilliantly, since she became a journeyman rider in 1981. "At first, we fought a lot. She had a nasty attitude. She'd walk into a barn with no respect and say, 'Why isn't my horse ready? *Get that horse ready.*' But she's grown up. She's a lot more mellow now," he said, as he eyed her chatting up Mott.

By 10 A.M. the workouts were done and Krone went off to rest. By noon she was back in the women's jockey room, dressing for her first race. Nothing much came her way, no excitement at all, until the 10th.

It was a big stakes race, and she was riding for Schulhofer. Suddenly, at the top of the stretch, a horse on the outside cut directly in front of her toward the rail, blocking her out. She braked sharply. "They clobbered her!" the trainer cried. There was an inquiry, and the interfering rider was disqualified.

I recalled hearing about a race in which Krone had blocked Pat Day, a Hall of Famer who won last year's Kentucky Derby. Furious, he had said to her afterward, "What kind of riding was *that?*" She had answered, "*Race* riding."

After this Gulfstream incident, I asked a steward, Donald LeVine, to explain the distinctions. He said: "If the horse next to you is boxed in and full of run, you don't have to move over for him. That's race riding. But you cannot interfere. That's against the rules.

"In this case, we established interference. Julie had to take up [rein in]. We got a lot of objections from bettors afterward. One said, 'You guys always side with Julie.' Which is ridiculous, but they get mad." Some sports writers say it is because Krone rides hard on others but is quick to protest when they do it to her. But in the women's jockey room, after the race, she was complaisant.

"It's a big purse and the guys get aggressive. It happens to all of us, so easily," she said. "You're hitting and hitting and your head's down low and you look up and think, 'Wow, I've drifted a long way,' and you look behind you and someone's right there; you know you've bothered him, but it wasn't intentional."

She was blow-drying her hair and discussing facial moisturizers with the jockey Craig Perret's wife, Janice. There was a cozy dormitory feel to the small room — leatherette sofa, clothes scattered, towels flung, boots piled. Krone's shelves held dehydrated health food, a bottle of Sheerly Coral nail polish and a Racing Form.

We went from the track to a health-food takeout shop, and then to her rented apartment. Since an attack of colitis two years ago, Krone has eaten with care. "I've also got to practice being less nervous," she said, but she was not sure how to do such a thing. "You go along and then something like that happens and you start thinking about your mortality. I was never scared like that before."

"Not on the track?" I asked.

"No. You don't feel afraid on the track. You don't feel anything. All that stuff about the wind in your face and the fear and the thrill — forget it. You're too busy running the race."

The apartment reeked of transience, all beige and Formica. Krone figures she's lived in a hundred such places, as jockeys do. Then, two years ago, she bought a house. It sits on ten acres of New Jersey horse country, with paddocks and a barn. She lived there with a fiancé for a time, but it did not work out. Now she's seeing another man, but lives alone with her two jumpers and her four cats, which for Krone does not mean living alone.

She had shipped the jumpers, Petey and Chicago, down to Florida and every Monday, when the track was dark, she jumped. On this Sunday evening, rain was expected. "I'll be depressed if I can't be with my jumpers tomorrow. That's the most fun I have all week," she said.

This woman does not spend much time away from horses, nor did she ever. On a horse farm in Eau Claire, Michigan, she and her older brother, Donnie, now an exercise trainer in Maryland, were toted around in the saddle by their mother, Judi, before they could walk. Judi Krone, who lives in Florida now, was a prizewinning show rider. "When Julie was two," she said recently, "I had her on a pony and I was leading him around the farm with just a lead rope on, no bridle. I dropped the rope for a moment and he really took off, bucking like crazy, but her little butt never left his back — and she was laughing."

At age five, Krone was being entered by her mother in horse shows for contestants age twenty-one and under — and winning, repeatedly. By fourteen, she was riding in 33 horse shows a summer and winning in horsemanship, showmanship, every category they had. Also, she was in love with Steve Cauthen, the eighteen-year-old wonder boy whom she had watched on TV as he rode Affirmed to a Triple Crown in 1978. "I'm going to be a jockey," she told her parents.

At about that time, after long marital discord, her parents split. She says little about it and is warmly attached to both of them now (her father, Donald, a photographer, lives in Michigan). But the strains then were heavy, and Krone herself took off.

The times were bad for women in racing. Just a decade earlier, the show rider Kathy Kusner had had to sue to get a jockey license. And when Diane Crump rode at Hialeah in 1969, some male jockeys boycotted the race. The only woman to achieve fame before Krone was Robyn Smith, who seems better remembered as the wife of Fred Astaire. *Sports Illustrated* ran a cover story on her in 1972, and the text, by Frank Deford, remains instructive: "She is never Miss Smith or Smith in the track vernacular; always Robyn or Robynsmith, run together, and occasionally The Bitch. The latter title is not pejorative, only vulgar recognition of the fact that she is the one member of her gender regularly around."

Into this nonpejorative climate strode Krone, with her mighty handshake. Now and then some trainer would let her ride, and by 1981 she was winning too often to ignore.

On June 5 at Belmont, when Krone came in from the winner's circle, Cooper was waiting. He had been waiting, I suppose, since 1981. He went with her to the news conference, and then she called her mother.

Krone: "Mom, isn't it wonderful?"

Mother: "Hey, kid, you're going to do this backwards." The Triple Crown in reverse — first the Belmont, then the Preakness, then the Derby.

Recently, I visited Krone in New Jersey. We went to see her friends Paula and Peter Freundlich, both dentists, who have Filly, the first pony Krone owned. As a child, she had trained this pony; then Filly had been sold and long since gone. Three years ago, Krone called every 4-H Club in Michigan and found the pony, now twenty-three and gone gray ("I didn't believe it was her. But I gave the commands, and boom! She's doing the tricks again"). Krone brought her east for the Freundlich children, Krista and Stefanie. Full circle.

"Come on, Filly," Krone said, snapping a whip. The pony sat, lay down, rolled over, quite as though she were a small dog, while the children watched in rapture.

Later we returned to Krone's home. In the front yard was the grave, marked by a weeping willow and a small statue of an angel,

of a beloved cat named Scagg L. Puss. She had just bought marigolds for the grave site. Downstairs were more cats and much
horse memorabilia. Upstairs was her bedroom with its canopy bed,
its mirrors, its crystal sconces — a girl's suburban dream. And on
the sun porch was a wooden horse. It was low, on wheels, with the
same girth as a racehorse and with a spring-loaded neck. Jockeys
use such horses for practice and exercise.

A bettor had said of Krone: "I've seen her yank on her right and
hit on her left, both at once. Amazing." I asked her to show me.

Krone mounts the horse. "Well, you see," she says, "when he
lugs out, I'm pulling him in with my right hand, like this, and hitting with my left," whacking hard, the two sides of her body sending totally opposite signals, "and if he still lugs, I start shoving him
with my body, too," now thrusting her weight to the left, making
the wooden horse clatter across the floor.

I ask, "But how can you push a real horse, a half-ton horse, sideways with your body?" She tsks, impatient that I don't get it. "But
he's in the *air*. I have all the advantage. He's *helpless*."

And now she crouches and she is really getting into it. To see
her from the clubhouse is one thing, exciting but remote. Here,
three feet away, I now see Rebecca of Sunnybrook Farm turn
abruptly into a killer, chin way down to duck the flying dirt, body
coiled, eyes narrowed to slits, fingers tangled in the mane. She is
talking fiercely to the horse, making fierce *chk chk chk* sounds, and
the whip snap is terrifyingly loud and mean. I don't know what
stretch she is on but she is no longer on this sun porch with me;
whack, goes the killer, whack, as my heart, I swear, beats faster. And
then, on a dime, she stops. "See?" she says, and dismounts, tosses
aside the whip, and goes outside to plant the marigolds.

WILLIAM NACK

The Rock

FROM SPORTS ILLUSTRATED

SHE SENSED what had happened the instant that she heard her mother scream. Sat frozen for a moment in her bedroom at the top of the stairs. Knew for sure what she had lost out there, someplace in the Midwest, out there among the cornfields in the dark.

Mary Anne was only sixteen then, but old enough to know the chances that her father had been taking, day after day, as he crisscrossed America in all those storm-whipped, wind-sheared private planes, often holding in his ample lap a grocery bag filled with $100 bills, as much as $40,000 a bag, looking like some pug-nosed desperado who had just knocked over a savings and loan. By then, by that late evening of August 31, 1969, Rocky Marciano was just a few hours shy of his forty-sixth birthday; it had been thirteen years and four months since the April day in 1956 when he had finally risen from the crouch and retired, at 49–0, as the only undefeated heavyweight champion in history. He had moved through those years as he had once moved in the ring, in a relentless, unremitting pursuit of what he desired — money and women, celebrity and respect, all that he ever wanted as the poor son of a shoe-factory worker growing up in Brockton, Massachusetts, during the Depression.

By that August night Marciano had become his own savings and loan, rich beyond his most extravagant boyhood dreams, a kind of wandering minstrel of money, in fact, dispensing cash loans with the careless facility of song. Indeed, he had accumulated vast stores of cash since he had quit the ring, mostly through personal appearances, and by 1969 he had at least $750,000 in loans on the street, not including the $100,000-plus he had lent to a loan shark linked to the Cleveland mob whose business he was helping to finance. He had even more money squirreled away in assorted hiding places — stuffed in pipes, in safe deposit boxes, in curtain rods, in all his favorite places — from Cuba to Florida to upstate New York to Alaska. He never paid for anything if he could help it; he could, for example, beat the telephone company by using slugs or a tripping wire to get his money back from coin-operated phones. Even if he had a round-trip commercial airline ticket, usually part of the deal when an appearance called him out of town, he would try to scrounge a freebie lift to his destination, often by calling on a network of private pilots who were willing, for the pleasure of his company, to bear him where he wanted to go. Back home in Fort Lauderdale, of course, he would hustle off to the airport to exchange the ticket for cash.

Mary Anne knew well the perilous edge on which he lived. In 1965, on a trip from Los Angeles to Honolulu, Rocky had hitched a ride on a cargo plane and loaded Mary Anne and a friend of hers in the hold in back. "They put little jump seats in for my friend and me, and my father and his friend were sitting on the top of the luggage," Mary Anne recalls. "A window blew in and we went into a nosedive and a red light came on and I thought, I'm twelve and I'm going to die. My father kept saying, 'Don't worry. You're gonna be O.K.' " He had escaped serious injury in a light-plane accident a year or two earlier, and for a long time his family and his friends had been importuning him to fly on commercial jets. "You are trying to save money in the wrong places," one of his closest friends and fellow skirt chasers, couch designer Bernie Castro, used to scold him. "You are risking everything. . . ."

On Sunday, August 31, Marciano was in Chicago with one of his oldest pals, Dominic Santarelli, and handling the logistics of his life as recklessly as ever. His wife, Barbara, had turned forty on August 30, two days before Rocky's forty-sixth, and he had promised her that he would be home to celebrate their birthdays on the day that fell in between, August 31, a family tradition. In fact, that afternoon, in the Marcianos' oceanfront home in Fort Lauderdale, the gifts had all been wrapped and the guests had already arrived. The sweetest gift of all was waiting there unwrapped. Unbeknownst to his father, the Marcianos' seventeen-month-old adopted son, Rocco Kevin, had learned how to walk while his father was gone, and Barbara had arranged a welcoming scenario that had the toddler carrying Rocky's presents to him when he walked in the door.

"We were all waiting with the birthday cake," recalls one of the friends, June Benson. "Then Rocky called from Chicago. He said, 'I'm gonna make an appearance in Des Moines, and then I'll fly right back. Hold everything.' "

That was the last his family ever heard from him. Frankie Farrell, the nephew of Marciano's pal Chicago mobster Frankie (One Ear) Fratto, was opening an insurance brokerage in Des Moines, and he had convinced Marciano to fly there with him from Chicago to make an appearance. Farrell had hired Glenn Belz, who had not been cleared to fly by instruments and had logged only thirty-five hours of flying at night, to pilot the single-engine Cessna 172 from Midway Airport to Des Moines. They took off at 6 P.M., despite warnings of a storm front billowing in front of them, and three hours later had made it as far as Newton, Iowa, when their plane was seen flying barely 100 feet off the ground, into a roiling bank of clouds. Reappearing once, it rose and disappeared again. In his laudable 1977 study, *Rocky Marciano: Biography of a First Son,* author Everett M. Skehan wrote: "The plane crashed into a lone oak tree in the middle of a cornfield. It was totally demolished by the impact, which killed all three passengers. A wing was sheared off and landed 15 feet from the tree; the battered hull skidded on and came to rest in a drainage ditch 236 feet away. Rocky's shattered body was found braced firmly in the seat of the wrecked Cessna . . . Belz and Farrell had been thrown clear. . . ."

It was late evening in Fort Lauderdale when the doorbell rang on North Atlantic Boulevard. Mary Anne heard her mother answer the door. She bolted to the staircase after she heard the scream. Jack Sherlock, the Fort Lauderdale police chief and an old friend of the family, was standing just inside the door. "Are you sure it's him? Are you sure it's not Rocky *Graziano?*" Barbara was saying, referring to the former middleweight champion of the world with whom her husband was often confused. "It can't be. Are you sure?"

Mary Anne started down the stairs. "Is my dad dead?" she asked.

"I'm sorry," Sherlock said.

Rocco Francis Marchegiano would have turned seventy years old on September 1, and by the time he died, almost a quarter of a century ago, the life he had created for himself outside the ring was quite as large and unlikely as the figure he had once cut inside it. Of course, Lord only knows what he might be doing today had he somehow survived his endless peregrinations; how many sacks of cash he might have wadded up and squirreled away in his far-flung caches; how big his lending business might have become; or how long he could have avoided arousing the serious curiosity of IRS agents, not only over his out-of-pocket lending business, for which he kept no books or paperwork, but also over his travels around the banquet circuit, where he insisted on payment in cash only. It was a strange, fantastic world he had built for himself, one shaped in considerable part by the obsessive, endless quest for $100 bills, for cash to feed his lending business, for cash to buy his way into multitudes of deals, for cash to toss onto Pasqualena Marchegiano's dining room table.

"He'd come home sometimes with two bags of money, and he'd give his mother one," Marciano's longtime accountant and traveling companion, Frank Saccone, recalls. "Five or six thousand dollars in each bag. His mother would count it, all over the goddam table." She would then stack it neatly in piles.

"What do you want me to do with it, Rocky?"

"Keep it, Ma, for spending money."

His idiosyncrasies were often so irrational as to drive Saccone to teary despair. One evening in the mid-sixties, Saccone recalls, Marciano had just delivered a speech at a large function in Montreal, when one of the organizers approached him and Saccone in the lobby of the hotel where they were staying. Thanking Marciano profusely, he handed him an envelope containing a check for $5,000. The Rock shook his head. "Can you cash the check for me?" he asked.

That would not be possible; the banks were closed. "I'll guarantee it," the man said.

"That's not it," Rocky said. "I don't take checks. I'd rather have the cash."

It was an awkward moment. "Look," Rocky said, "do you have $2,500 in cash? I'll take that. You keep the check."

Saccone took Rocky aside. "Why don't you let *me* take the check, and *I'll* cash it," Saccone said. "Then I'll give you the cash."
Rocky insisted. "I want the cash, right now!"
"But, Rocky, you're throwing $2,500 away!" said Saccone. "I know these people. I know this check is good. It's a cashier's check. *It is cash in the form of a check.* Try to imagine that."
There was no trying. "These are my deals," Rocky said. "If I want cash, it's my business. Don't interfere."
Marciano turned to the organizer. "Can you get me $2,500 in an hour?" he asked. An hour later the man was back with the money, as bemused as Saccone at Marciano's thinking. "Is this really what you want?" Saccone asked.
"That's great," said Rocky, happily handing the organizer the check.
Saccone traveled the world with Marciano, on hundreds of trips, and he never knew the man to want it any other way. "He had this crazy, crazy need for cash," Saccone says. "He loved the sight of cash. A check was just a little piece of paper. I remember times he'd get a check and lose it. He'd put it somewhere and forget about it. He'd reach in his pocket and pull out checks that were all tattered. I've seen him give away checks for $50,000, $100,000. I'm talking big money. He didn't even associate that with money. To him a check was just a piece of paper. But if he had $40,000 in $10 bills, there was no way he'd give any of that away. He *believed* in green stuff."
There was always plenty of it flowing his way and far more abundantly in the days after his retirement than during his years in the ring. Marciano was an enormously popular champion, and more than his complexion lay at the source of the appeal. The archetypal working-class stiff from blue-collar Brockton, he brought to the lights a boxing style edited down to its barest essentials, an unearthly power of will and tolerance for punishment, particularly around the chin; and he had what columnist Red Smith called "a right hand that registered nine on the Richter scale," and a left hook that trembled the upright like an aftershock. Stir into this mix an incomparable appetite for work, a quality of meekness and humility that was often affecting — after knocking out his boyhood idol, Joe Louis, in the eighth round of their 1951 fight in

New York, Marciano wept openly in Louis's locker room — and that crooked smile on a darkly handsome mug, and what you had was the ideal composite for the central character in a cartoonlike Hollywood movie.

None of this was even remotely foreseeable in the beginning, back in the days he spent at the James Edgar Playground, in the rough-and-tumble Irish-Italian streets of central Brockton, where he dreamed of escaping the want of his childhood by making it as a catcher in the big leagues. Slow afoot, without a major league catcher's arm, he worked hours on his short, powerful stroke. "There were forty or fifty of us shagging balls for Rocky," says Nicky Sylvester, a boyhood friend and later the court jester in his entourage. "He wouldn't give anyone else a chance. Two hours of hitting!" Marciano used to run lunch down to his father, Pierino, a laster at a nearby shoe factory, and the sight of his father standing at his machine, his undershirt drenched, both legs and arms moving at once, a dozen tacks held in his lips, spoke to him of a life he did not want to lead. "I'll *never* work in a shoe factory," he told his family, according to his brother Sonny. "I have to find a way out."

Climbing out of Brockton and leaving the dread privations of his boyhood behind was the theme with variations that ruled him the rest of his life. "He was deathly afraid of being broke," says former world featherweight champion Willie Pep, one of Marciano's best friends. "He used to say to me, 'I'll never be broke again.' He was a tough guy with a buck, Rocky. He was afraid."

Marciano was drafted in 1943 and began boxing in the Army, chiefly as a way to avoid KP and other schlock details. He devoted all his considerable energies to it only after his discharge from the service, in 1946, and an abortive tryout with a Chicago Cub farm team in North Carolina in the spring of 1947. By then, fighting under an assumed name, Rocky Mack, to protect his amateur status, he had knocked out one Lee Epperson in the third round of a bout in Holyoke, Massachusetts, and earned $35. He fought as an amateur the rest of that year and into the next, and at five foot ten and less than 190 pounds, with only a 68-inch reach, shorter than that of any other heavyweight champion who ever lived, he appeared on his way to Palookaville. One afternoon in '48, Goody Petronelli, who would one day train Marvin Hagler to the world middleweight championship, was leaving the gym on Center Street in Brockton when he ran into Marciano. Goody had seen him in the amateurs and was surprised when Marciano told him that he was turning pro.

"I never thought he'd make it," Petronelli says. "He was too old, almost twenty-five. He was too short, he was too light. He had no reach. Rough and tough, but no finesse."

But he had that hammer, that Cro-Magnon chin and that fearless, unbridled instinct for the attack. He turned pro on July 12, 1948, when he scored a first-round knockout over Harry Bilazarian in Providence, and then fought ten more times before Christmas, all the matches ending in knockouts, seven in the first round. Brockton is only twenty-five miles from Providence, where he fought 15 of his first 17 fights, and a Brockton cheering section soon began showing up to witness the mayhem. Recalls Sylvester: "When Rocky had a guy in trouble in Providence, all the Italians from Brockton would stand up and yell, 'Timmmmmberrr!' "

They were shows bereft of art. Trainer Lou Duva, who would take Evander Holyfield to the heavyweight title some forty years later, recalls driving with Vic Marsillo, the manager of Sugar Ray Robinson, to see an early Marciano brawl in New England. The word *footwork* does not make it in describing what Duva saw that night. "Rocky kept falling down," he recalls. "He kept missing and going through the ropes. I said to Vic, 'He's as strong as a bull.' Vic said, 'Are you kidding? He can't fight at all.' It was Charley Goldman who straightened him out."

Charley trained fighters for Al Weill, the New York manager and promoter, and that fall he had Marciano and his Brockton trainer, Allie Colombo, begin working with him in Manhattan. Goldman was the training guru for a young Angelo Dundee, later the trainer of Muhammad Ali and Ray Leonard, and Goldman seemed apologetic about how the young man looked. Says Dundee, "So Charley told me, 'Ange, I gotta guy who's short, stoop-shouldered, balding, got two left feet and, god, how he can punch!' I remember going on the subway to the CYO gym, and in walks Rocky with a pair of coveralls and a little canvas bag." Goldman knew that Marciano had trained hours as a baseball catcher, and he taught him to swarm and slide and throw from a crouch, rising as though he were pegging to second base.

"Charley taught the technique that if you're tall, you stand taller," Dundee recalls. "If you are shorter, you make yourself smaller. Charley let him bend his knees completely to a deep knee squat. He was able to punch from that position, come straight up from the bag and hit a heck of a shot. . . . It was just *bang-bang-bang-bang-BANG* and get him outta there. And he was the best-conditioned athlete out there."

No one understood his limitations better than Marciano himself, and his whole monkish existence in the gym and on the road was geared to making up for them, to developing what gifts he had. He thought nothing of walking the seventy-five blocks from his room to the gym to train. A health buff long before it became the fashion, he ate veggies, sipped only an occasional glass of Lancer's rosé, always with dinner, and carried a jar of honey in his pocket to sweeten his coffee. He chewed but never swallowed his steak, and left the ruminated chaws in a bowl next to his plate. And Marciano may be the only fighter in history who exercised his eyeballs, obtaining for this purpose a pendulum that he rigged above his bed. Lying flat on his back, with his head still, he would follow the pendulum back and forth with his eyes — convinced, of course, that stronger eyeballs did a better fighter make. More than once he sparred 250 rounds for a single fight, 100 rounds more than normal, and there was never anything in his ring work to suggest a hesitation waltz.

Marciano never met an opponent, particularly among the 43 he knocked out, who did not leave the ring with a fairly intimate knowledge of that fact. Even long after Goldman had straightened out his feet and taught him how to slip a punch and make a weapon of his left, there was a merry unpredictability about what would happen next when Marciano was in the ring. He threw punches from every conceivable point on the compass, and the legal ones landed everywhere from the navel to the top of the head. Some even found the chin.

But it was in the fights in which Marciano was in trouble, behind in points or cut and bleeding, that he created the persona he would carry with him all the way to that fatal field in Newton. And his signature moment in the ring, the instant when the myth was born, came at the single most dramatic turning point of his life. It was the night of September 23, 1952, in Philadelphia, in the 13th round of his 15-round title fight against the world heavyweight champion, Jersey Joe Walcott, and the time was growing short for an increasingly desperate Marciano. A beautiful boxer, clever and resourceful, Walcott had built up an easy lead in points, and all he had to do was keep Marciano away. Marciano had chased but not quite found, had thrown but not quite landed, had struck but not quite hard enough. By the thirteenth round he knew there was only one way to win it. He waded in yet again. And then, as Walcott feinted back toward the ropes, Marciano suddenly stepped in and threw a short, overhand right that struck Walcott on the jaw with such force that it distorted his face, dropped him to one knee and left him slumped forward, kneeling unconscious, with his left arm slung through the ropes.

So Marciano's long journey out of Brockton was finally over, and the belief in his indomitability became a kind of article of shared faith among his ardent followers. Marciano defended his title only six times in the three and a half years that he held it, but he did nothing to discourage the belief that he was invincible and much to embellish it. In fact, in his second fight against Ezzard Charles, in New York, on September 17, 1954, he once again turned imminent defeat into sudden, stunning triumph. Like one of those Benihana chefs butterflying a jumbo shrimp, Charles hit Marciano with a blow in the sixth round that split his left nostril down the middle; blood spurted everywhere. At the end of the round no amount of work could stanch the bleeding. Marciano's corner was in a panic. The ring doctor let it go through the seventh, with Marciano bleeding heavily, but by the eighth round the corner sensed that time was short. They were all screaming at the champion to press the attack. Marciano fought with a fury. A right hand floored Charles. Glassy-eyed, he climbed back slowly to his feet. Marciano rushed back at him, landing thumping lefts and rights, until Charles at last fell for the count.

No matter what happened, in the end the Rock would find a way.

When Marciano retired on that April day in 1956, seven months after knocking out Archie Moore in nine, he had not only fulfilled his father's most oft-expressed wishes — "Don't do anything to disgrace the family name. Don't do anything I'll be ashamed of" — but he had also brought honor to it beyond the old man's unlikeliest hope. More than undefeated, he left the ring utterly untainted, and this despite one underworld figure's efforts to coax him to hit the water in his May 16, 1955, defense against Don Cockell, an Englishman, in San Francisco. One of Marciano's closest California friends, Ed Napoli, recalls the day he sat with Marciano in a hotel room in that state and listened as a gangster made him an offer to throw the fight. Cockell was a long shot, at 10–1, and Marciano could always win back the title in a rematch.

"Rocky, you can be set the rest of your life if you throw this fight," the mobster told him.

At which point Marciano got angry, Napoli says, and ordered the mobster out. "You disgust me," the fighter told him. "I'm ashamed that you're Italian. Get outta here and don't come back." The fight ended in the ninth round with Cockell, out on his feet, sagging in the arms of referee Frankie Brown.

As celebrated and mythic a folk hero as he became to the workaday Italian-American across the land, Marciano found himself to be an even larger, more respected figure among members of the underworld, a life-size icon whose company and favor were sought by hoodlums wherever he went. Over the years, with all the running around he did, Marciano kissed the cheeks of many of the major crime-family bosses — Raymond Patriarca, Carlo Gambino, Frank Costello and Vito Genovese, who when he was dying put out the word that he wanted Marciano to visit him in prison. Rocky paid the call. "Rocky went to Leavenworth to show Genovese films of his fights," says Richie Paterniti, one of Marciano's best friends during the last twelve years of his life. "Wherever we went there were mob guys. They loved him because he represented what mob guys really want to be, the toughest guy in the world, right? A macho guy. They all had respect for him. They all wanted to be with him. They kissed his ass. Every mob guy. He was an Italian, and he beat up every guy he faced. He exuded power, an air of authority. That's why they wanted to bask in his sunshine."

They could not indulge him enough. They bought him dinner and gave him money and set him up with their tailors. When Saccone first went to New York with Marciano, he found himself among all these shiny suits. "We'd go to these elaborate restaurants and sit with fifteen, twenty underworld characters, but I didn't know it," he says. "I was a naive accountant from Brockton. I thought they were just friends of Rocky's and they liked him. Rocky finally told me who they were. They couldn't do enough for him. They'd say to him, 'I got a beautiful tailor. Let me take you down there and get you some suits.' They'd buy him six suits, three dozen shirts. He loved it and *they* loved it."

In spite of the casual social contact he had with hoodlums, he feared the violence and notoriety of the underworld, and he made it a point not to get involved in their businesses. "Let's keep our distance," Marciano used to tell Paterniti. In fact, according to an underworld source, one of the most feared hoodlums in the history of organized crime, Felix (Milwaukee Phil) Alderisio, saw Marciano not only as a venerated Italian-American folk hero whose reputation had to be protected, but also as a kind of naive, innocent bumpkin from Brockton who had to be watched, lest he stumble blindly into trouble. "He was an Italian champ, and they wanted him to be clean," the source said. "All the boys. That came out of Chicago. Milwaukee Phil said, 'Keep him clean. Don't get him dirty. Protect him at all costs. He's a goofball; he doesn't know what he's doing.' Chicago had an umbrella over him."

The only time Marciano ever faced serious trouble with the law was after he began quietly investing vast sums of cash, $100,000 at a crack, in the loan-sharking business of Pete DiGravio, with whom he often stayed in Cleveland. "If you've got some cash and want to make some money on it," DiGravio told Rocky, "I've got the outlet. Guaranteed. No bad debts in my place." The Rock was in. Marciano never felt that he was involved in anything illegal, says Saccone, and justified his investments on the grounds that he was merely lending to the shark and not involved in the dirty end of the business, on the street itself.

Of course, there was never anything in writing, since the Rock did not believe in paper. "All unsecured loans," says Saccone. "Never secured. Never-never. No piece of paper. No note. Nothing signed. All in his head. I can recall him saying to me, 'Jeez, I know I loaned somebody $5,000 in New York, and I can't remember who it was. But I'll remember it.' He never did. It was gone. Rocky was a very articulate, intelligent man, but when it came to business, he was so, so stupid."

This nearly got him into trouble in Cleveland when the Internal Revenue Service started looking into DiGravio's affairs. When the IRS asked him where he had obtained some large sums of money, DiGravio told investigators, "Rocky Marciano loaned it to me."

And when they asked to see the contracts, DiGravio told them, "We don't have contracts. He just gave me the cash." With nothing on paper, Marciano grew anxious when the Cleveland IRS office invited him in for a visit to explain his ties to DiGravio. Marciano was an extravagant evader of taxes, never declaring any income unless it left a paper trail, but until the Cleveland inquiry, Saccone had finessed all IRS queries by having them transferred to the Brockton office, where "they loved Rocky," says Saccone. "It wasn't difficult to get rid of the cases. He was a great charmer, Rocky. We'd spend two minutes discussing the case, and the rest of the time Rocky would tell stories about his first fight with Walcott. The IRS guys would eat it up."

Cleveland was another matter. Marciano and Saccone made the trip together to Ohio, and the morning they arrived they called the IRS office to tell investigators that they were in town. "Forget about it," the agent told Saccone. "Pete DiGravio just got killed." DiGravio had been cut down by rifle fire on the 16th hole of a golf course outside Cleveland. Marciano, Saccone says, never saw a dime of the thousands that he had given the shark — fearing that word of his loan might leak out, he never made a claim on the estate — and this was not the first time that one of his investments had evaporated. Marciano raced around the country looking for deals to sink his money in, and he lost hundreds of thousands in ill-chosen ventures. Taken in by the hoariest of scams imaginable, he once actually bought swampland in Florida. He lost nearly $250,000 on some coal company in Pittsburgh, even more than that investing in component parts for telephones, and once confided to a Florida friend, Jim Navilio, that he had found an investment that couldn't miss: "I got a guy who can cure arthritis," said the Rock.

When he wasn't chasing after these and other phantoms, he was spending an inordinate amount of time trying to collect bad debts. At times he enlisted in this enterprise his wide variety of friends, from a law-abiding New York State judge, John Lomenzo, to his old Chicago pal Frankie Fratto, a reputed syndicate terrorist. In the early sixties when Marciano grew tired of waiting for repayment of a $75,000 loan to a Toronto businessman, he appealed to Judge Lomenzo, who shed his robes and headed north with Marciano to Canada. A distinguished jurist who would later serve as

New York's secretary of state, Lomenzo made a plea for mercy and compassion on behalf of his poor client, Marciano. "Rocky is having hard times, and he loaned you the money," said the judge. The businessman wrote out a check immediately. Waiving his own private rules, Marciano took the paper and cashed it.

Fratto was persuasive in his own quiet way when Marciano sent him collecting. "If people did not pay Rocky back, I would help him," he says. It was all very simple: "I went to them and told them, 'You owe my friend some money. I suggest you pay it back.' They did not give me a hard time."

Mostly, though, Marciano did his own enforcing. Saccone remembers the time he and Marciano were strolling through Brockton when Rocky, pleading business, excused himself and ducked into Brockton Eddie Massod's pool room and gambling hall on Center Street. Massod owed Marciano $5,000, and he hadn't made a payment in months. Worse, he had been hiding from him, a no-no at the Marciano savings and loan. "If you couldn't pay it back, be a man and face it," Saccone says. "You could never hide on him." The Rock found him on the third floor, from where Saccone, standing on the sidewalk below, could hear the rising shouts. Glancing up, he saw Brockton Eddie hanging halfway out the window and the former heavyweight champion of the world leaning over him, a hand clutched around Eddie's throat.

"I've waited long enough!" Marciano screamed. "No more stalling. I want my money. Now. . . . Now!"

"I need a little more time," gurgled Eddie.

"No more time. . . . No more time!"

A few minutes later Marciano stepped from the door counting a sheaf of $20 bills, the first of dozens of installments that Saccone would be in charge of collecting monthly from Massod. The CPA was only one in a vast and intricate mesh of people, friends and followers of unusual ardency, who worked what lives they had of their own around the odd, often nocturnal, unpredictable movements of the Rock. Marciano had been married to the same woman, the former Barbara Cousins, the daughter of a Brockton cop, since December 31, 1950, but the union unraveled long before the decade was done. Barbara tended to obesity, had a serious drinking problem and smoked heavily — she would die of lung cancer in 1974 — whereas her husband's tastes ran more to svelte, statuesque blondes, that single glass of wine and smokeless rooms. "He couldn't stand his married life," says Saccone. "He loved his daughter, and she loved him, but he had no relationship with his wife. There was nothing compatible between them. He wanted to do things, and she didn't."

So the mesh included people, such as the late Lindy Ciardelli on the West Coast and Paterniti on the East Coast, whose job was to help feed Marciano's prodigious sexual appetite. "Rock liked girls, know what I mean?" Paterniti says. "Nobody wants me to tell you about it, but Rock was insane about girls — all the time. Rocky was the heavyweight champion of girls. Forget about the fights. He was crazy about the girls; that's all he wanted to do. Rocky constantly had orgies and parties, night and day. . . . A friend of mine in New York got me and Rocky thousands of girls. Honestly, literally a thousand girls. We had girls every single day and night. I carried a suitcase full of vibrators. I mean, we used to call Rocky the vibrator king. I had a suitcase that I took all over, filled with vibrators and electric massagers and emotion lotion and all kinds of creams and oils. . . . We went to Pennsylvania and we were with these mob guys and they were bringing us girls and Rocky said, 'Don't let 'em know we got all that stuff. They'll think that we're weird or somethin'.' "

There were women for Marciano everywhere he went in those days after his retirement. That a woman be waiting for him was as requisite for his appearance as the folded $100 bills. "He never had an affair," says Santarelli, his Chicago underworld pal, who booked him to make appearances and advertisements all over. "I don't think he had sex with the same girl twice. Never, that I know, and I knew him a long time. Any girls he had sex with, you couldn't bring her to dinner no more. That's it. Get rid of her. He never wanted to see her again. For dinner, or even a cup of coffee. If he ever went to some place and there was not a girl waiting for him, he'd never come back."

So it was this lust for women and the hunger for making deals and the quest for cash that drove the Rock to the road. He had the whole mesh linked together perfectly, his life and travels so arranged that he never had a need for anything. There was the network of pilots, of course, and then all those eager aides-de-camp awaiting him with cars and limos at whatever airport he was headed for. He was, by consensus, the world's worst driver.

On one of his occasional sojourns to the family home in Fort Lauderdale, he did a commercial for a car dealership and for his fee asked for a gold Firebird 400. He gave it to Mary Anne so she could pick him up at the airport. She remembers a comic interlude of her youth when a motorcycle cop pulled her over one day and discovered she not only did not have a driver's license but also was only thirteen. She told the cop who her father was and where she lived. The cop roared off to fetch Rocky. "I waited until they came roaring back," Mary Anne says. "My father in his Bermuda shorts, no shirt, bare feet, baseball cap, black hair blowing, with his arms around the cop, holding on. The cop asked my father for his autograph and drove off."

The cop no doubt left thinking he had saved Fort Lauderdale from this adolescent menace. "The world's worst driver drove me home," she says. "My dad did not even have a license."

So he had all his chauffeurs in place. He had rooms and places to stay all across America — at Ed Napoli's in Los Angeles, at Lindy Ciardelli's in Santa Clara, California, at Ben Danzi's twelve-room apartment in New York, at Bernie Castro's estates on Long Island and in Florida, at Santarelli's in Chicago, at any hotel he chose in Las Vegas and at scores of homes all over Providence and Brockton, Buffalo and Boston. Santarelli recalls one night in Las Vegas when they were watching Jimmy Durante on stage and Durante announced, "Ladies and gentlemen, in our audience tonight we have the undefeated heavyweight champion of the world — and *America's guest* — Rocky Marciano." Touchy on the nerve of his parsimony, the Rock got all indignant. "Can you imagine this guy?" he said to Santarelli. "He ties a rope around his suitcase so his clothes don't fall out, and he says that about me?"

But that was what he was, America's guest. In all the years, going back to the championship days, there was never a single reported sighting of Marciano picking up a check. One evening, at a table of twelve in a Chicago restaurant, the waitress passed by the seat of businessman Andy Granatelli, the manufacturer of STP motor oil additive, and unknowingly gave the check to the Rock. In a hot panic he tossed it over his shoulder, onto the floor, and demanded of Santarelli, "How could she bring me the check with Andy Granatelli sitting here? Who owns this place? He's trying to be a smart guy." Marciano never ate there again. He knew all the restaurants where he did not have to pay — dozens of restaurateurs sought him out to decorate their tables — and when he was dining with any of his innumerable fat-cat associates, which was quite often, his immediate entourage of traveling friends was under orders never to buy as much as a round of drinks. Just about every such friend suffered Marciano's rebuke for offering to pay for something.

One night, after watching Castro pick up the umpteenth straight dinner check at an expensive New York restaurant, Saccone asked for the tab. Marciano grabbed him and took him aside. "Don't ever, *ever* do that!" Marciano scolded. "When you're with me, you don't pay a nickel. When you're with me, and you're my friend, you don't touch anything: never, never, never." Saccone protested that he felt uncomfortable freeloading all the time. "I'm capable of paying my own way," he said.

"Doncha understand?" said Marciano. "These people *wanna* be around me. Let them pick up the tab. They enjoy it. They wanna do it."

The freebies, as Marciano saw it, were among the benefits a man received for being part of the entourage, for being there when Rocky needed him. In all the hours in all the years he worked for Marciano, Saccone never dared send him a bill, never received a dollar for his services. The adventures were the payment, and the bonus was all the business that Marciano nudged his way. "He introduced me to people who were very substantial in my getting work," Saccone says. So it was for all the professionals, the lawyers and bookkeepers alike, who served Marciano's needs.

"Rocky was a door-opener, the greatest door-opener in the world," says Santarelli. "I'm an Italian guy from the old neighborhood in Chicago. I'd go to parties with Rocky and meet nice people, businesspeople. 'How you doin', Mr. Santarelli?' Businesspeople would contact me to get ahold of him. Many people called me: 'Do me a favor. Set up Rocky for me.' Rocky was a great guy, everybody loved him — if a favor was needed, Rocky would be there — but he was being used all the time. In every walk of life, every friend. Everybody used him. Even the priests used him, restaurant owners used him, women used him, movie stars used him, mob guys used him. . . ."

Knowing this, of course, Marciano refused to go anywhere for free, and the only exception involved the occasional favor for a friend, as when he showed up one day in Michigan to referee some fights, at no charge, for Goody Petronelli, when Goody was running a boxing program in the U.S. Navy.

"You had to pay him to show up for fights," says Santarelli. "He got $250 just to step in the ring to be introduced as the former heavyweight champion. If you wanted Rocky, you had to pay for it. In cash."

If Marciano thus beat the IRS out of some taxes, Santarelli says, that was not the only reason he insisted on payments in cash. On numerous occasions, he says, Marciano complained to him that, under his contract with Al Weill, his former manager, he had to pay Weill fifty percent of all his earnings — not only from his days as a fighter but also from his years in retirement. "He took fifty percent of Rocky in and out of the ring," says Santarelli. "That's the reason Rocky retired. That was the conflict. He didn't want to pay Al Weill any more money. Even for a personal appearance, Weill wanted fifty percent of it. He wanted cash because he didn't want Weill to get a dime."

The whole object of Marciano's daily existence, the reason for the network that moved and sustained him from place to place, was to get him from one sunset to the next without spending a dime. "There wasn't anything he ever needed that he couldn't get with just a phone call," says his brother Sonny.

On occasions it was only the phone company that stood between Rocky getting through a day in which he got away free and a day in which he was forced to spring for a coin. Marciano worked on correcting that nettlesome problem by using those slugs to make calls, or by feeding that wire contraption into the coin deposit in an apparent attempt to lobotomize the system. He had an unfathomable hostility toward phone companies, and more than once he was observed hammering a phone cradle as though it were Jersey Joe Walcott's nose in the thirteenth round at Philadelphia. On one occasion, says Napoli, Marciano lost a dime and went berserk, pounding on the phone with the receiver.

"It took my dime," he cried.

At New York's La Guardia Airport one day a phone did not return his dime after he got a busy signal. He screamed at the operator, "You sonuvabitch! I want my dime back!" When that failed, he ripped the receiver out of the phone, threw it on the floor and then began walking past the bank of pay phones along the wall, pressing the coin-return buttons, then fingering the empty coin slots and then ripping all the receivers out of the machines.

"I thought, My god, what is he doing?" says Saccone.

For as much as he coveted the cash, of course, the paradox is that he did not need it, never used it to buy himself anything, never put any but a small part of it to any other use but in the service of his own dark, meretricious underground of unsecured loans and fanciful investments. In fact, it is difficult to imagine anyone handling money more cavalierly or treating it with such unconscious contempt, dating back to the days when, according to his biographer, Skehan, he used to stuff it in plastic bags and tape it inside the water tanks above the toilet bowls in his hotel rooms; or when, one night, he took off and left $27,520 in a plastic bag among clothes mildewing in a suitcase in Napoli's care; or when, too impatient to sit through a stage performance of *The Great White Hope*, he told his daughter, who was sitting next to him, that he would meet her for dinner later at La Scala and then bolted out of the theater, leaving a brown paper bag mashed in his seat. Mary Anne happened to notice it and stuck it in her purse before she left. They had just settled in for dinner when Marciano said, "Oh, god, I'll be right back. . . ."

"You left something?" she asked, removing the bag.

It contained $40,000.

This was Marciano, impulsive and restless, distracted and eccentric, who climbed into the Cessna that night at Midway Airport, and it was fitting that he left for Des Moines with a paid Chicago–to–Fort Lauderdale airline ticket tucked in his pocket. When he called home to say he was heading west to make that appearance, his family life had become a lie, and his life had more hiding places than his money and more secrets than hiding places. When Santarelli and Benny Trotta, the Baltimore mob associate, saw him off at the Butler Aviation terminal that day, Marciano had no intention of returning to Fort Lauderdale anytime soon. "I'll see you in the morning," Santarelli recalls Rocky telling them. All Farrell needed to do, to get him on that plane, was play on his weaknesses for cash, in the form of a $500 fee, and women. "They promised Rocky a young broad, seventeen or eighteen years old, to help little Frankie Farrell," Santarelli says.

That was all it took to lift him off toward the distant storm.

No one knows what eventually happened to the $40,000 that Mary Anne recovered from the theater seat that night in New York, just as it is hard to imagine what might have happened to all the rest of the cash, perhaps more than $2 million, he loaned out and stashed away. Most of Marciano's friends and family believe that the bulk of his savings ended up in the bomb shelter on the Ocala, Florida, estate of Bernie Castro, who died two years ago. Mary Anne used to go there with her father, and she vividly recalls him placing his hand on a pipe that ran through the shelter: "He told me, 'Remember this spot, Mary Anne. A great place to hide money. Remember this pipe.' "

A year after the accident, Mary Anne says, she and her mother went to Castro's estate to ask him if they could search the shelter. "He told us, 'Don't be silly,' " she says. They never got inside. Mary Anne figured that some of the money was in safe deposit boxes, under assumed names, and she found doodlings of Rocky's that suggested he might have used two names: Mr. Rocco and Mr. March. She tried to make sense of code words he used to write down, such as *powerless* and *insecure*, but got nowhere. "For many years I tried to put it together," she says. "I even had a CIA friend who helped me search Swiss bank accounts. Nothing."

Believing himself to be immortal, Marciano had no use for life insurance, and wills were only for people who foresaw an end he simply could not imagine. He died intestate, and his family had a terrible struggle at first. The taxes and expenses to maintain the oceanfront house were "so astronomical," Mary Anne says, that the family had to move two miles inland in Fort Lauderdale, to a more modest, four-bedroom ranch house. "It was rough," Mary Anne says. "My mother sold her diamonds for us to live. There were all sorts of liens on the estate; it wasn't settled for five years."

Mary Anne lives in the ranch house with her grandmother Betty Cousins, whom she calls Nana, and Rocco Kevin, twenty-five, who goes by Rocky Jr. An electrical engineering student at Florida Atlantic University, in Boca Raton, Rocky Jr. bears a resemblance to his father, and Mary Anne thinks that he was born out of a relationship that her father had with a Florida woman. Barbara had had five miscarriages after having Mary Anne, and she had become "desperate to adopt." Magically, a lawyer who was close to Marciano found a mother willing to give her child up for adoption.

"I think it was all arranged," Mary Anne says.

"I have my suspicions," Rocky Jr. says. "My one regret in life is that I didn't get to know my father."

Mary Anne has nothing but fond memories of him and the time they spent together. "To me he was gentle and caring," she says. "He'd pick me up and spin me on his knee. He'd come in off trips and he'd yell, 'Barb, can you get me a glass of water?' And then he'd walk into little Rocco's room and pick him up and say, 'My son! My son!' " His death shattered the family. "When he died, a piece of my mother died," Mary Anne says. In her last days Barbara lay in bed and hallucinated, seeing her husband beckoning to her. "Rocky, I'm not ready to go yet," she would say. "I have to take care of Mary Anne and Rocky." Barbara died in 1974 and was entombed next to her husband in a Fort Lauderdale mausoleum.

Mary Anne is sitting at the kitchen counter in her home, sipping iced tea and smoking a cigarette. She has not had an easy few years. On August 4, 1992, she was released from the Broward Correctional Institution after serving eight months of a 22-month sentence for her part in a robbery at a club in Fort Lauderdale. "I made a few mistakes," she says. "I just got mixed up with the wrong people. It's been rough for me, very rough. I never hurt anybody. The only people I ever hurt were myself and my family. I was brought up very well. I had a good family background. The mistakes I made are my own. I went the easy way instead of toughing it out. I felt so bad when those articles came out about me. I didn't want his name to be tarnished: Rocky's daughter. What a nightmare. I'm still on probation, but I've come a long way. I was made to look at myself and make some serious changes."

Marciano left a large and lasting legacy as a prizefighter, as a historic force and presence in the game, but that was not all he left in Fort Lauderdale. Nana Cousins, eighty-nine, feels angry and bitter toward him for the kind of life he lived, for his long absences as a husband and father, for what he put his family through. In a living room scattered with photographs, in a house where his son and daughter live, there are no photos of the former undefeated heavyweight champion of the world. Twenty-four years after his death, he is still old business, unresolved. Mary Anne is telling that story about how Rocky loaded her and her friend into that freebie cargo plane bound for Hawaii when she was twelve, and how the window blew in and the plane went into a dive. Mary Anne laughs.

"You should *never* have got on that plane," Nana scolds. She is standing with her back to the kitchen window, facing her grand-daughter. "God, he was tight!"

Mary Anne tosses back her hair and turns to smile sweetly at her. "But, Nana, I could get anything I wanted out of him."

"And me?" Nana says. "I even bought my own ticket to see him fight Joe Louis. And he lived with us! Everything I say is true. We could write a book. Too bad. We really did like him in those days. . . ."

"I loved him and I always did," says Mary Anne.

"You should. He was your father. But he wasn't a good father."

Mary Anne shakes her head. "He was a wonderful father."

"O.K.," says Nana. "All right, have it your way."

"I think he *was* wonderful. I only had him sixteen years."

"Did you have a father, Mary Anne?" Nana says, softly.

"Yes, I did."

"He was gone!"

"So what? We went everywhere together, and we spent quality time, and we did, so, I mean, yes, we did," says Mary Anne. "Some people can live a lifetime and not have what I've had. They don't communicate. I was very lucky. My mother and father were two wonderful people, and I was very fortunate."

"Say it your way," Nana says.

"That's the way I remember it."

Nana drifts toward the door. "Barbara should have gone through with her divorce."

Mary Anne looks down, shaking her head. "Oh, brother," she says. "Would you let out the dog, please? She's locked in my room."

"You're just trying to get rid of me."

"No, I'm not."

Nana starts out the kitchen door. "It's all coming out in a book some day."

"Fine, write a book."

"Maybe I'll be six foot under, but ... when I get to the other side, I'll tell loverboy a thing or two."

GARY CARTWRIGHT

The Old Man and the Tee

FROM TEXAS MONTHLY

DISCIPLES OF GOLF who regard *Harvey Penick's Little Red Book* as a revelation on par with the tablets of Moses will be reassured to learn that God still works in wondrous ways. A sequel to the book, *And If You Play Golf, You're My Friend,* arrived from Simon and Schuster last month. Moreover, the experience seems to have redeemed both the 89-year-old Penick and his 62-year-old coauthor, Bud Shrake.

Though Harvey's body is as fragile as an autumn leaf — he's nearly deaf and can't walk unassisted — his mind is as keen as ever. You can find him several days a week at Austin Country Club (his resident shop since he hired on as its golf pro in 1922), seated in a golf cart next to his young nurse, Andrea, signing books, shaking hands, offering an occasional tip to the steady procession of adoring fans who stream past. People say that he never forgets a name or a face. Not long ago, famed heart surgeon Denton Cooley — who played basketball at the University of Texas when Harvey was coaching the UT golf team — showed up at the club and asked Harvey if he remembered him. "Yeah, you used to play basketball at Texas," Harvey said. "What have you been up to since then?"

As for Bud Shrake, a writer of considerable reputation, his career wasn't exactly sagging when he teamed up with Harvey, but he had never before had a book at the top of the *New York Times* bestseller list, much less one that stayed on the list for 54 weeks. The *Little Red Book* has become the best-selling sports book of all time, if you exclude perennials such as encyclopedias and record books.

It has sold nearly one million copies, more than Bud's previous nine books combined. And as a bonus, Bud's golf game has improved, at least marginally. "I've gone from shooting in the upper eighties to shooting in the lower eighties," he says. Somewhat apologetically, he adds, "I'd be in the upper seventies if I'd listen to Harvey and spend three quarters of my time practicing my short game instead of banging away with my driver." In a chapter of the book that addresses the pigheaded tendency of most golfers to showboat their strength while ignoring their weakness, we are reminded that about half of any player's shots are struck within sixty yards of the flag stick. "Bobby Jones said the secret of shooting low scores is the ability to turn three shots into two," Harvey (and Bud) tell us.

In the year and a half since its publication, the *Little Red Book* has become a literary and cultural phenomenon, a sports version of the best-selling melodrama *The Bridges of Madison County* — but without that book's sappiness and pretense. This shouldn't really amaze us, but it does. Harvey Penick is one of the best-loved figures in golf, one of its last living pioneers. His influence has radiated across the world of golf for seventy years, directly or indirectly affecting the lives of thousands of players. Serious golfers from Texas to New York, from London to Madrid and Melbourne know Harvey by reputation, but until the *Little Red Book* appeared in print, no one fully realized the magic that his name would conjure. Here was a voice from the dawn of creation. Harvey started caddying at the original Austin Country Club in the Hyde Park section of the city in 1912, just twenty-four years after the sport was introduced in this country. (ACC claims to be the oldest country club in Texas, though Galveston Country Club makes a similar claim.) Harvey played on the Texas Professional Golf Association tour in the twenties, sharing transportation and hotel rooms and competing for meager prize money with the likes of Jack Burke, Sr., and Lighthorse Harry Cooper. He was president of the Texas PGA when two youngsters named Ben Hogan and Byron Nelson applied for membership. Harvey Penick may be the only person on the face of the earth who could offhandedly remark — as I heard him do recently while correcting a flawed backswing — "Walter Hagen had that same problem."

In his thirty years as the golf coach at UT and in his decades as a club pro and an instructor at PGA schools, Harvey has taught some of the greatest golfers who ever lived — 1992 U.S. Open champion and all-time leading money winner Tom Kite, 1984 Masters champion Ben Crenshaw, Don Massengale, Mickey Wright, Betsy Rawls, Kathy Whitworth, Sandra Palmer, and many others. Seven of the thirteen members of the Ladies Professional Golf Association Hall of Fame took lessons from Harvey. But he was much more than a teacher; he was a spiritual force and frequently a surrogate parent. They used to call the UT golf team Harvey's Boys. When Sandra Palmer was struggling to make it on the women's tour, Harvey and his wife, Helen, took her into their Austin home.

Along with grip and stance, Harvey taught honesty, integrity, and character. He was justifiably proud when Tom Kite won the U.S. Open, but he was even prouder when Kite sacrificed an opportunity to win the Kemper Open by warning New Zealander Grant Waite, who eventually beat him by one shot, that Waite was about to commit a two-shot penalty. "There is nothing guaranteed to be fair in either golf or life," Harvey teaches. "You must accept your disappointments and your triumphs equally." Harvey has always taken a deep satisfaction from the results of his teachings, not only when some former pupil won a major tournament but when an average weekend player hit a good shot and for one shining moment knew what it felt like to be a champion. "My greatest reward has always been the look of pleasure in the eyes of pupils who have just made a perfect shot," Harvey says. This is not an exaggeration: Harvey has been known to shriek with joy and break out in goose bumps.

Almost from its inception, the *Little Red Book* seemed blessed with timing and an extraordinary reserve of goodwill. In May 1992, the same month the book went on sale, ABC commentator Jack Whitaker gave the book a lengthy and extremely complimentary plug during a lull on the network's telecast of the Liberty Mutual Legends of Golf tournament in Austin. The following month, *Golf Digest* ran an excerpt and featured Harvey on its cover. A short time later Kite won the U.S. Open and immediately sent his trophy to Harvey. And then Crenshaw won the Western Open. In a matter of days everyone interested in golf was talking about the *Little Red Book*. The president of Pine Valley Country Club in New Jersey, one of the most famous and most exclusive golf courses in the world, confessed to Shrake that he had never read anything more interesting. An Austin couple taking a vacation cruise down the Amazon reported seeing another passenger engrossed in the *Little Red Book.* The owner of a New Age bookstore in South Austin began practicing the slow-motion drill described in the book instead of t'ai chi. Harvey's son, Tinsley, went to Ireland partly to escape the hoopla of the book and immediately found himself cornered in an Irish pub by a native who couldn't believe his luck at having encountered the son of the master.

Before the Ryder Cup in England in September, the *London Daily Express* devoted two of its seven pages of coverage to a story on Harvey — and on the *Little Red Book,* which was scheduled to be published in Britain the next month. The author described Harvey as "a mystical holy man" and wrote, "The *Little Red Book . . .* is only a manual of golf if *Moby Dick* is about angling and *The Merchant of Venice* is a guide to investment." Predictably, the book's warm reception has spawned a sort of cottage industry. So far there are audiocassettes and videocassettes, a calendar, and a newsletter. Harvey turned down several other offers, including an extremely lucrative one from Johnnie Walker Red Label scotch, which tried to buy 100,000 copies of the *Little Red Book* to use in an advertising campaign. Harvey explained to Bud, who would have received half of the royalties, that he didn't want to encourage young people to drink. "Good for you, Harvey," Bud said. One golf magazine wrote recently, "We're getting *Little Red Book*ed out. We've got the book, the video, the audio. What's next, a 32 oz. drinking glass and Harvey Penick umbrellas?" "*Hmmmm,*" Shrake mused, "Harvey Penick umbrellas!"

That the book was ever published in the first place is a small miracle. Harvey didn't write it for publication. For sixty-something years, usually after a session with a pupil, he had jotted down tips and observations in a small red notebook that he kept in his briefcase. Most of the entries were spare and deceptively simple, homespun snippets of wisdom such as "take dead aim" or "swing the club like you would a weed cutter" or, alternatively, "swing it like you would a bucket of water." To nongolfers such pointers no doubt sound mundane, almost moronic, but every word in the book had, according to Harvey, "stood the test of time." "Paralysis by analysis" is a phrase you hear frequently around a golf course: What Harvey has done is remind us that the object of this game is to hit a ball with a stick.

Until about three years ago Harvey had never showed the notebook to anyone except Tinsley, who had replaced his father as the pro at Austin Country Club when Harvey retired in 1971. A genuinely modest man, Harvey never dreamed anyone else would be interested. The notebook was to be Tinsley's legacy, a compilation of knowledge and experience passed down from father to son. Harvey thought that he didn't have long to live, and he believed that when he died, the club would fire Tinsley and hire some young hotshot who taught golf as though it were nuclear physics and broke down a golf swing into forty-five distinct and separate movements.

In 1989 the end did indeed seem near. Harvey was admitted to St. David's Hospital in Austin, suffering from a fractured spine, prostate cancer, disorientation, and severe depression. "Every day when I left the hospital, I thought it was for the last time," recalls Tinsley, who is now in his mid-fifties. The depression was made more acute by Harvey's feeling of uselessness. Then something wonderful happened. Messages (and money) began to pour in from club members and touring golf professionals. One message from Jack Nicklaus read, "Get well — we need you." For the first time in days, Harvey responded to life. "Can you imagine Jack Nicklaus, the greatest golfer who ever lived, saying he needs me?" Harvey asked his family. "It's unbelievable." With the money that had been contributed, the family was able to hire a private nurse, and Harvey went home.

In the spring of 1991 Tinsley contacted Bud and asked if he could meet Harvey at the country club. Bud occasionally played at the club and had taken a lesson or two from Harvey. Mainly, his connection to Harvey was through Bud's brother, Bruce, who had been one of Harvey's Boys when he played golf at UT in the late fifties. Bud drove to the club and was directed to the practice tee, where Harvey and his nurse were waiting in the golf cart. The nurse stepped aside while the two men talked, first about Bud's brother. Then Harvey said, "I'm about to show you something I've never showed anyone except my son, Tinsley," and he produced the dog-eared notebook. "Do you think I could get this published?" he asked. Bud read a few pages and said that he probably could. Harvey continued, "Would you help me get it in shape?" Bud said that he would be honored. "How much do you think it will cost me?" Harvey asked, and Bud smiled and replied that he'd see what he could do.

Bud immediately called his literary agent, Esther Newberg, who was less than enthusiastic about the prospect of selling a book about a sport in which she had no interest, by a regional golf instructor whose name she'd never heard. Bud suggested that she get in touch with an editor at Simon and Schuster named Charlie Hayward, whom Shrake knew to be a sports enthusiast. Hayward passed the proposal along to the editor in charge of the sports books, Jeff Neuman, who instantly recognized the potential. Within a matter of hours, the publishing company offered a $90,000 advance. Bud telephoned the good news to Helen, who takes all of her husband's phone calls since his hearing has failed. Maybe something got lost in the translation, but Shrake got the impression that Harvey was strangely noncommittal about the deal. The following day at the club, he learned why. Harvey asked Bud to sit beside him in the golf cart. In a voice so soft and feeble that Bud could hardly hear it, Harvey confessed that he'd been awake all night worrying about the proposal. "With all my medical bills and everything," he said, "I'm not sure I can afford to pay ninety thousand dollars."

The serendipitous philosophy that led Harvey to seek out Bud in the first place — "When you're trying to decide which club to hit, the first one that comes to mind is the right one" — persuaded the old man to put himself in Bud's hands for the run of the project. In the beginning, nobody connected with the book believed it would make a lot of money: The publisher projected sales at 50,000, but hedged its bet by ordering an initial distribution of just 17,500. Still, it was apparent that Harvey and Bud were a match made in heaven. Shrake had published seven novels, including the classic *Blessed McGill*, written dozens of screenplays, and authored two best-selling as-told-to books with Willie Nelson and Barry Switzer. Publishing was a territory that Shrake knew well. And the subject was dear to his heart. "What Harvey had to say was so important that it had to be preserved for all golfers everywhere for all the ages," Bud told me. "It happened to fall to me to make it happen."

Since there wasn't enough material in the notebook to fill even a thin volume, Bud began a series of tape-recorded interviews with Harvey. The interviews were slow and tedious. Bud had to sit facing Harvey and speak slowly so that Harvey could read his lips. Harvey's voice was so weak that at times Bud had to hold the small clip-on microphone to the old man's lips. Using the notebook as a starting point, the writer asked questions and the teacher elaborated on what he had already written, thinking of new things along the way. Once the tapes were transcribed, Shrake began writing short chapters, some only a paragraph or two, each on a subject that could be covered with a simple heading — "Hand Position," "The Grip," "The Waggle," "The Right Elbow," "How To Tell Where You're Aimed." "I wanted it to be like eating peanuts," he said. "You read two or three chapters and you can't stop." Bud made several requests of the publisher, all of which editor Jeff Neuman supported. He wanted the book jacket designed to look as if it had been published a hundred years ago, he wanted it to be roughly the same size as the original little red book, and he wanted it priced at no more than $20. "Everyone who plays golf has twenty dollars and will spend it on anything that he thinks will help his game," Bud reasoned.

As each chapter was typed, Bud gave it to Harvey to read and correct, another painfully slow process, but one that was absolutely essential to success. In the introduction to the *Little Red Book*, Ben Crenshaw writes, "What sets the great teachers apart from the others is not merely golf knowledge, but the essential art of communication. . . . Harvey has spent a considerable part of his lifetime . . . not thinking about *what* to say to a pupil, but *how* to say it." A single word can make all the difference. Harvey tells students to *place* their hands on the club, the implication being not to grab or twist or wrap the hands around it. The success of the book can be attributed to Harvey's clear, concise voice, abiding wisdom and integrity, and what Shrake calls "the purity of Harvey's soul" — but it also owes much to Shrake's skills as a writer and his own deep love of the game. Shrake told me, "The very thought that some serious golfer might take instructions from something that came from me rather than something that came from Harvey was terrifying."

As a kid growing up in Fort Worth, Shrake used to follow his daddy around the golf course at Colonial Country Club, where the senior Shrake was a charter member. "My dad wasn't a great golfer — he shot in the seventies — but he was good enough to play in tournaments," Shrake says. "I loved the game, but I had no talent for it." In the mid-sixties, when he was on staff at *Sports Illustrated* in New York, Shrake played occasionally with Dan Jenkins and some of the other editors, and he played in the annual 5:42 P.M. Open, a tournament staged at Wing Foot Country Club in Westchester County for the regulars at Toots Shors, the famous Manhattan bar.

After moving to Austin in 1967, Shrake continued to play sporadically, but he didn't take up the game seriously until 1984 — when his diabetes was diagnosed and he was ordered by his doctor to give up drinking. "I had to fill up my time doing something else besides drinking, so I took up golf," Shrake says. With old friends Willie Nelson and Darrell Royal, Shrake played almost every day, from early morning until dark, fifty-four holes or more. Each golf shot is new life, new hope, Harvey teaches his pupils: A bad golf shot is a little death, but in golf there is life after death. There certainly was for Shrake: In the past nine years, golf has become more than a recreation — it has become his reason to be. "I love the way P. G. Wodehouse put it," Shrake says. "Some people say that golf is a microcosm of life, but just the opposite is true: Life is a microcosm of golf."

As the book zoomed to the top of the bestseller list and stayed there, Harvey was inundated by success and having the time of his life handling it. He looked ten years younger. Normally when a writer publishes a book, he is expected to go on tour to promote sales. In Harvey's case, the tour was coming to him. He was signing as many as 250 books a day and still requests were stacking up in the office behind the pro shop. "Harvey wrote so slowly and with such painstaking care that it took him about ten minutes to sign each book," Bud recalls. "I bought him a signature stamp — it said 'Take Dead Aim, Harvey Penick,' and it was indistinguishable from the real thing. But Harvey wouldn't use it. He said it wasn't legitimate." Many adoring fans, some traveling hundreds or even thousands of miles, popped by the club. So did old friends, some from Harvey's school days. Invariably Harvey recalled their names.

A man carrying a handmade golf club that his father had given him came by one day: Harvey didn't recognize the man, but he recognized the club. "I made that club for a fellow in 1927," he said. "You must be his son." He was. Letters poured in too, dozens of them every day. Many were simply messages of congratulations, but Harvey insisted on personally answering every letter that required a response. Two handwritten letters arrived from President George Bush. Harvey wrote back, "May I suggest that you are over-analyzing your swing."

Wealthy golf nuts telephoned almost daily, wanting to fly to Austin in their private jets to take lessons from Harvey. Fielding the calls, Tinsley tried to explain that his father no longer accepted new pupils, that he was eighty-seven, deaf, disabled, unable to follow the flight of the ball down the fairway. Moreover, the callers needed to understand, Harvey's teaching methods were not what most pupils expected. A lesson might consist of Harvey's reaching out with his cane, moving a ball back a few inches, then driving away in his cart even as the student was asking questions. When he analyzed a student and decided he couldn't help, Harvey simply drove away in his cart without a word. Sometimes he preferred hiding behind bushes while studying a pupil's swing. Tinsley would tell the callers all these things and still some would persist. A textile heiress from North Carolina said that she didn't care what it cost, this was her husband's birthday and nothing less than a personal lesson from the incomparable Harvey Penick would do. Tinsley sighed and told her to come on down.

Watching Harvey autograph books one day, Shrake noticed that he was using the phrase "to my pupil and friend," even when addressing someone he had never seen before. Shrake asked him why and Harvey replied, "If they read my book, they're my pupil — and if they play golf, they're my friend." Shrake mentioned this to Neuman later, and the editor said, "There's the title for our sequel!"

And If You Play Golf, You're My Friend is much like the red book in appearance, style, and substance: It is a compilation of tips, observations, and snippets of wisdom. The main difference is that the cover is green. No doubt it will come to be known as the Little Green Book. Material for the new book was collected from stories about Harvey that golfers had told Shrake after the first book was published, filtered back through Harvey himself for verification, and retold in his own words. "If Harvey didn't remember a story, I didn't use it," Shrake said. This time the publisher did not hedge its bet: The initial printing was 300,000, and the company decided to bump that another 50,000 before the books were shipped. This book also costs twenty dollars. "It may sell as well as the first book," Neuman told me, "but it will never feel the same. You only fall in love for the first time once. The *Little Red Book* is the happiest publishing story I know."

Curious to learn how Harvey and his family were dealing with success, I dropped by the club one morning in early October. Harvey was on the patio outside the clubhouse, seated as usual in his golf cart beside his nurse. Seven or eight women of various ages were clustered about, fawning over Harvey, and the smile on his face suggested that he was adjusting to life in the fast lane. "Imagine me, a caddie from Hyde Park, a C student who found it hard to write a single page of a theme in school, writing a bestseller," Harvey said, beaming. Harvey and Helen continue to have a modest lifestyle, in a one-story townhouse near the club. Reluctantly, Harvey has agreed to a sevenfold increase in the fee he charges for a lesson — from $5 to $35. Teaching pros with half of Harvey's reputation think nothing of charging $500.

Tinsley was more circumspect: The book has obviously changed his life but in ways that are not yet fully apparent. The success of the book has made Tinsley's job more difficult. "People demand more than I can give," he said. "I'm not like my father. Even though I know it's the best advice I could give, I can't bring myself to tell a pupil, 'Swing it like you'd swing a bucket of water — fifty dollars, please.' I just can't do that."

After lunch I walk over to the practice tee and watch Harvey give a lesson to Don Massengale, who lives in Conroe and plays the senior tour. Massengale is pushing his tee shot off to the right rather than hooking it like he wants to. Harvey instructs Massengale to lighten his grip and move his hands back. "Keep the club face square," he says, "and try to hit the ball over the shortstop's head." After about half an hour, Massengale is hitting the ball perfectly.

Later that same afternoon, Shrake is alone on the practice tee when Harvey drives up behind him just as he lurches at the ball and sends it dribbling down the fairway. "Oh, my, we've got a lot of work to do," Harvey says. He has Bud take a few practice swings, then tells him, "You need to get back on your heels." Bud tries it Harvey's way and discovers that he is swinging smoothly instead of diving at the ball. "Now hit the ball like you're mad at it," Harvey tells him.

"Like I'm mad at it?"

"Like it's your worst enemy."

Bud crushes his next drive straight and true down the fairway, maybe the best golf shot he has ever hit in his life. He can't believe what he's just done. "*Owwwww!*" Harvey shrieks. And you can see the goose bumps popping out on his arm.

JOHN PAUL NEWPORT

They Might Be Giants

FROM MEN'S JOURNAL

THE HARDEST-WORKING man on the Space Coast Tour is Gene Jones, Jr., a.k.a. Gene the Machine. Granted, that's not saying an awful lot, since many of Jones's peers, especially the youngsters, spend as much time honing their personalities as honing their games. Unlike on the PGA Tour, where wit and colorful behavior are relics of the past, in bush-league professional golf personality counts for a lot. That's because most of the players are just giving the pro game a shot for a few years before moving on to their true life's work: conducting golf seminars for the plaid-pants crowd at backwater country clubs or selling universal life-insurance products for Prudential.

Jones is like the nerd in your college lit class who always read every assignment. After a tournament round, he will pound balls at a driving range, go home to videotape his swing in the search for tiny flaws and then practice putting and chipping for an hour or two. On days when the Space Coast Tour doesn't stage an event, he finds another tournament to enter. On Sundays he practices some more and then usually takes his ten-year-old daughter, Amberly, out for a round of golf. What drives Jones to pursue golf so maniacally is a matter of considerable speculation among his fellow competitors. But obviously, he's very serious about the game.

I first encountered him as I was standing near the scoreboard during the first round of the DeBary Plantation tournament, north of Orlando, last fall. Around me, young Space Coast cadets were offering preposterous excuses for why they had scored so poorly. "I'd have shot a 68 if I hadn't triple-bogeyed number eight," a curly-haired fellow from Colorado assured me, explaining his round of 77. Another player, this one from Georgia, pointed toward the neat, handwritten row of 4s, 5s, 6s and 7s that appeared after his name on the scoreboard and complained, "How could someone as studly as me have shot a dip-shit round like that?" He didn't seem overly upset, however, as he lounged in his golf cart, feet on the dash, guzzling a Coors. He was young and good-looking, he had a rich sponsor somewhere paying all his bills, and there would always be tomorrow.

This was when Jones drove up, making the turn after nine holes of play, his eyes scanning the scoreboard like antiaircraft sensors. At thirty-five, he is a short, sturdy-looking man, with blond hair, plump cheeks and a forlorn, distracted air. In baggy black shorts, a Nike cap and saddle-oxford golf shoes, he looked more like a schoolboy than the tour's leading money winner. Nevertheless, his arrival silenced the cadets.

"What's the low score?" he asked in a taut North Carolina accent.

The question was precisely worded. Not "Who's in the lead?" because Jones didn't care about the person attached to the score. Not "What's in the money?" because finishing high enough to earn a check is not the issue; Jones almost always does. Rather, simply, "What's the low score?" What number precisely did he have to beat to take the lead?

"Uh, three under, Gene," someone said.

"Thanks," Jones replied and gunned the cart up the path. No one dared ask after his score, which happened to be even par.

After a pause, the banter resumed. "No one can play well *all* the time," my pal with the Coors continued in defense of his dip-shit round. But then he added, with a none-too-friendly edge in his voice, "Unless your name is frigging Gene the Machine."

The Spalding Space Coast Tour is golf's version of Bull Durham baseball. Most of the players are in their 20s, and every one thinks he is on the brink of Big Tour stardom. Pitted against them is a handful of cagey veterans and downward-spiraling former tour pros with names like Tony Cerda and Doug Weaver. The latter group almost always cleans up.

The biggest difference between Bull Durham–style minor

league baseball and the Space Coast Tour is that in baseball the players earn a living. On the Space Coast Tour, which operates most of the year except for the hot summer months, probably fewer than a dozen golfers actually support themselves out of winnings. The rest, mostly the young guys, hit up Mom and Dad for cash transfusions, wangle financial-sponsorship deals from wealthy sportsmen who might otherwise back a racehorse, hustle amateurs at the approximately 140 Orlando-area golf courses or work part time.

The Space Coast Tour is essentially an open-air golf casino: Players put down their bets in the form of $300 to $350 entry fees, and the top few finishers walk off with most of the loot. The Spalding Company, hoping to curry favor with the club professionals of tomorrow, kicks in $100,000 a year to the kitty. And the house — in the person of J. C. Goosie, sixty-four, sole owner and proprietor — sweeps away twelve percent after course expenses. Last year the total purse was about $1.2 million, compared with more than $54 million on the PGA Tour.

"Our operation is simple," Goosie told me over the telephone. (He doesn't show up at Space Coast events when he qualifies for tournaments on the Senior PGA Tour.) "We want ex-college players to come down here and spend about $16,000 to $17,000 — that's for everything, entry fees, living expenses, everything — and play for a year. If a guy's good, he's gonna make $12,000 or $13,000 of that back. If he's very good, he may break even. So for 15 to 30 cents on the dollar, next to nothing, he's gonna get experience he can't buy nowhere else."

J. C. Goosie invented the minitour concept twenty years ago, basically because he and his pals who couldn't get on the regular tour needed a place to play. The idea caught on. Over the years quite a few Space Coast alums have made names for themselves on the PGA, including stars like Paul Azinger and Craig Stadler. Recently, however, the best subtour talent has gravitated to the PGA Tour–sponsored Nike Tour (formerly the Ben Hogan Tour) and the four-year-old T.C. Jordan Tour. That leaves Goosie and a few other upstart minitours, like the Golden State Golf Tour, in California, defending the honor of single-A golf.

Conditions are what you'd expect: spiky greens, sprinkler systems that occasionally burst to life in the middle of a player's back-swing, passing motorists yelling "Fore!" as a joke and no sign of a gallery anywhere. The absence of fans has advantages: Players feel free to relieve themselves in the woods whenever they like and to indulge in the same colorful expletives that golfers everywhere enjoy. The day-to-day manager of the Space Coast Tour is a former pro and real estate agent named Bobby Simpson, who has an odd way of holding his head, like a turtle peeking out of its shell. The starter is an affable Cajun nicknamed Crow, who spends the balance of his week at the dog track. And the rules officials include retired old pros who disperse around the course in golf carts and can often be spotted snoozing.

Such is the sweet narcotic bliss of golf, however, that nobody seems to mind.

I followed Jones around the back nine at DeBary, and it took me a while to identify his value-added as a golfer. His drives, though accurate, were not particularly long, and his swing, though serviceable, was brusque and pared down, pistonlike — not at all the elegant, modern Fred Couples ideal. He did appear perfectly comfortable standing over the ball, which is not always the case with golfers on the Space Coast Tour, many of whom bounce up and down neurotically and back away from the shot so often you begin to wonder if they might be afraid of hurting the ball.

After a few more holes, however, I began to understand that Jones's distinction is not his ball-striking ability so much as his raw animal hunger to score birdies. He works the course like a perpetual-motion machine, darting after his balls with the ferocity of a terrier, swinging extra clubs to groove the right feel, pacing like a CEO in a doctor's office whenever he has to wait, sizing up putts from every angle of the compass. On the eleventh hole he missed a seven-foot birdie putt and stayed on the green for several minutes afterward, inspecting the turf around the hole with the disgust of a surgeon trying to comprehend a botched operation.

Jones's attitude stood in marked contrast to that of his playing companion for the day, D.W. Smith, forty-two, a courtly Mississippian wearing a straw fedora. Smith, a very fine golfer himself (during one 17-round stretch last summer he shot 90 under par), lolled about in the cart between shots chatting with other golfers

like a pastor at a church social. "Look at D.W.," Jones said deri-
sively, nodding as Smith nonchalantly got up to arch his back like a
cat enjoying the sun. "If *I* was two over, I'd be eyeballing down the
fairway to see how I could get me a birdie."

During a brief delay on the fourteenth tee, Jones took me aside
to apologize for a minor display of temper — he had tossed a
club — on the previous hole. "I expect a little more out of myself
is all," he said. "When you're playing this bad, it just gets under
your skin, that's all. You gotta get after yourself, gotta get a little bit
mad." The day before, he said, he had shot 67 in a hurricane to
win the $1,000 first prize at a tournament in Lady Lake.

With that he stepped up to his ball, mumbled something like
"Come on, now, just gimme a chance" and sizzled a three-iron
straight down the center of the fairway. "Whoo-ee, Jethro," Smith
cooed in appreciation. Jones acknowledged the compliment with
a tight-lipped smile and stood aside, practicing his hip turn as the
others hit.

"Personality-wise," I jotted in my notebook, "this guy's a natural
for the PGA Tour."

I had hoped to talk with Jones more extensively after the round.
But before I could collar him, an entertaining golfer named Billy
Glisson asked me for a ride to his car. I had met Glisson a few days
earlier. He claims to be the World's Leading All-Time Minitour
Winner, and he probably is, though many would consider that a
dubious honor.

"I come down here for one thing and one thing only, and that's
to win," he told me in his hurry-up South Carolina accent as we
barreled down a derelict stretch of highway. He was dragging on a
Viceroy and blowing smoke out the window. "Coming in second
don't cut it. That's why I've won 91-plus minitour events. I reckon
it's like Nicklaus."

Glisson, forty-six, is a friendly, lackadaisical mess of a man. He
has a broad, blunt nose, longish, dirty blond hair that curlicues
out the back of his golf cap and such a monster belly that he never
even tries to tuck his shirttail in. He tends to wear the same pair of
baggy gray shorts day after day and leaves a butt trail of Viceroys
around the course which Hansel and Gretel would envy. I estimate

he smokes three packs per round. Glisson also engages in the disturbing habit of popping his ball in his mouth between holes despite all the insecticides around.

If the Space Coast Tour attracted media attention the way the PGA Tour does, Glisson's personal history would be the stuff of legend. During the early years he supported his golf habit by working as the night manager of an Orlando brothel that operated out of a beauty salon. He got so good at golf, however, that by the early eighties he was supposedly winning more than $50,000 a year on the minitours. In 1981 he made it to the big tour and did pretty well. "Got on TV four or five times," he bragged matter-of-factly. Unfortunately, he soon suffered a nearly fatal stroke — "Too much drinking and carrying on, I reckon" — and so, after a couple of years' recovery, it was back to the minors.

Glisson lasted long enough on tour to make a mark, however. He is remembered, among other reasons, for confusing the courtesy-car volunteers with his frequent requests to pick up more than one "Mrs. Glisson" at the airport. At one tournament, the real Mrs. Glisson spotted her husband strolling the fairway holding hands with a Mrs. Glisson not herself and stole his Corvette out of spite, leaving only his street shoes in the parking space.

Despite a too-quick backswing and constant exasperation at slow play, Glisson still wins his share of minitour events. That's why the 79 he had shot that morning was such a thorn. "Couldn't make a putt," he grumbled as we drove. "When you play golf for a living, you gotta have total concentration. All I could think about was my damn car."

His car, a black 1983 Eldorado with an I'D RATHER BE GOLFING bumper sticker in the rear window, had broken down that morning on an I-40 exit ramp. He had had to hitch a ride, by chance with Gene the Machine, to make it to the tournament on time. We found the car, apparently repaired, tilting half-in, half-out of a muddy ditch beside the weather-beaten combination garage and sign shop where he had left it. The proprietor charged Glisson only $35. "Hot damn," Glisson said, beaming like he'd just holed out a pitching wedge from 100 yards. "I thought they'd take me to the cleaners."

Even so, he had to borrow $20 to make it back to the friend's apartment where he stays, sleeping on the couch, while competing in Orlando. And a few days later the Eldorado broke again. This time the repairs cost $800.

Glisson has a new wife and two children back in South Carolina. I asked him why he still plays tournament golf. "It just gets in the blood, I reckon," he replied, "and you can't get it out."

The next day, back at DeBary Plantation, Gene the Machine failed to win the tournament. He cranked out what for him was another disappointing round of even par to finish three shots off the pace. The winner, in a sudden-death playoff, was Doug Weaver, another former tour pro like Glisson but unlike Glisson in nearly every other possible respect. I realized this immediately when I offered to buy him a drink at the clubhouse bar to celebrate his exciting victory, and he enthusiastically accepted by ordering milk.

Weaver, thirty-three, is a solidly built redhead with a deep southern voice and a lightly pocked face. I thought he was joking about the milk, of course, but he wasn't. He ordered a tall glass of it, took one sip, then dashed off to a telephone to tell his wife the good news of their $4,300 payday. "God must be teaching us to be very dependent on Him," Weaver said when he returned, "because every time we get almost broke, I win a tournament."

Two years earlier, he said, the family had been in a similar pickle. Their bank account was practically zero, his wife was pregnant, his swing was incoherent, and he had just shot 81-82 in a pro-am tournament at Pebble Beach. After the tournament, he and his wife, Patricia, walked down to the beach below the course and prayed. "Dear God," they beseeched, "if we're going to play golf in 1991, You're going to have to put the money in our hands because we're too embarrassed to ask anyone for it ourselves anymore." Sure enough, a few days later Weaver received an offer from a potential sponsor — one of his partners in the disastrous Pebble Beach pro-am, no less — of $30,000 over the next two years. He was back in business.

I asked Weaver what keeps him golfing when the financial abyss yawns. "I realize I could go back to South Carolina and get a good job," he replied. "But the Bible says a young man without vision shall perish. That doesn't mean really perish, but he just won't have a good life." He paused to take his last gulp of milk. "This is the dream God has laid on our hearts."

The shocking thing about the pro-golf scene in Orlando is the sheer number of men, like Weaver and Glisson and all the cadets, who manage to arrange their lives to play golf every day "for a living." Because in addition to Goosie's operation, two other, even lesser minitours operate in the area: the Tommy Armour Tour and the North Florida PGA Winter Tour. Together the three tours qualify Orlando, without a doubt, as the Bush-League Professional Golf Capital of the Universe.

I called on the Tommy Armour Tour one Saturday during its one-day tournament at the Overoaks Country Club. First-place prize money was $1,000, and the second-place check (which went to Gene the Machine for shooting 67 again) was $600. When I arrived, the players who had already finished were standing around in a grove of live oak trees, the branches hung with Spanish moss, sipping beer or soft drinks and chatting amiably amongst themselves. It looked a lot like a big southern picnic or family reunion. "No offense," a competitor recently arrived from New Jersey told me, "but this is the lamest tour I've ever played on."

The man who owns the Tommy Armour Tour is a perplexed-looking 49-year-old named Terry Fine. Fine plays in his own tournaments as a way of tuning up for the Senior Tour. The day I visited, he shot an 81. "The biggest complaint the players have down here in Florida," he said, "is the blatant stealing out of the purse that takes place on some of the other tours." By "other tours" he was clearly alluding to Goosie's, though Fine later said he did not mean to suggest by "stealing" that Goosie was doing anything illegal — merely that he was keeping too high a percentage of the pot for himself.

No love is lost between Fine and Goosie. For Goosie, the Tommy Armour Tour is "kind of a sore thumb." He claims not to mind the competition — "good, honest competition we can handle" — as much as the way Fine "slipped around behind my back, giving my players his cards, that sort of thing," when Fine was getting his tour off the ground three years ago.

As for Fine, he likes to portray himself as the golfers' true friend.

He prides himself on keeping a higher percentage of the players' money in the pot, after expenses and profits, than does Goosie. But since his major sponsor, the Tommy Armour Golf Company, contributes less to his tour than the Spalding company does to the Space Coast Tour, the players still get a better return with Goosie. To compensate, Fine was working on a deal to offer all Tommy Armour Tour members in good standing a ten-percent discount at Wolf Camera outlets across the South. "One thing we're trying to do at the Tommy Armour Tour is add a little dignity," he said. Earlier, the tour had been known as the Hooters Tour, after a restaurant chain that features busty waitresses in tight T-shirts and hot pants. So dignitywise, that's progress right there.

I wandered over to the clubhouse porch, where a number of competitors were loitering after their round. They constituted the usual assortment of oddballs one finds in bush league golf: a bartender and occasional dancer at a Chippendales-like club, a frightened-looking kid from South Africa who appeared to be no older than twelve, a 41-year-old tenured Delta pilot who competes regularly by virtue of his eighteen off days per month and a surly, ponytailed, practice-range pro who was griping about how much Fred Couples earned for switching to Parallax clubs (supposedly $4 million) and showing off his own abnormally long driver. This club's head weighed about ten pounds and was made of Kryptonite or plutonium or something and if manipulated correctly could propel the ball, he said, 339 yards. He let me try it on the range. It was like swinging a maypole with several small children attached. My best attempt almost reached the 100-yard marker.

As I was preparing to leave, a 24-year-old golfer named Joe Shahady took me aside to suggest privately that I might want to mention in the article how much he enjoys eating PowerBars. PowerBars, according to some information Terry Fine made available, provide delicious, nutritious, *sustained* energy to help golfers maintain the focus required for hitting straight drives and making crucial putts. I forgot to mention earlier that the PowerBar company is an official sponsor of the Tommy Armour Tour. Any player quoted in the press singing the praises of PowerBars gets a $500 bonus.

I finally had a chance to sit down and talk with Gene the Machine after the first round of the next Space Coast tournament, a two-day affair at the Kissimmee Bay Country Club. He had just shot a 66 but couldn't resist complaining about a couple of knee-knocker putts he missed. "I just couldn't get anything started on the front nine," he grumbled.

Off the course Jones is not nearly as daunting as he is when stalking a golf ball. He has a mild, fidgety manner and a hang-dog vulnerability. During the interview, whenever a subject arose that he didn't feel comfortable with, such as the past, he flitted off to something more benign, usually golf. "I used to be down on my-self because I didn't have any money and all, but the insight I had was that the more failures you go through, the higher you can achieve," he said. "You can work hard in golf and make it."

Reportedly, Jones was a superstar in high school in Orlando. He won the Florida PGA Junior title and the U.S. Olympic Junior championship before turning pro at eighteen. Then something happened, all the details of which I could not discover. A car wreck was part of it; for five years he wore a neck brace. Apparently, too, he didn't get along with people; he was introverted and, as he puts it, "too hard-core" about golf. For a long time he drifted. He sold pots and pans in Fort Worth, cleaned swimming pools in Orlando and mowed the grass at a country club in South Carolina. "I had went as low as I could go," Jones says; "but I won't say I was going crazy, because I still always believed that I could play."

His rescuer was Malcolm McDonald, an Orlando-area surgeon and friend of the family. Dr. Mac, as Jones calls him, remembered what a fine player Jones had been as a youth and convinced him four years ago to move back from South Carolina. To make that fi-nancially possible, McDonald bought Jones and his wife a trailer and a few acres of land outside Orlando and encouraged him to reconcile with his dad, a teaching pro.

The turning point for Jones, golfwise, seemed to come last year when he qualified in a preliminary round to compete in the Greensboro Open, a PGA Tour event. "At Greensboro, you'd hear 10,000 people giving you the clap, and it was really motivating," Jones said. "I'm not gonna say I belong out there on the tour, but that experience made me think I might."

In 1992, by the time we were talking, Jones had already won sev-enteen tournaments on the minitour scene. "It scares me how well I'm doing," he said. "Right now I'd be afraid to take a week off."

Then he excused himself to go home and practice for the next day's final round. He was tied for the lead.

To get to Kissimmee Bay from DeBary Plantation, you motor down the interstate past the fantasy factory at Universal Studios and the counterfeit reality of Walt Disney World. Then you turn left into a nightmare strip of bogus American roadside attractions. You pass Gatorland, Pirate's Island, Medieval Times and Fun 'n Wheels. By the time you reach the county jail, where you turn right, Long John Silver's seems like a high-class seafood shoppe.

I mention this because it occurred to me as I drove to Kissimmee that it's no coincidence that the Bush-League Professional Golf Capital of the Universe should be in a city like Orlando, which is wholly predicated on the suspension of disbelief. Because that's what golf is all about, too. For ostensibly mature adult men to persuade themselves that the possibility of slicing a dimpled ball into some completely artificial, blue-dyed lagoon is a risk with as dire and pulse-quickening consequences as being eaten by a bear or ambushed by the Viet Cong demands not only the suspension of disbelief but also the collusion of an entire social ecosystem. That the players are engaged in *professional* golf (albeit third-rate professional golf) only adds to the gravitas and urgency of the adventure. The delusion grows that these rounds really matter, that the players' very careers hang in the balance on each and every shot. This, I concluded, could be the ultimate source of professional golf's dark and addictive thrill and possibly the key to understanding why men of the bush league so willingly sacrifice all the nice things that their wives would like them to buy with the money they don't earn, such as new drapes for the living room and higher-quality knickknacks.

That was my thinking, anyway.

For the final round of the Kissimmee Bay tournament, Jones was paired in the next to last foursome with three cadets named Scott Pleis, Bo Fennell and Chris Hehmann. Hehmann was a rookie who had apparently never before been so high on the leader board for a final round.

Diluting the potential tension of the round was the observational presence, in a golf cart, of Steve Pleis, Scott's brother, and

Brad McClendon, a brawny, crew-cut, good old boy from Louis-iana. Steve Pleis and McClendon, having gone out in the first group of the day, had already finished their rounds. They had zipped around the course in near record time — "They played like they were in some kind of hurry to take a shit," a rules official told me — and now had a bad case of the giggles, especially when it came to Hehmann.

"He's playing out of his ying-yang," McClendon chortled at number 11 when Hehmann mis-hit an approach shot but then chipped in from 50 feet for a birdie. On 14, when Hehmann left a 40-foot putt almost 15 feet short, Steve said, "There's a lot of chicken left on that bone," and he and McClendon sat stifling their laughter like Sunday schoolers in a church pew. Eventually Hehmann self-destructed.

Jones, of course, was having none of it. He continued to play nearly flawless golf, hitting most greens in regulation and rolling his lag putts to within inches for tap-in pars. If Jones even noticed Pleis and McClendon trailing the group, he didn't show it. The Machine was focused, readying himself for what he had told me the day before was his primary focus and favorite part of a tourna-ment: the final three holes. Coming off the fifteenth green, Jones said he figured two birdies out of three would give him a chance to win. "We'll see what we can do," he said.

He got one birdie at the par-3 sixteenth, draining a 40-footer. On 17, a 416-yard par 4, he parked his approach shot five feet from the pin, and I had no doubt the Machine would hammer home the putt. But he didn't. The ball gave the hole a smell but then lipped out. On 18, all Jones could muster was a routine par.

His 69 tied him for fourth. "One of those days," he said tersely and walked off the course.

In the clubhouse bar afterwards, a couple of dozen players were waiting around to pick up their prize checks. Roger Rowland, a towheaded cadet from nearby Ocala, was hunched over his beer at the bar and shaking his head from side to side. He had just won the tournament with twin 66s. "Man, I'll tell you," he was mutter-ing, "you plain gotta play some golf to win one of these things."

Billy Glisson was there, chain-smoking Viceroys and throwing back Seven and 7s as he regaled the Pleis brothers with tales from the good old days. "There was a lot more going on in those chairs than just blow-dries, I guarantee" was one line I overheard, presumably in reference to the beauty parlor/brothel where he used to work. For some reason he was carrying a jumbo driver and waggling it, Bob Hope–style, as he delivered his shtick. The Pleis brothers seemed only mildly amused.

To my surprise Gene Jones walked in and took a stool at the bar. I had the impression that drinking with the boys was not something he did very often.

"Hey, Machine," someone called out. "There's a rumor going around that you're making so much money you don't even cash your checks."

The barroom grew quiet to hear his response. "That's right," Jones said and took a long sip of beer. "I just go home every night and stare at 'em."

The line got a laugh, and that seemed to relax him. When a relative old-timer sauntered by and said, "Hey, Gene, what happened out there? I'm not used to seeing your name that far down the list," Jones smiled and seemed to relish the implicit compliment.

I took the stool next to Jones and offered to buy him a beer, but he bought me one instead. I asked him about his round. "Golf's a tough business," he replied with a shrug. "It's all about making the short ones."

He got out a pencil and calculated on a cocktail napkin that the missed five-footer on number 17 had cost him $800. "But I still had a $2,000 week. I'll be getting $1,400 from Goosie and another $650 from the Spalding bonus pool. That's pretty good money for a country boy." Then he began pulling jewelry out of a pouch that he carries around in his golf bag: a gold Rolex, a gold pinky ring with a gaudy dollar sign on its face and a key ring hung with a tiny gold golf club and a spike wrench.

Finally, the tour manager, Bobby Simpson, began circulating with the checks: large, yellow Space Coast bank drafts signed by J. C. Goosie himself. Jones folded his neatly into quarters and tucked it in his wallet beside two suspiciously similar-looking pieces of paper. "What are those?" I asked.

He took them out and showed me: uncashed Space Coast checks for $3,000 and $1,000. "I guess I am getting a little behind," Jones admitted sheepishly. But as he returned the checks to his wallet, he held my glance for a moment, and I could see how powerfully proud he was of winning checks that large. He was proud of all that he had accomplished with his life in the last few years. Maybe he does take the checks home and stare at them, I thought.

The instant Jones left the bar, a journeyman pro named Dan Oschmann said: "The son of a bitch. I wish he'd get the hell out of here and let the rest of us make some money." He meant it as a joke, but he was serious, too.

In the PGA Tour Qualifying Tournament, which began two weeks later, Jones obliged. He was one of only 43 players out of nearly 900 entrants — including a large proportion of the Space Coast irregulars — to win a coveted tour card for 1993.

I talked to the Machine by telephone afterward. "I'm looking to earn a million dollars," he said. As of late April, however, Jones had made the cut in just two tournaments, earning a total of $4,340.

Only $995,660 to go.

Running Man

FROM VANITY FAIR

EVEN THOUGH NIKE is a shoe company, shoes must be removed in the chairman's office. For it is here, in Oregon, in a town called Beaverton, that the Pacific current most sweetly touches American shores. "Despite all that crush of people, the Japanese have such wonderful ways of creating a peaceful environment," Phil Knight says as he sweeps his arm around his bright and airy office. "That influenced me." Even more, though, people who have studied him say that his immersion in Japan and other places Asian has more particularly influenced him in his ability to be inscrutable and manipulative.

Really, nobody yet seems to have gotten a handle on Knight. He has made the greatest fortune ever from athletics, and when the *Sporting News* named the "most powerful" person in the world of sport earlier this year, it chose not an athlete, or a team owner, or a commissioner, but a shoemaker — Phil Knight. His every move is now scrutinized as carefully as the glamorous superstars who wear his sneakers. Why, after Knight met with Michael Ovitz of the Creative Artists Agency recently to blue-sky about what Nike and CAA might be able to do together, the announcement of their new joint venture was front-page news in the *Los Angeles Times* and sent reverberations all through the insecure realms of athletics and agentry.

Really, what are you up to, Phil?

"The target now," he replies without cracking even an Asian smile, "is to invent a new game."

*

To the people who work here in Beaverton, Nike is *inside the berm,* so the rest of the world is, by extension, *outside the berm.* The berm is a hillock, constructed to run around the Nike property, which is itself never called the headquarters or the complex or — God forbid — the offices. Rather: the campus. This takes to its logical conclusion how a major executive once played on Frank Zappa's description of Hollywood to describe this particular place of business: "Nike is like high school, only with money."

It is self-sufficient inside the berm. There are three restaurants, a beauty salon, a laundry service. There is a child-care center. There is even a radio station — KAOS (get it?), Radio Free Nike. There is a basketball gym, a tennis court, an exercise facility, a jogging track — a way of life. It is, in fact, a great deal like Disneyland, the major difference being that Disneyland is a make-believe place where people visit occasionally, while Inside the Berm is a make-a-living place where people go to work every day.

Inside the berm, the analogues to Fantasyland and Frontierland are shiny, glassy buildings (set around a shiny, glassy picture-postcard lake) that are named after famous Nike endorsers. There's your Nolan Ryan Building and your Bo Jackson Sports and Fitness Center and your John McEnroe Building. That is where the chairman's offices are located, for the irascible McEnroe remains Phil Knight's favorite living athlete. Knight's wife, Penny, reports that when Mac was upset at Wimbledon one year the esteemed chairman of Nike went into such a funk that he sequestered himself in a darkened room and played Donkey Kong for seven hours straight.

And no one ever forgets, inside the berm, that it is all thanks to sneakers. Imagine that. In two decades Knight has taken Nike from a bunch of neophytes making sneakers with a waffle iron to a $3.7-billion-a-year worldwide juggernaut that employs 6,500 human beings, and Michael Jordan too. No less than the *Harvard Business Review* has declared that the Nike "brand name is as well-known around the world as IBM and Coke." But, even now, notwithstanding what Knight is up to with Mike Ovitz, Nike is still mostly sneakers. Imagine that. Imagine a man becoming a billionaire (nearly twice over, yet) off sneakers. But now sneakers are a $6 billion wholesale business annually in the United States alone, forty percent of the footwear market — and rising, inexorably. "I wouldn't want to be in shoe polish," says Peter Moore, ex-Nike, now the creative director of the newly constituted Adidas America.

"You know what Ovitz told me?" Knight asks. "You know what he said? Nah, I better not say this."

Aw, go on, say it.

"All right. He said sports is bigger than entertainment now. *Sports*. Can you believe it? Ovitz said that."

That is spoken with buttons-busting pride. Knight, like virtually all the folks in the athletic-shoe end of things, falls over himself swearing how much he loves the business because he loves sports. After a while, it sounds like some kind of loyalty oath. But it's true enough; sneaker people are admitted jock sniffers. For fun, Knight just loves to jet off with Penny to his favorite sports events. After the Olympics last summer, he bundled up Michael Jordan, Charles Barkley, the other Nike Dream Teamers and their wives and took them all to Hawaii on the company jet. Jordan and Barkley, of course, would go on to lead their teams to this year's NBA finals, giving Nike the real championship even before the series started.

This year, at the Australian Open in Melbourne, Knight made the local columns for dancing on the tables at a nightspot. He also earned a byline for himself as a cub reporter for the company newsletter, filing this exclusive back to Beaverton: "Mary Joe Fernandez looked terrific in her new Nike clothes. Her beauty, olive skin, graceful lines and moves made her a perfect model for our stuff. She went out in the quarters to Arantxa Sanchez Vicario, who is the opposite of a perfect model for the competition's stuff."

Bitchy, bitchy. But it was little Arantxa's singular misfortune that she happened to be playing in Reeboks. Never mind that she whipped the luminous Nike standard-bearer. "Phil is absolutely blinded by loyalty," says Howard Slusher, Knight's friend and right-hand man for many years. Knight is even on record as once baldly declaring, "The most sophisticated piece of research equipment Reebok has is its Xerox machine," and he still beams for Michael Jordan's stand last summer. At that time, Jordan essentially chose Nike over country, publicly protesting having to wear the U.S. Olympic uniform just because it was made by the evil Reebokian empire. Of the firestorm of mail and calls — 200 to 1 questioning

Jordan's patriotism — Knight says staunchly, "I'll accept the blame for Michael."

As with this case, Knight and other sneaker people tend to be hopelessly schizophrenic. Oh, how they profess to love the purity of sport, the deeper meaning; how they love running around the berms of the world, sweating pretty, communing with nature. But, of course, starting in 1956, when young Horst Dassler of Adidas started co-opting Olympic runners by handing out free shoes, nobody has done more to muck up the purity of sport than have the sneaker hustlers. It is instructive that *Blue Chips,* the new movie from director Ron Shelton (*Bull Durham, White Men Can't Jump*), which was originally written about a scumbag alumnus who leads college basketball players astray, has been rewritten to turn the villain into big business, including a scumbag sneaker pimp. Meanwhile, the whole sporting universe has professed to be apoplectic about Nike's unprecedented multimillion-dollar contract with a college basketball coach, Mike Krzyzewski of pristine Duke.

To be sure, there's nothing constitutionally evil about what sneakers have wrought, inasmuch as everybody and his or her brother has been mucking up sports since 1956 — and usually to the betterment of athletes' lives. It's just that sneaker people feel they must act so high-toned. For instance, now Nike is going after women in a big way. Women are the last frontier for Nike. But instead of merely pushing distaff sneakers like detergent or panty hose, Nike people have to go on about women being "more introspective athletes" than men. Also, "they have embraced running in a healthier way." Dear, wise women are not "diverted by endorsements" the way dumb, shallow guys are. Even Knight himself prattles on about women's new "self-empowerment" vis-à-vis Nike. Sneakers? Self-empowerment? Hey, cutie, you come here often?

But then, for years at Nike the only female of prominence was Nike herself — the winged goddess of victory, whence cometh the brand name. A decade ago, when Reebok suddenly appeared out of the blue with a flattering aerobics shoe, the men of Nike were buffaloed; they sat around, one insider recalls, and "just laughed at these dumb broads, listening to pretty music, watching themselves in the mirror."

Geoff Hollister, one of the most senior employees (who is still celebrated for telling Knight that seeing — just seeing! — a runner in Nikes cross the finish line was "better than sex"), remembers, "We wouldn't listen. We wouldn't even listen to our own wives."

And so, all of a sudden, Knight was driving to work one day, and . . . "It was between quarterly reports, but you could see how the lines were going, the graphs, see how Reebok and us were doing, and nothing was happening to change that, and I came out of the driveway, and I remember I just said to myself out loud, 'Well, this is the day. This is the day they pass us. This is the day we're not number one anymore.' "

Even though Nike climbed back on top of the market, it still has not conquered the women. Yet. The female gross profits at Nike were up 17 percent last year, the company is starting a bathing-suit line this summer, and although everybody inside the berm swears women are too smart to fall for celebrity endorsements, they've signed on several star female athletes anyway and have considered launching a whole line of clothes and shoes for Mary Joe Fernandez. Moreover, presaging, perhaps, what may come from congress with CAA, Nike has signed its first nonsports huckster, Jennie Garth from *Beverly Hills, 90210,* strictly to pitch to impressionable teenage girls, and hired Sigourney Weaver to be the dulcet voice over adult commercials.

But not to laugh, not to be cynical. This is the way it was before, back when it was the men who were pure, the men who were self-empowered, back when it was men like Phil Knight who were running — running, running, running through Oregon . . .

Runners then were truly insufferable zealots, drawing smug strength from the idea that "we were pariahs." That is what Jeff Johnson, the first man/runner hired by Knight (in 1964), says. When young Phil Knight — "Buck" he was called then — took up the sport, it was assumed that any boy who ran did so because he couldn't make a *real* team; in the vernacular, he was "twerpy." Or as Michael Jordan would say of Knight years later, "This is one weird scientist."

Nonetheless, if distance running was respectable anywhere in the United States, it was in the independent state of Oregon, in the inner-directed town of Eugene, where the University of Oregon's track team — the Ducks, so-called — was coached by an even weirder scientist. Bill Bowerman wouldn't even permit the boys to call him "coach"; instead, he identified himself as Professor of Competitive Responses. No glamorous sprinters wanted to be Ducks. The Oregon climate was too damp, and the Spalding track spikes would get soggy, full of cinders, sometimes even crack in the oatmeal weather. But the hardier distance lads were attracted to the ennobling Oregon experience.

This you must understand: Nike comes from its earth as much as the rice in Japan or the cedars in Lebanon, and, well, the goddess Nike herself was not born of woman, but birthed by the river Styx.

Professor Bowerman was unusual in one other way: unlike virtually all other athletic instructors, he was of a mechanical mind. He created a lighter track shoe himself, which was dubbed "the Vagina" because, the Duck sophomores all smirked, it might not look like much, but it certainly was terrific if ever you could get yourself inside it. Ultimately, Bowerman's tinkering would build Nike for Phil Knight as surely as Oregon had bred Nike for him.

Although young Buck was a city boy from Portland, the son of a lawyer, he looked like a hayseed, and when he went down to Eugene in '55 he was nicknamed "White Mole." But he was a good enough student, president of his fraternity, and an honest journeyman on the Duck track team. In most photographs, he can be spied back in the pack as it comes around a turn. Out front always was Jim Grelle, classmate, four-minute miler, Olympian-to-be.

Bowerman would often use the expendable Knight as a guinea pig to try out his homemade spikes. So Knight's interest in equipment was piqued, and one day a teammate named Otis Davis laced on a pair of Bowerman's latest homespun spikes and, as Knight watched, "beat a runner he had no business beating." Knight didn't actually say, *It's gotta be the shoes.* But he knew that it was.

The epiphany passed, though, and when he graduated he enrolled in the Stanford School of Business. But there, one fine day of destiny, a professor, Frank Shallenberger, assigned a term paper on the subject of starting up a new small business. Knight still remembers vividly what Shallenberger casually suggested: "Write about something you know. And something you like."

It was the same sort of charge that helped Fred Smith invent Federal Express in a class at Yale. But Smith got a C. Shallenberger so much liked what Buck Knight wrote about sneakers that he gave him an A. It simply seemed to make good sense.

The athletic-shoe market is a lie, of course. Everybody knows that eighty percent of the product is used for purposes other than athletic. Still, sneakers have come to matter so much. Last summer, Reebok paid $3 million to a seven-foot, twenty-year-old basketball player named Shaquille O'Neal on the assumption, evidently correct, that smaller men would buy the same shoes. Athletic shoes possess much the same proportion and styling as fast cars. See? They've really become sort of miniature status symbols for the masses.

There was even something of a brouhaha three years ago, with critics claiming that Nikes had come to mean so much to the children of the inner cities that violence, even murder, had been committed in order to obtain the high-priced Air Jordans. And, whatever the actual blood shed, the language was savage. Columnist John Leo, writing in *U.S. News & World Report*, asserted that the Nike slogan, "Just Do It," was a nihilist battle cry for the "people mired in the ghetto" to do almost anything, while Spike Lee, who has made several Nike commercials, fired back at critics that such assaults were "thinly veiled racism . . . a scam, a segment of the media trying to dig at some positive BROTHERS." Ironically, although many sneaker commercials, Nike and otherwise, play unashamedly to the African-American audience, sneakers are about as cross-cultural as anything this side of a Big Mac. People who share no common interest in clothes, music, earrings, comedians, or, for that matter, dress shoes crave the same sneakers.

"A lot of things have come together," Knight says, trying to explain it. "Our more casual way of life today. A desire to dress more comfortably." Suddenly he brightens. "But I'll tell you, above all, it's basically sports. It's just the sports. Remember what I told you Mike Ovitz said?"

A few apostates protest. "Ah, it's just the fashion business," says Peter Moore of Adidas America. "No, it's not runways in Paris or Milan, but it's the fashion business all the same. Look, you don't become a $6-billion-a-year industry in this country selling to athletes, because there just aren't that many athletes."

But Knight keeps saying that it's all sports and fitness.

"Sure he says that," Moore replies, just this side of a snort. "Because that's fashionable to say. And sometimes technology is what's fashionable. Like back in the mid-eighties, when the new Nike Air was selling, it was the exact same time BMWs and Apple computers were hot. Technology was fashion then. It's all just fashion."

Whatever the cause, health or vanity, the march of civilization down through this, our twentieth century, has gone from head to toe, from an emphasis on fedoras and bonnets to sneakers. Why, until very recently, whenever people bought shoes they rarely even got into the name of the brand. Especially among men, shoes were shopped for almost exclusively by model. I'd like a wing tip. Pair of brogues, please. Hey, lemme see your saddle shoes. Shoes didn't go by brand names any more than chickens did before Frank Perdue.

Well, yes, the exception proves the rule. Every red-blooded American boy who played basketball yearned for only one brand: the Converse All Star. To wear All Stars on the court — instead of something twerpy like Keds or P.F. Flyers — was to be a player, to be a man. Converse owned more than ninety percent of the basketball market. "Remember what they meant to you?" Knight absolutely rhapsodizes. "God, remember. . . ?" For any boy, owning his first All Stars was like a girl getting her first bra.

The little track-and-field spike market was hardly so symbolic and fuzzy. It was just old Spaldings. But among worldly aficionados, a distinctive shoe with three stripes, made in a little Bavarian village, was catching on. By the time Buck Knight made the Duck varsity, the three-striped shoe — properly spelled lowercase, adidas, properly pronounced ah-dee-*doss* — was still so rare in America that it was spelled Adidas and pronounced uh-*dee*-duss. It didn't matter, though. In his dorm room, Knight actually kept his first Adidases on the shelf above his desk, the better to commune with them.

This was the start of a pattern, too. Just as Converse never saw Adidas sneaking up with its German technology, so would Adidas fail to see Nike coming on with its geeky joggers, as later Nike would not acknowledge that Reebok was for real with its sex appeal to women. He who sells sneakers is doomed to ignore history. Tom Carmody, an early Nike official, is now vice president of the

Sports Division at Reebok. Sports Division, Mr. Carmody? What other division is there at Reebok?

Carmody snickers. "The only other one is the froufrou, the fitness. I'm on the side that's attacking Nike."

Ah, that would be the one with the Shaq, with Emmitt Smith of the world-champion Dallas Cowboys, with a powerful Wimbledon champion, Michael Stich, with a gritty French Open champion, Michael Chang, and, of course, Mary Joe Fernandez's conqueror, Arantxa Sanchez.

"Yeah, we're going to beat them at their own game. We're going to be more authentic than they are, more credible with men. Phil's playing right into our hands, you see. He's out there, looking around for more challenges. Phil's getting more Oriental again. And now he's back into his Dimension Six mode."

How's that?

"Dimension Six. If Jeff Johnson hadn't come up with the name Nike, Phil wanted to call the shoe Dimension Six. Really."

Dimension Six?

"Yeah. It means: One, the fan. Two, event. Three, uh, arena. Four, players. Five, uh . . . equipment. Of course. Can't forget that. Shoes. Apparel. And six, media. See? The six dimensions of sport. Phil loves that kinda crap. Of course, he's conquered about half the dimensions already, hasn't he? Now he's going after 'em all. There he is, hanging around with Michael Ovitz down in Hollywood. Fine, Phil, fine. New challenges. Yeah — and we got the Shaq."

Just do it.

"Heh, heh, heh. How much longer has Michael Jordan got? Two, three years tops? And already kids are putting up Shaq posters, and they'll go through a glass wall for their Reeboks. You know what we're gonna do this summer in Japan?"

No.

"O.K., you know that sumo wrestler, whatshisname, Hawaiian descent? We're going to bring Shaq to Tokyo and have them meet in public. We have to get permission. You know why?"

Well —

"Because it is going to shut down Tokyo in August when we do this. It is going to *shut down the city*. The sumo wrestler and the Shaq, just standing there. While Phil is going to Hollywood. Now, listen, please understand: I have a tremendous respect for Philip Knight. In fact, I'll tell you an ironic thing. He must be one of the great entrepreneurs of our time. Nike. But I think he's even more valuable now. Phil is better suited to leading a large company. He can get people in the right slots, and he can plan. Long-term. His leadership will be even more felt now.

"But the way I see it, Reebok and Nike, we're about the same as Coke and Pepsi were back in the twenties, ready to take over the soda business. We're going after the men's market now, and Nike's going after the women's, and if we both succeed, then, effectively, Reebok and Nike are just going to lock everybody else out of the stores."

But Reebok is the one going to be Coke, not Nike?

Carmody just chuckles, devilishly.

The Stanford term paper, the $3.7 billion blueprint, has long been lost, but Knight can well remember the substance. It went like this: Adidas has the worldwide soccer market sewn up, and track nearly so. It is making inroads into tennis, even into U.S. basketball. Unless Converse finally wakes up, Adidas is going to take over the world. Except . . .

Except . . .

Except if you were going to start a sneaker company from scratch, you would never locate the factories in Western Europe (or the United States). You'd put them in Asia, where the labor is cheap.

But it was all just a term paper, and Knight still planned to become an accountant. Serendipitously, though, he decided to take a world tour first, and the moment he arrived in Japan he fell in love with it. He even climbed Mount Fuji — which, Japanese lore has it, will make you a wise man — and when he came down, he sagely detoured to Kobe, to visit a company named Onitsuka, which had started manufacturing an Adidas knockoff named Tiger. If there was a lightning bolt in the bashful American's life, this was it. In fact, in *Swoosh*, a history of Nike written by J. B. Strasser and Laurie Becklund, the wife and sister-in-law of Rob Strasser, the cagey number-two man who broke with Knight in 1986, the authors even write, "Later . . . his colleagues at home would wonder whether he had shared basic personality traits with the Japanese from birth. . . . Or whether he had been the greatest imitator of all, imitating the imitators."

Knight has forced himself to come out of his remote Asian mode for public appearances, but he remains an exceptionally private person, even enigmatic, and uncomfortable, too, in some of the most quotidian social situations. He recedes behind his scraggly beard and his Kabuki sunglasses and the Bowerman-trained, light padded step of a cutpurse. Rob Strasser says Knight often told him, "I really don't like people." Yet, as with the Japanese, Knight is most at his ease going out after work with a bunch of sports colleagues, drinking and laughing, gossiping. "Well, certainly," he says, "my social life and business life are closely tied."

Penny Knight rolls her big eyes. "Oh?" she asks. "Does one ever stop before the other starts?"

Her husband smiles back at her, but he doesn't dispute her.

And just as the business of Japan, with its pragmatic friendships, suits Knight's personality, so does the meditative side of the Oriental coin. When associates criticize him, it is invariably for "drifting," going off on another Asian walkabout. And when praised, it is universally for possessing nearly occult powers of vision, some Oregon form of dark Eastern mysticism.

Knight can bridle at the general subject, forcing it back to the snug haven of sports. "O.K., everybody talks about the Asian influence on me," he begins, "but look at it from another frame of reference — a classically Western one. What we say is that the Japanese way is collaborative. All right, and what is the equivalent model for that here? [Pause, the setup:] It's a team. The Japanese collaboration is no different from a football team when you go back to the huddle and you say, 'Hey, help me out — I can't block this guy by myself.'

"So, fine, you can say we've borrowed a lot of Japanese concepts. And I say, Read the language of sports. You'll see it all there. You don't have to go to Tokyo."

Still, indisputably, Knight was instantly captivated by Japan, and when he returned to Oregon he had already decided that he would try importing Tigers from Kobe. Bowerman was delighted to throw in with his former runner in this side venture, especially since he sensed that something new was, ahem, afoot. The poig-

nant loneliness of the long-distance runner was about to give way
before hordes of witless New Wave disciples, clogging the byways,
jogging, and (worse) boring everybody else to death by talking
about jogging.

Soon enough, it was a certified cult. But, per usual, none of the
major athletic-shoe firms caught on. And so, in February 1964,
Buck Knight took his first order of Tigers. On sales of $20,000 that
year, the new company he named Blue Ribbon Sports made
$3,240.

He kept his day job as an accountant.

Phil Knight still runs for exercise, and enjoys playing tennis even
more. This day, though, he is just relaxing in the desert, proving
yet again that money does not buy elegance. "Buck can put on the
finest new suit, but in ten minutes it looks all rumpled," Penny
says, and all agree that Knight's most felicitous fashion epoch was
what is generously described as his "Beaverton Vice period." He
favored white linen then; linen rumples on everybody — ergo,
clotheswise, a level playing field. Prime among the many well-
remembered fashion statements of the chairman of Nike was one
made during a lobbying trip to Washington when he met with Sen-
ator Bob Dole and then budget director Richard Darman while
wearing a suit and tie, no socks, and untied Nikes. Most times,
though, as on this day, he merely features Oakley shades and builds
his wardrobe, such as it is, around them.

Penny is with him, along with their Manx cat, whose name is
Moles. The Knights' two sons have gone off to college, and Penny
now travels to most places with her husband. They are happy together, and with Moles. Penny says, "Let's tell about Christina."

He ducks his head. For Buck Knight, this is getting dangerously
close to the bone. But he nods in his beard, and Penny talks about
how Christina is a teenager from Colombia whom the Knights
took in as their foster child. Christina has her own apartment with
her own car now, but she remains their child. Not a whole lot of
people have known about Christina, for even if Knight were not so
naturally covert, his sudden great wealth has taught him to be wary
even when he is giving money away. The odd passel of friends he
goes to games with are distinguished by the fact that they don't try
to hit him up. And that they are loyal.

In the beginning, when Nike started signing up stars, it was much simpler. Cash on the barrelhead. Jordan himself desperately wanted to go with Adidas — would have if only the Germans had upped the ante — and as recently as five years ago, when Knight rejected a new Jordan business proposal out of hand, Jordan stormed out of the office, telling a friend that Knight was a "racist" and that "I was so mad I almost hit him."

In Europe, Adidas was known for paying off not only in shoes but also in cash, women, and Omega watches, and while Converse could usually just get by bartering precious All Stars in the United States, a streetwise promoter named Sonny Vaccaro convinced Knight that Nike had to seed the U.S. market. Vaccaro was authorized to pay coaches to put their teams in Nikes, and to give Nikes away to good players, even down into high school. "Sports is a street game," Vaccaro explains, "and they understood that at Nike then. They let me swing."

Tennis was the other key terrain, for it is an international sport that enjoys upscale prestige and is perfectly showcased for marketing purposes: two players, four shoes, on a court for hours at a clip. Nike's paradoxical strategy, born of necessity, was to go against the social grain, signing a succession of scruffy rogues to tread the sainted courts — first "Nasty," Ilie Nastase, then "McNasty," John McEnroe, and most recently "the Punk," Andre Agassi. Nike was so strapped in the early seventies that it had to pass on one young star whose agent was demanding the whopping sum of $1,500.

At that time, in fact, all that was keeping Nike alive, barely, was a Japanese trading company named Nissho Iwai. Penny Knight was trying to feed her new family on a $25-a-week food budget. Her only comfort was that, although her husband had given up his accounting jobs, he still had his CPA license.

And it got worse. There wasn't a bank left in the great state of Oregon that would give Phil Knight so much as a nickel. Then the Bank of California not only pulled his loan but threatened to turn the company in to the Feds for bouncing checks. And on top of all that, Nastase's game fell down to the level of his charm, while, in 1974, the kid player whose agent had demanded $1,500 won Wimbledon. His name was Jimmy Connors, and his feet were everywhere to be seen.

But here is the kicker. Here is what happens when, as Nike's head of tennis, Ian Hamilton, postulates about his boss, "sometimes you gotta think the whole thing is a horseshoe stuck up your ass." After Knight passed on Connors, his agent pawned him off at the shoe company of last resort, a Romanian firm named LK. Communist shoes! So bad that Connors ignored his contract with the Commies and started wearing another brand. He won Wimbledon in Nikes. For free. And everybody in the world saw it. For free.

Just a few years later, Knight recalls, when McEnroe hurt an ankle, he started wearing an obscure three-quarter model that had sold all of 10,000 pairs that year. Because of McEnroe's strained ligaments, the model sold a million two the very next year. It was about that time when Buck Knight woke up one morning worth $178 million.

Knight had had good luck at Portland State University. His wife had walked into an accounting class he had been teaching there on the side. And there was another young woman at the college who preferred graphics. Her name was Carolyn Davidson, and he called her, and asked her, for thirty-five dollars, to whip up some ideas for a logo for a new shoe he was making. She handed in a dozen proposals, all of which nobody liked, so they picked the one they disliked the least, which was passed off as "a fat check mark."

Shortly thereafter, it occurred to the Nike boys that production of the shoeboxes was beginning the next day *and they didn't have a name for the shoe.* That night, Jeff Johnson had a vision in bed. "Nike!" he yelled. Nobody liked it and almost no one knew who Nike was. But . . . any port in a storm. At least it was better than Dimension Six, which the boss was pushing.

And that is how Nike shoes went on the market in 1971 — an American product made and financed in Japan with a name and logo nobody in the company could much abide. Fittingly, the company's legendary technological breakthrough came about the next year in the same goofy way when Professor Bowerman took out his wife's waffle iron while she was at church, poured rubber into it, and thereby created square cleats.

After Nike's haphazard creation, the company was hardly more inspired in planning the commercial techniques — promotions and advertising — that have become as much a part of Nike as the shoes themselves. Signing Jordan in 1984 was the quantum leap, but Nike really wasn't any brighter than any other company in understanding that buying an athlete's endorsement should only be the start. A mere nine years later, it all sounds so textbook — sign a big star, promote him, make him into a personality, name a product after him. But until Nike rolled the dice on the number 3 draft choice in the NBA, there had probably been only one product in the history of sport that had sold well under a star's imprimatur: The Jack Kramer–model tennis racket, for Wilson.

Not only that, but all the while Nike was changing the rules on endorsements, bidding up, scuffling for kid basketball players, lionizing scruffy anti-Establishment heroes, Knight and many of his associates from the Oregon track milieus remained curiously, situationally purist. To paraphrase Oscar Levant on the subject of Doris Day, some days Phil Knight was a virgin.

Advertising was strictly outside the pale. Advertising was not only phony but adversarial, placing itself as an intermediary in the middle of the romance that the runner had with his shoes (and, by extension, with the good folk who made the shoes). Knight considered it only barely athletically correct to advertise in the peer-group running journals, but they were, after all, published by purist runners. However, in the ads Nike placed in these insider magazines, Knight wouldn't allow either models or hyperbole to be employed. "As pragmatically as Phil approaches everything he does," Howard Slusher says, "there is always this Aristotelian idealism that pervades it all."

Dan Wieden, the president of Wieden & Kennedy, the little Portland advertising firm that would stand the industry — the country — on its ear with *Bo Knows* and *It's Gotta Be the Shoes* and *Just Do It* and rock 'n' roll tennis and Michael Jordan hanging around with Bugs Bunny and now Sigourney Weaver pushing self-empowerment through sneakers, remembers the first time he met the man who would be his spiritual partner in these commercial devotions. The fellow walked into the ad agency, stuck out his hand, and this is exactly what he said: "Hi, I'm Phil Knight and I don't believe in advertising."

*

It is gospel that companies that explode from nothingness, like Nike, must be the inspired work of one man who also holds full dominion. But here's another Nike contradiction: from the beginning, the firm was a strange collaborative effort — Oriental or teamlike, whatever your pleasure — in which Knight would often disappear into the background, if not out of the picture altogether. He himself is the first to say, "I was only a part of what became the Nike culture. I was never even a majority."

But the stars were aligned, the horseshoe firmly lodged, and the young men who chanced to come to work for Nike were oddballs who operated best without direction or approval. Knight regularly switched them around to new, different, unfamiliar tasks before they could discover they really weren't qualified for anything. Once, for example, when Nike started up an apparel division, the man appointed to head it was chosen simply because he dressed better than anybody else. Knight would send off his colonels to perform tasks, ignorant, and with little advice save "Now, don't fuck it up." To anyone who succeeded exceptionally, he would say, sotto voce, "Ah, not bad." That was it. That passed for passionate commendation.

In return, the others ran roughshod over the leader. For example, one of the early principals was a man named Del Hayes, who had himself been Knight's boss, back when he held a square job in an accounting firm. One day, a Nike discussion broke up with Knight telling Hayes, "O.K., whatever you do, Del, don't buy that plant in Saco." But almost immediately Hayes called the broker and bought the factory.

When Knight heard, he just smiled. "You just can't do anything with old Del, can you?" he asked. That was the usual tenor of his response to the most blatant insubordination. Nobody can ever recall him firing anybody. And yet, it was this generous distribution of genuine responsibility that delivered him respect. "You guys decide," he would say, leaving the table.

Says Jeff Johnson, who walked away from Nike eleven years ago, took his millions, and settled in the wilds of New Hampshire, "Phil was like an aloof father figure who couldn't stand to show his affection. But the very fact that he withheld his praise and direction, that somehow made us scared to fail — not for ourselves, but for him. You see, we understood he was letting us decide his fate. I have such affection for Phil. Always did. But I really don't know yet if he knows how much we cared about him."

And Rob Strasser says, "Phil told me once, 'If I have to have a friend, you're it.' " Then suddenly, one day in 1981, Knight called Strasser in and dispatched him to Europe. Strasser was stunned. "What do I do?" he asked.

Knight shrugged. "You know: Sell shoes. Be a businessman. And don't fuck it up."

Everybody understood that Strasser had gotten too big for his britches and had been exiled. Like that, just when they thought they might have the boss figured out, Knight would throw them a curve. No one could ever put him all together. "He has friends," Tom Carmody of Reebok says, "but only chips of friendships. But, damn, did he do it right. You look back, we were all fools. But we were on a mission, and even if Phil didn't know anything about running a company, he was smart enough to let us think we could take over the world. People always ask me, Is he really worth all that money he's made? And every time I say, Oh, hell yeah. If Nike had had some typical entrepreneur dominating us, it never would've worked."

Still, such a romantic, helter-skelter organization was almost destined to come a cropper once past the first blush and the first generation. As early as 1980, like some recreation director on a Caribbean cruise ship, Knight was walking around asking his old buddies, "Is anybody having any fun?" In fact, nobody much was anymore, but their emotions were complicated by the stock allocations, which had made an awful lot of them guilty rich. Nike might have muddled through this transition from teddy bear's picnic to Wall Street listing had it not been for one external happenstance; coincidentally, at this time, there was a stroke of Nike luck.

Only, it hit Reebok. Some aerobic shoes were made, by mistake, with soft garment leather. They were a sensation. Reeboks seemed so stylish; they made women's feet look smaller. And suddenly Reebok was a bandwagon. Knight was confounded. "We think we got it all figured out, and the shadow moves," he says. "*We* had described the game: product, with athlete endorsement. Then they caught up with us with image and design." He shakes his head. "I just didn't understand Reebok. Look, I still don't. We'd have focus groups, and women would tell us that if they bought six pairs of Reeboks that fell apart on them, they'd still go back and buy a seventh. That was just beyond me: styling one hundred percent, performance zero." Even now, Knight's woeful tone suggests that somehow Reebok didn't play by the rules.

At the time, his response was just to vanish — by turns barricading himself behind his desk or literally hiding away. Sometimes he even threatened to cut and run for good. "I'm leaving this turkey farm," he would tell Strasser. Just as he was befuddled by Reebok, he was lost in the lonely crowd that he had wrought at Nike. "There were all these middle managers now," Jeff Johnson remembers. "And Phil just didn't know how to deal with them. So he wouldn't leave his office. He was scared to. You could see that in his eyes."

"Or he'd be in China or somewhere, meditating," says Peter Moore.

Rob Strasser adds bitterly, "A lot of guys never got over his drifting away when the Reebok challenge came. I never understood it. Never will. Phil was always such a competitor, and he wouldn't even *try* to compete then."

Knight shifts uneasily in his chair before these grim memories. It looks as if he wishes very much that he had his Oakleys on for cover now. But, at last, he stirs and goes on the attack. "Yeah," he says, "everybody said, Compete with Reebok. Copy them. But this is what I *ask* when I get this question when I go to speak in business schools, and none of the students ever answer my question. They get very uncomfortable because I ask them, All right, if you were the leader in the market — any business — and a competitor came along with a product that was inferior to yours but outsold you, would you make a product to compete with a brand that's inferior by being inferior yourself? And nobody likes that question. No, it's much easier to play that old sound bite about the bunch of male dopes at Nike, with no understanding of women, who didn't know what to do."

In the end, nobody ever truly answered that question at Nike, either. Instead, the company's pre-eminence was restored by a deus ex machina, the heaven-sent Michael Jordan. Moreover, his shoes — Air Jordans — profited by a new technology that permitted a secret gas to be pumped into the soles, a gas with molecules larger than air so it can't escape. Air Jordans have no air! But who cares? And Knight bucked the trend toward specialty models by pushing something he called a "cross-trainer." Essentially, despite the highfalutin name, a cross-trainer is no more than a sneaker you can do a bunch of stuff in, but about a day after Knight made the decision, a bundle named Bo Jackson, the cross-trainer nonpareil, was left on the Nike doorstep.

Nike signed Charles Barkley to give it a rough edge in basketball, and Jim Courier to be the all-American boy in tennis. It signed pole-vaulter Sergey Bubka and sprinter Irina Privalova and two score more Olympians to appeal to Europeans. It signed baseball-and-football-playing Deion Sanders to be an imitation Bo Jackson, only with jewelry and a do-rag. Meanwhile, Wieden & Kennedy made the Nike characters Disneyesque, while Reebok's advertising campaign — U.B.U. — was, providentially, a disaster of the first order. Slusher took Knight's campus dream and built the berm, and the campus in it. A daughter walked into Penny and Phil Knight's house. And, most extraordinary of all, the new men of Nike started inviting Nike women to the men's meetings when they were going to talk about women.

By 1989, Nike had passed Reebok again, by 1992, sports had passed entertainment, and so by 1993, Buck Knight was back to searching, long-term, for his own Dimension Seven.

Paradoxically, even as Knight revels in the fact that his company is still idiosyncratic, still Oregon, he is himself searching for more control. He has grown furious that Nike athletes can sign endorsements with other companies without Nike's approval, that, for example, Andre Agassi could sully his Nike image by declaring flat out in dreadful Canon commercials that he's a phony, that "image is everything" — especially when every mother's son should know that loyalty is.

Ultimately, it is obvious that Knight believes that only Nike agents should ever represent Nike athletes. Last fall, Alonzo Mourning, an NBA rookie from Georgetown — a tight Nike school with a basketball coach, John Thompson, who sits on the Nike board — was *assigned* an outside agent by Nike. Said agent then held Mourning out from signing with the Charlotte Hornets until well after the season started. Why? The Hornets needed their first draft choice more than their first draft choice needed them. After all, he was the one who had the shoe contract. Even once he had signed, when a reporter asked Mourning point-blank whom he worked for, the Hornets or Nike, Mourning didn't hesitate for so much as a beat. "I work for Nike," he answered.

And then Buck Knight went out and met with Michael Ovitz.

Knight has also started to construct huge museums-cum-emporiums that sell only Nike paraphernalia. (And can you imagine how much more business Nike and its Asian-minded boss can do when it starts putting sneakers on those billions of Chinese feet?) Essentially, the new Nike Towns threaten Foot Lockers and other U.S. athletic-gear retail outlets, just as Nike's greater control of the athlete threatens agents and teams and ultimately leagues. "We want to work more closely with existing organizations," Knight says blandly.

If that sounds benign, no one knows better than Knight how Adidas, in its palmy days, became such a controlling presence behind the throne of international sport that it is widely credited with being the surreptitious force that installed the rulers of the soccer and track federations, as well as the International Olympic Committee itself. But Horst Dassler died of cancer in 1987 when he was only fifty-one, and the Adidas *Macht des Sports* has all but unraveled around the world by now. At the Olympics, there used to be three institutions that, in addition to the IOC, fought for power: the U.S. Olympic Committee, the world media, and the Communist consortium. Last summer, at Barcelona, there were still three: the U.S. Olympic Committee, the world media, and Nike. It is not facetious to say that, basically, Nike has replaced Communism in the sports universe.

Power bases change, of course. In the past, there have been important individual businessmen in sport, but most of them have been promoters or administrators. Of manufacturers there have really been only two: Horst Dassler, in his relatively brief span, and Albert G. Spalding, an egocentric ex–baseball pitcher, who was an immense presence in American sport until his death in 1915. Knight is clearly in a position, at age fifty-five, to derive more power from a product than any man ever in sport. "I prefer to think artistically now, rather than financially," he says — inscrutably, one is tempted to say.

He's back in the desert now, outside the berm for a few days, delighting in watching his Nike tennis heroes compete for the greater glory of Swoosh. He is reminiscing about all the years, the three decades since first he came down from Fuji, the two decades since he reluctantly put the name Nike on the shoeboxes. He runs his hand through his scruffy hair. "Nike has become a good company," he declares proudly. "I mean that. Not just a good product — good advertising, good service. Good. Like, well [pause]. Disney is a whole force for good, you know." Disney seems often to sneak into the conversations about Nike. It's not forced; it just happens to come up all the time.

Looking outside, where his wife lies in a bikini, tanning, Buck Knight shakes his head. He doesn't bother with the sun much himself; you can take the boy out of Oregon, but etc. "I mean . . ." He beams. "I mean, it's a wonderful thing just to think, My God, if you could just leave a Disney."

He turns back then. "You know what I always feared? That years from now my grandchildren would hear that I was the founder of Nike and they'd say, What's a Nike? That's what scares me."

Howard Slusher, who is one of the larger chips of a friend to Knight, says, "I've tried to figure Phil out a thousand times. I mean, I've wrestled with it. And I still don't know. He's changing some, you know. I've heard him say a couple times that the real test of a great businessman is if he's an artist. And what's interesting about that is twenty years ago — maybe even ten — if Phil'd made that statement, he'd have said 'scientist,' not 'artist.' And there is this one thing, and that is that very few people in this world can choose what they want to be, and Phil is one of those, and he chooses to be Nike."

Another time, quiet, a contemplative place, maybe like somewhere that he retreats to in the Orient, and Knight starts talking about Dick Donahue, whom he brought on as president to tend to the short term. Donahue has eleven children. "I asked Dick once," Knight says, " 'Can you ever stop worrying about your children?' And he said, 'Sure.' And I said, 'You can?' I mean, I was surprised he said that. But then Dick laughed and said, 'Yeah, three days after the wake.' "

And Buck Knight cracks a little smile, because he knows that you know that he isn't talking only about his two sons and his foster daughter. He is also talking about his other child, his baby, still and ever.

Biographical Notes

Notable Sports Writing of 1993

Biographical Notes

Oxford-born MARTIN AMIS was educated in Britain, Spain, and the United States. A regular contributor to the *Independent*, Amis is also widely considered to be one of the most important voices in contemporary British fiction. His books include *The Moronic Inferno and Other Visits to America*, *Einstein's Monsters*, and *London Fields*.

ROGER ANGELL is a writer and editor for *The New Yorker*, where his year-end summation of the year in baseball is required reading for baseball enthusiasts. Angell served in the Air Force during World War II, and lives with his wife in New York City.

IRA BERKOW is a sports columnist and feature writer for the *New York Times*. He has a bachelor's degree from Miami (Ohio) University, and reports several degrees of hard-earned experience from his previous employment at the *Minneapolis Star-Tribune* and the Newspaper Enterprise Association. He was a runner-up for the Pulitzer Prize for Distinguished Commentary in 1987 and a finalist for an Edgar Award for his book *The Man Who Robbed the Pierre*.

JOHN ED BRADLEY worked as a sports writer for the *Washington Post* and was on the staff of the *Washington Post Magazine* until 1987, when he left to write fiction. Since then, he has published four novels, *Tupelo Nights*, *The Best There Ever Was*, *Love and Obits*, and, most recently, *Smoke*. A contributing editor to *Esquire*, Bradley is also a special contributor to *Sports Illustrated*.

BRUCE BUSCHEL has worked for the *Philadelphia Inquirer*, *GQ*, and *Philadelphia Magazine*, where he is currently a contributing editor. A previous winner of the ASCAP Deems Taylor Award for a profile about Wynton Marsalis and a Golden Quill award for an article about Mickey

Mantle, his work has appeared in a number of national publications. Buschel lives in Riverdale, New York.

GARY CARTWRIGHT has contributed stories to *Harper's, Life,* and *Esquire.* In 1986, he was a finalist for the National Magazine Award for Reporting Excellence. He is the author of several books, including *Confessions of a Washed-Up Sportswriter* and *Dirty Dealing.* He is also the coauthor of two movie scripts, "J.W. Coup," and "Pair of Aces." Cartwright is currently a senior editor at *Texas Monthly.*

BUD COLLINS has been an NBC sports commentator since 1972 and a columnist for the *Boston Globe* since 1963. A native of Berea, Ohio, Collins is a graduate of Baldwin-Wallace and attended graduate school at Boston University. He lives in Boston.

FRANK DEFORD was guest editor of *The Best American Sports Writing 1993.* Deford is the author of ten books, including the novel *Love and Infamy,* published in 1993. A contributing editor to *Vanity Fair,* Deford appears regularly on National Public Radio and ESPN. He is currently at work on a novel about a young woman with polio just before the discovery of the Salk vaccine in 1955.

JOHN HEWITT has written exclusively for *Gray's Sporting Journal* since 1976, where he is now senior editor. A native of Topeka, Kansas, he has lived in Fairbanks, Alaska, for twenty-five years, where he coaches his daughters' two softball teams and hunts ducks.

MARK KRAM, JR., has been a sports writer for the *Philadelphia Daily News* since 1987, and is also a contributing writer for *Philadelphia Magazine.* He previously worked at the *Detroit Free Press* and the *Baltimore News American.* Born in Baltimore, he lives in Haddenfield, New Jersey, with his wife and two daughters. A story by his father, Mark Kram, appeared in *The Best American Sports Writing 1993.*

MARTHA WEINMAN LEAR is a frequent contributor to many publications, among them *Mademoiselle* and *Ladies' Home Journal.* A native of Malden, Massachusetts, she is a graduate of Boston University. Lear is the author of the critically acclaimed chronicle of her husband's battle with heart disease, *Heartsounds.*

JOHN MCPHEE has been a staff writer for *The New Yorker* since 1965, and the Ferris Professor of Journalism at Princeton University since 1975. He is the author of over twenty books, most recently *Assembling California.* He received the Award in Literature from the American Academy of Arts and Letters in 1977 and the John Burroughs Medal in 1990.

DAVIS MILLER is a contributing editor at *Sport* magazine. His fiction and nonfiction have appeared in *Esquire, Sports Illustrated, Rolling Stone, GQ, Men's Journal,* and many other publications. He wrote a film documentary about Bruce Lee for Warner Brothers and is at work on a second documentary about Lee which is being produced for distribution in mainland China. "The Zen of Muhammad Ali" was nominated by the *Miami Herald* for a 1994 Pulitzer Prize. Davis lives in Winston-Salem, North Carolina, and Louisville, Kentucky.

LEIGH MONTVILLE worked as a reporter and columnist for the *Boston Globe* for twenty-one years before joining *Sports Illustrated* as a senior writer in 1989. He is the author of *Manute: The Center of Two Worlds,* a biography of the Sudanese basketball player Manute Bol.

WILLIAM NACK was a reporter and sports columnist for *Newsday* before joining *Sports Illustrated* in 1979. One of America's leading writers on thoroughbred racing, Nack has earned six Eclipse Awards for his coverage of the Sport of Kings. He is the author of *Secretariat: The Making of a Champion.*

JOHN PAUL NEWPORT is a contributing editor at *Men's Journal.* He was born and raised in Fort Worth, Texas. A graduate of Harvard, Newport previously worked as a reporter for the *Fort Worth Star-Telegram* and as an associate editor at *Fortune.*

SUSAN ORLEAN is a staff writer for *The New Yorker.* Her work has appeared in a number of publications, including *The New York Times Magazine, Rolling Stone,* and *Vogue.* She is the author of *Saturday Night* and *Red Sox and Bluefish,* a collection of her columns from the *Boston Globe.* A Cleveland native, Orlean retains her allegiance to the Cleveland Indians.

DAVE PARMENTER is well known in the surfing community as a surfer who writes, rather than a writer who surfs. While traveling on the world professional surfing circuit, Parmenter began writing features, and his work has appeared in a number of surfing magazines, including *Surfing, Surfer, Australian Surfing Life,* and *Surfer's Journal.* Parmenter, currently a surfboard designer, splits his time between San Luis Obispo, California, and Makaha, Hawaii.

CHARLES P. PIERCE is a contributing writer to *GQ* and *Boston* magazine. He previously wrote for the *Boston Phoenix,* the *Boston Herald,* and the *National Sports Daily.* This is his third appearance in *The Best American Sports Writing.*

GEORGE PLIMPTON is known for doing things most people only dream about. He is a special contributor to *Sports Illustrated,* editor of *The Paris*

Review, and a columnist for *Esquire.* The most recent of his twenty-some books is *Chronicle of Courage: Very Special Artists,* with Jean Kennedy Smith.

S. L. PRICE is a native of Stamford, Connecticut. He graduated from the University of North Carolina in 1983, and spent four years as a columnist and feature writer for the *Miami Herald* before joining *Sports Illustrated* in 1994.

JOHN SCHULIAN is a television writer and producer in Los Angeles. Among the programs he has been involved with are *Wiseguy, Miami Vice,* and *Midnight Caller.* Formerly a columnist for the *Chicago Sun-Times* and the *Philadelphia Daily News,* Schulian is also a frequent contributor to *Sports Illustrated* and *GQ.*

A senior writer for *Sports Illustrated,* GARY SMITH has also written for *Rolling Stone, Inside Sports,* the *Philadelphia Daily News,* and a number of other publications. His story about high school basketball on a Crow reservation, "Shadow of a Nation," appeared in *The Best American Sports Writing 1992* and won the 1992 National Magazine Award for Feature Writing.

Notable Sports Writing of 1993

SELECTED BY GLENN STOUT